RAGE

Reviews of the first edition

"... The book by Itten is... a very interesting read, the writing is lively, and it is full of information about people familiar from literature or cultural history." Psychologie heute 6/2008

"... Theodor Itten ... has written the first German-language book on the topic of rage." Brigitte Nr. 13, 4.6.2008

"... Theodor Itten, psychotherapist and author, has engaged with sudden rages from both writerly and therapeutic angles..." Die Presse 19.4.2008

"... "Your own feeling of self-worth, self-assurance, personal responsibility, are fed by the truth of your emotions," as the Swiss psychologist Theodor Itten puts it in his splendid, recently published book "Jähzorn" (Rage) Wiener Zeitung 4.4.2008

"... Individual case studies provide new social, psychological and psychotherapeutic insights, as well as specific prompts for psychotherapists, doctors, educators and other supportive professions. This book brings a focus to sudden rage for the first time in the German-speaking world..." Salzburger Nachrichten 2.2.2008

"... a recommended read..." Deutschlandradio Kultur 21.1.2008

"... "Jähzorn" is the first German-language book there has been on the subject, and is published by the renowned Springer-Verlag in Vienna." Saiten 11/2007

"... The Swiss psychotherapist Theodor Itten highlights ... the positive and negative aspects of rage..." www.derstandard.at 15.11.2007

"... In his book "Jähzorn", Theodor Itten gives psychotherapeutic answers to this unpredictable emotion..." St. Galler Tagblatt 27.10.2007

RAGE
Managing an Explosive Emotion

SECOND EDITION

Theodor Itten

Translation by Ruth Martin

Translation from the German language edition *Jähzorn* Theodor Itten © 2007 Springer-Verlag Wien New York, all rights reserved.

English translation *Rage* first published in 2011 by Libri Publishing.

Second Edition published in 2021 by Libri Publishing

Copyright © Libri Publishing

ISBN 978-1-911450-78-8

Translation by Ruth Martin

The right of Theodor Itten to be identified as the author of this work has been asserted in accordance with the Copyright, Designs and Patents Act, 1988.

All rights reserved. No part of this publication may be reproduced, stored in any retrieval system or transmitted in any form or by any means, electronic, mechanical, photocopying, recording or otherwise, without the prior written permission of the copyright holder for which application should be addressed in the first instance to the publishers. No liability shall be attached to the author, the copyright holder or the publishers for loss or damage of any nature suffered as a result of reliance on the reproduction of any of the contents of this publication or any errors or omissions in its contents.

A CIP catalogue record for this book is available from The British Library

Cover painting: Raphael Grischa Itten
Cover design by Helen Taylor
Design by Carnegie Book Production

The publisher and author would like to thank a Swiss Foundation, which prefers to remain anonymous, for the generous translation grant.

Libri Publishing
Brunel House
Volunteer Way
Faringdon
Oxfordshire
SN7 7YR

Tel: +44 (0)845 873 3837

www.libripublishing.co.uk

Contents

Where does rage come from?   1
    The Well   1
    The Language of Rage   3
    Rage by Numbers   11
    The Reasons   23
    The Basic Fault   37

How does rage manifest itself?   57
    The Triggers   57
    Rage in a Cultural and Religious Context   66
    Social Psychology and Society   97
    Perpetrators   106
    Victims   129

What can we do?   139
    Psychotherapy   139
    Insights   154
    Children and Parents   162
    From Victim to Perpetrator   168
    Routes Out of Rage   181

New episodes of rage   193

Tips for therapy and self-empowerment	201
Help!	201
Creating a scale of emotions	204
The code word	207
Expanding the repertoire of your own emotional regulation	210
Tips for victims of rage	212
A few remarks on psychotherapy	214
Appendix	217
Acknowledgements	219
Bibliography	221

To My Sons
Dimitrij, Anatol and Raphael

And for Francis Huxley

Meanwhile, the emotions that disturb the soul are those of the underworld demon within us, whose vital sap – called rasa *in India – is held to be the essence of consciousness and, when suitably prepared, the drink of immortality called Soma.*

Francis Huxley, 1990

Preface

Ever since the evening of 9th July 2006, the FIFA World Cup Final, billions of people who watched the game know how suddenly an outburst of rage can happen. Zinedine Zidane, the "Buddha of Football" as the filmmaker Stephane Meunier once called him, was subjected to such offensive and demeaning provocation by one of his Italian opponents that he could no longer contain his extreme rage. The awful incident, totally unexpected and alarming for us as spectators, was over in nine seconds. The Buddha had head-butted his agent provocateur to the ground. He was up, his opponent was down. That was it: instant retribution from a god of football. A few seconds later the Buddha was given the red card. Back to his old introverted self, he left the pitch with his head bowed and tears in his eyes. A humble, masterful and self-contained man, calm and emotionally reserved, a role model – as many writers have described him – had failed to show his anger in a sensitive, age-appropriate manner.

According to the papers, Naomi Campbell has had another outburst of rage. The fashion icon, too, loses her cool time and again, seeming even to get pleasure out of throwing tantrums. Campbell and Zidane are two of the 25 out of every 100 inhabitants of their respective civilised countries who tend towards outbursts of rage. Violent rages are things that break loose suddenly and cannot be restrained. There are triggers that unleash these outbursts, and certain people are temperamentally predisposed to them. A rage can erupt out of a person like a volcano's lava out of the earth. When someone's emotional tension becomes too high, and they have no means of dealing appropriately with these intense feelings, they erupt with rage. Enough is enough. Their emotional life is ruled by a habit.

In the world of psychology and psychopathology, this expression of rage is viewed as an affective personality disorder, as one of a total of eight criteria of Borderline Personality Disorder, and as a marker of an unbalanced, choleric character. However, rage doesn't count as a mental disorder in either of the two current trend-setting international systems of classification, the ICD-10 and the DSM-IV/2. This isn't a bad thing, and I hope it remains the case, even though I have made a public issue of rage for the first time in the German-speaking world through this study.

Where does rage originate? How does it manifest itself? What can we do to rid ourselves of it? Many individuals experience sudden rages as a personal, and often inherited, emotion. The destructive power of these rages, bursting unannounced into our daily lives, is well-known and yet often treated by society as taboo. Many children of raging parents, and many partners of raging men and women, suffer the psychological and physical injuries caused by these uncontrollable bursts of emotion. We are witness to outbursts of rage within the family, in relationships, on the road, at work, and in schools and institutions. We stand helpless before the open secret of a veritable plague to society.

In the interests of gaining some clarity on this, a team of researchers surveyed 481 pedestrians in eastern Switzerland between March and June of 2006 about their experience of outbursts of rage. In addition, another 94 people serving as a control group were surveyed by phone in August 2006 in three cities: Bern, Zurich and Basel.

In the first part of this book, the results of these surveys will be presented, discussed and put into context. Rages will be analysed in relation to culture, religious history, and social psychology. Christian and Jewish biblical narratives, and Greek and Germanic myths will show rages as part of the human condition, and illustrate how they were dealt with in ancient times.

In the second section we will consider the triggers, the outbursts and the characteristics of these outbursts. What function do rages serve in the social building-blocks of our lives, like family, school, work and leisure? How do the perpetrators and victims of rage relate to each other? And what happens when former victims become perpetrators?

In the third part we will look at the options open to us – in particular the methods used in psychotherapy – for releasing ourselves from rages. A few case studies from my psychotherapy practice show how we can free ourselves from these sudden outbursts. How does our way of dealing with the feeling of rage change when a form of therapy is employed that integrates body and mind? What self-help methods exist to help us escape from the vicious circle of sudden rages? How can this powerful feeling, this integral part of our life, be kept in check? How can we hold onto it so it can be used in an assertive and responsible way? What can I do to prevent rage from returning once I have released myself from it? Why can't some people live without it?

Preface to the 2nd English edition

I have been given the chance to write a foreword for this book for the third time (two English, one German) – what a surprise! In the third part of the book ("What can we do?"), I make various suggestions for taking a healing approach to this impulse-control disorder, based on the principal results of my investigation. And yet both my publisher and I have received repeated requests to provide further self-help tips. What effective options exist for the self-treatment of rage? For this new edition, I have written a new chapter on this pressing issue, based on my experience as a psychotherapist with women and (predominantly) men who suffer from these sudden fits of rage. In it, I describe the interventions and self-help exercises that have proven most effective.

When the idea for this book first arose in 2005 – a book that is still the only German-language work on this powerful emotion and its socio-psychological consequences – neither publisher nor author intended it to be a self-help guide or an aid to resilience. It was and remains a social, phenomenological overview of the subject, based on an empirical study.

The Covid-19 pandemic, and the self-isolation imposed by politicians worldwide (and in some places enforced by the authorities) has resulted in whole families staying inside their own four walls. And this has produced a massive increase in domestic violence, from China to Brazil, from Greece to Berlin, from Switzerland to Africa, mostly committed by men against women and children. A measure intended to protect the population against the spread of this severe respiratory infection has caused a pandemic of psychological and emotional violence within the family. And we now know how many of those in power with megalomaniac tendencies also dress up the exercise of their power with a fit of rage.

There are people who prefer to "swallow" their feelings of resentment, anger and rage. Others try to drink or smoke them away, or repress them by some other means, instead of expressing these vital, physical impulses in words. For many people, men in particular, showing your true feelings is often a risky undertaking. In the mathematics of gender stereotypes, showing your feelings is often equated with "showing weakness".

In the morning, a top businessman would get horribly upset over the mess on his desk that he had left there the night before. The temptation to externalise his own chaos was a strong one. If one of his senior management team should disturb him as he was tidying up, with an urgent matter they needed to discuss, "it" – as he put it in his psychotherapy sessions with me – would usually erupt out of him in a fit of rage, shouting and screaming. Together, we explored various potential routes out of such embarrassing, overly sensitive behaviour. He decided that from then on, every evening he would make a to-do list for the following day in neat handwriting, and leave his desk tidy. This was something he could do for himself as an act of self-respect and self-care. And voilà, that was an end to these vexatious rages. He also managed to improve his handwriting, and became more serious, calm and respectful towards himself and others. This exercise, as part of his new, mindful way of life, in which he did not leave himself in the lurch when he needed his own support, helped him to rebalance his repertoire of emotions.

Many social and personal emotions, and the way we regulate them, are set out for us by our culture, family and social history, and inherited from one generation to the next. There is a whole range of emotions and feelings, such as uncertainty, injury, offence, a sense of inferiority, anger, aggression, imperiousness, vengefulness, malice, grief, guilt and feeling lost, that emerge as triggers and features of an attack of rage. The psychotherapy that I describe in this book, and in the new chapter containing tips for help and self-help, is an effective practice for anyone wanting to learn socially acceptable and psychologically healthy ways to regulate the difficult emotions related to sudden rages. Even just summoning up the courage to make this change has a positive effect.

Sankt Gallen **Theodor Itten**
May 2020

Where does rage come from?

The Well

I saw the pitchfork flying towards me. In a split second the quivering, three-pronged spear would bury itself in my five-year-old back, at the exact height of my pounding heart. It was a humid afternoon in late summer. I ran for my life, and for the first time, I felt the weight of the world upon me. I screamed blue murder. The world between me and my uncle Hannes was silent. With all my remaining strength, I dived behind the well; the fork landed in the gravel in front of it. My whole body shook – I was out of breath – I was almost nothing *but* breath. My heart thudded, pumping the blood around my small body, and slowly tears welled up in my eyes. My scream, and the screams of my cousins, brought other adults running outside from the parlour. When I finally poked my head slowly over the lip of the well, I saw them gripping my uncle on both sides, man-handling him into the house. I saw a face contorted by pain and rage. I was thankful to be alive. Looking back, this is my first conscious experience of rage in my extended family.

How could something like this happen? How could my uncle, who earlier had been chatting, laughing and joking with us kids over tea and cake, come to throw a pitchfork at me? How could he have lifted it over his shoulder with his powerful, tanned right arm, like a hunter or a warrior with a spear, with the intention of plunging it into the innocent back of one of his family? Was he out of his mind? Yes, said the other grown-ups, he was in a rage. It was a moment of madness.

We, the children, had triggered the sudden outburst. I learned immediately that the victim is the guilty party. And what had I done? We – ten or so children between the ages of four and ten – had been playing hide-and-seek, a favourite game. The big well in the middle of the courtyard was "home". We hid all over the farm, which branched out in all directions. There was one place I particularly favoured: the manger in the cattle shed. Nobody would find me underneath the freshly cut grass. The cows had not yet been let in from the pasture. Uncle Hannes had told us twice already that we shouldn't make the delicate grass dirty with our muddy feet. We were asked not to hide in the manger. My feeling at the time was that he hadn't forbidden it in the same way he had forbidden us from hiding in, on, under or behind the combine harvester in the yard. I didn't regard his request as an order. And so I went back to my favourite hiding-place. Uncle Hannes came into the barn, unnoticed by me, to get the stall ready for the cows. "OH, COME *ON*", he shouted after me, when I tried to scamper out of my hiding-place as quickly as possible to make a dash for "home". He already had the pitchfork in his hand. He was about to lift the grass that he had cut that morning and brought into the barn, to feed to the cows who would soon be coming in from the pasture. It was at this moment that I turned around briefly in fright. My uncle Hannes was gripped by rage. I had no idea there could be an anger so powerful and so deadly. He had gone mad, as my Grandma said later. He was so overwhelmingly angry because I, a small child, had not followed his instructions. He felt ignored and disrespected. I had overstepped his boundaries. He had let his own emotional barriers down. His threatening gestures were at this moment focused entirely on me, the little boy who he felt had disobeyed him. By throwing the pitchfork, he wanted to "get me out of his way". He was possessed by an inner force of rage, which had come upon him so suddenly he himself could not stop it. In a single moment I was expelled from the paradise of childhood. I felt the most awful fear and trembling. Seventeen years later, I was astonished to rediscover these feelings characterised by Søren Kierkegaard – in his consideration of Abraham's willingness to sacrifice his son, Isaac, on God's command (Kierkegaard 1941).

The events of this Sunday afternoon in 1957 remained incredible, incomprehensible, to me for a long time. This first experience of a sudden rage shook my foundations and the feelings of safety and love the farm provided. As a two-year-old, I had seen how Farmer Scherer, in whose immediate neighbourhood my first home stood, sometimes whipped his stallions in anger. I had seen his farm boy angrily throwing down his hammer. I had noticed them both swearing at their cows when the animals couldn't stay still to be milked, and tried to push the farmers' hands away from their udders with their back legs. But a sudden outburst of rage like the one I witnessed on this summer afternoon was a completely new experience. Grandma saw it as her duty to tell me off on the way home, which gave me the impression it was my fault that this uncontrollable rage had burst forth from my uncle. I learnt an important lesson that day: sometimes we shape our lives; sometimes our lives shape us. A notable detail in my recollection of the situation: the deathly silence that fell over the whole yard from the moment the fork began its flight through the air.

The questions of why these sudden outbursts of rage happen, and why people lose control, are ones I want to explore in this book. As a depth psychologist, I am also fascinated by the three-pronged fork. It is both a symbol of the psyche and the sceptre of the sea-god Poseidon. If my uncle had been holding a hammer, like Thor, he would no doubt have thrown this at me instead. The point is to take note of the flying objects that are thrown at us in rage: the items that smash against the wall, the floor, the ground. The power of a sudden rage destroys the products of our civilised culture, the things that constitute and signify the human world. Raw materials brought forth from the earth are shaped and become the man-made objects that make up our reality. The smashing of objects is also the smashing of the world. And when people are killed in a fit of rage, the epicentre of that world is also destroyed.

The Language of Rage

> Then shall he speak unto them in his wrath, and vex them in his sore displeasure. (Psalms 2:5)[1]

Languages, as we know and use them, have been around for a good 40,000 years. Even the early hunter-gatherers who formed themselves into groups had a complex language at their disposal.

---

1 Using the King James Bible as a standard edition, except where references to different, contrasting editions are required.

Our language, with its words, sentences and melodies, communicates facts and opinions, and allows others some access to our mental images. "Nobody knows how and why this magnificent system came into being. It seems to be connected to some sort of evolution of the species, since no other animals speak, but all humans do [...] Human languages are the most highly developed, most flexible systems of communication we know. They are distinguished through their ability to be used for conveying messages of any degree of complexity, and by doing this incredibly quickly and efficiently" (Janson 2006 p. 13).

Our emotions, our thought patterns, and the psychological concepts that come to light in verbal expressions, are free creations of our thought and operative actions, and cannot be obtained directly from our sense-experience. Language derives words from human experience. The vernacular is full of words that help us to uncover our psychological phenomena. The truth – in Greek, *alatheia* – is "naked". Words, which we use to define the feelings in our bodies, always take us closer to emotional phenomena (Kluge & Seebold 2002).

The word "rage" dates from around 1300 AD, and comes from the Old French *raige*. It also has roots in the Latin *rabia:* madness, rage or fury. "Rabies" or hydrophobia also comes from this root, and the physical symptoms of this – frothing at the mouth, lashing out in fury – are like an extreme outburst of the kind of rage this book seeks to understand. In the French word for rage, *colère*, (irritation), we hear additional images. *Ira* (ire) is portrayed by Seneca as the worst and at the same time most unnatural emotion (pure feeling as opposed to reason).

The goal is to annihilate or combat the feeling; boiling with rage, *fou de colère*. During outbursts of rage we are, according to the pre-Enlightenment way of thinking, possessed, fanatical, and even possessed by the devil. The devil has the wrathful man in his power.

In German, the term for this kind of explosive rage is *Jähzorn* – the original title of this book. *Zorn* is rage; the prefix *jäh* means "sudden". There is no English equivalent for this, so instead I will distinguish between sudden outbursts of rage (*Jähzorn*), a violent, unpredictable and uncontrollable emotion, and a protective, defensive rage (*Zorn*), which it can be healthy to release.

The word "anger" originates in the 12th century AD, from the Old Norse *angra*, "to grieve or vex". It also has a root in the Greek

Where does rage come from?

ankhein, "to squeeze", and the Latin *angere*, "to throttle or torment". We talk about being "choked up" with anger: an angry person is strangled by his emotion, whereas the person who succumbs to a sudden rage has a valve to release the pressure. "Wrath", the German *Wut*, is commonly associated with gods, and is a more creative fury. Wotan, whose name is associated with *Wut*, is the god of both war and wisdom. Rage that can be harnessed is a powerful and useful force: the phrase "go berserk" comes from the feared Norse Berserker warriors, who fought in a state of trance-like fury reportedly brought on either by psychological training or drugs. The milder form of anger is irritation, when things don't work out the way I'd imagined. A bellyful of anger comes from a sense of having been treated unjustly. Anger is a healing power for injuries to the soul (Kluge and Seebold 2002).

Sudden rages are a cruel army, mobilised quickly and powerfully from a primordial inner strength. Rage connotes one of the four primary emotions in our animal nature – a brilliant or fulminant feeling that breaks into our everyday lives. In his study of Michelangelo's sculpture of Moses, Sigmund Freud (1856–1939) writes of a gradually awakening rage. A sudden outburst of rage is an untameable feeling of anger. If I were able to contain such a powerful emotion as anger, I could very probably also quell an outburst of rage. I could take my anger into safe keeping and tend to it, so that it could be given its freedom through a physical expression of emotion. Anger and rage, as this book will show, are all about observing and drawing boundaries, and protecting your territory. Anger defends the boundary; rage oversteps it. Anger is a part of our emotional life in the same way as joy, passion, fear, hunger, sadness etc. When the inner tension becomes too great, when the well of emotion overflows and the pressure gets too much, repressed anger bursts into the civilised world as rage. In our survey, many people described the suddenness of a fit of rage as: "going straight from 0–60"– an immense, powerful acceleration.

An outburst of rage brings out feelings that are normally suppressed by religion, morality or ethics in order to maintain a good impression of us amongst our fellow men. A rage is an anger that barges into our normal relationships. Everyone who suffers from rage ("ragers", as we will call them here) knows that this can happen at any time. Everyone who knows them knows this too. If we call this the rage-potential factor in a relationship, then it is children of all ages who know best how careful they have to be to avoid possible outbursts. Rage restricts a person's space to breathe and space to live, and has a limiting effect on the rough-and-tumble of family life. Rage is an emotional relic from an archaic time, when we first developed into Homo sapiens. This is very interesting from the point of view of evolutionary psychology. Demonic tendencies can be punished, but – and this may be both fatal to the process of civilisation and interesting from an evolutionary perspective – they cannot ultimately be quashed or sublimated.

Is rage stored in or nourished by the unconscious? If so, it would be an expression of the "anima mundi", correcting individual mental tensions brought on by the process of civilisation.

The Protestants' iconoclastic riots were driven by Luther's anger and by three or four other monks (like Zwingli or Calvin) who wanted to put themselves in charge of definition. The result of this was that they achieved the redistribution of the goods and benefices of the Pope and the Catholic Church amongst the emerging bourgeoisie and their rulers. So, they went from destruction to the restoration of newly-established power. Luther himself was quick to use words of violence, and said nobody would be saved who didn't leave the Catholic Church and follow him. His lust for power fired his crazed anger against himself, his surroundings and his situation in life, and against the devil, of whom he was terribly afraid (Erikson 1972).

Things are much the same today as they were at the time of the Reformation. Terrorists, anarchists, power-crazed military coups or religious fanatics motivate their subordinates, soldiers and sympathisers to destroy the status quo, and the things built by previous generations; to destroy everything, just not their own power. This is reminiscent of the Luddites, the craftsmen who destroyed the new machines in the factories. The fear of losing their own existence gave them the strength to express their anger destructively. Hidden anger gave them the energy for sabotage. Noise, as for the punk movement, is a negative form of creativity. Negative because we break the thing that's breaking us, stop what's stopping us and smash what has hit us. So it goes in the scientific debate around the use of technology. Holy wrath, like holy war, is a religious legitimation of one's own wickedness. Everything is allowed in the name of God – every man for himself, and God against all. Here, sudden rage and the completely irrational behaviour that accompanies it become clear.

Where does rage come from?

For example: driving too close to the car in front on the motorway to bully or intimidate other drivers has cost more than one tailgater their lives. Or sportsmen who kick off at players on their own football team, like Oliver Kahn, the former German National goalkeeper, who has a tendency to smack his defenders round the head and punch them in the back.

The modern world is so vast and inter-connected that only as a collective can we be aware of everything that's going on right at this moment. Perhaps we can contribute to the store of human knowledge through social dreaming. We each reach the limits of our own understanding and achievement. We are up against the wall: where should we go if we don't know how to go on? A dead-end metaphor. In an impossible situation, a sudden outburst of rage can bring a momentary sense of freedom, found in the resulting emotional exhaustion, in the same way epileptics sometimes report a new-found calm before the storm appears.

The existentialists had a feeling of "thrownness". How could Jean-Paul Sartre, such a notorious liar in his private life, bring such intellectual liberation to us, the younger generation? We were taken in by the theatricals between him and Simone de Beauvoir, and believed what we saw on the surface – having power over the powerful, and impressing us with the offender-victim position (his visit to Stammheim prison). Negative heroes destroy heroes. Were Atlas, Hector and Achilles filled with rage? They were certainly angry warriors.

Annaeus Seneca was born in Cordoba, in about the 4th century AD (he was for some time a tutor to Nero, the Roman Emperor noted for his outbursts of rage). Seneca gave a number of definitions of anger in his books on the subject: anger is the desire to take revenge for injustice; anger is the mental stimulation that causes us to harm what has harmed (or threatens to harm) us; anger is the desire to reciprocate pain (Laktanz 1919).

In many studies of the five basic human emotions – curiosity, fear, anger, sadness and joy – sudden rages are often treated as a variant of anger, along with bitterness and disappointment. Luc Ciompi has spent many years looking at affective mental phenomena (emotions). His concept of "affect-logic" defines an affect as "an integrated psycho-physical mood brought on by inner and outer stimuli, with varying qualities, lengths, and proximity to the conscious mind" (Ciompi 1997).

Now that I have explored a few words that will become the key concepts of this study, using their etymological roots, I will allow myself to be led by this language and present the theories on rage I wrote down before the empirical data for the study was collected. I look on these as a structural diagram to help you find your way through this complex and diverse area of experience.

Theory 1

Sudden rages develop in the context of human civilisation. The wrath of the Almighty and Everlasting God, and other gods and goddesses, is used principally for the immediate punishment of a people, a tribe or an individual who has done something weak, evil or wrong in the eyes of the wrathful god. The authors of the Judeo-Christian bible were intensely preoccupied with the wrath of the creator. That which is godly is wrathful, and rage is as natural in the act of creation as is the shining of the sun. "Holy rage" is the human justification of the deadly dangers which humanity faces. Sudden rages are useful in the exercise of power; the threat of rage is made in an attempt to ensure obedience. Rage is deployed as an educational tool, to make people obedient to a given ideology, morality, ethics, or dogma. Cain slew Abel in a fit of rage, because his path through life and his truth were not valued as highly as his brother's. Steven Mithen's study (1996), *The Prehistory of the Mind: A Search for the Origins of Art, Religion and Science*, which looks at pre-civilised conditions, makes it clear how important it was for humans to be allowed to show their basic feelings openly, in their new world order of agriculture and settlement. Just as food was shared and dreams were narrated in the morning at a dream school, feelings, too, were shared as a matter of course. At some point in the history of Homo sapiens a feeling arose in us. The specific history of this feeling – be it rage, anger, joy, love – has the tendency to become a history of heredity. Rage is a global human phenomenon.

Theory 2

The more densely populated, industrialised, computerised and alienated from human nature the social, economic and psychological conditions of a western civilisation are, the more severe attacks of rage will be. A person's sense of self-worth, self-confidence, and self-responsibility are fed by the truth of their feelings. Their inner and outer feelings carry on developing until their last breath. In the great tribe of humanity every man and woman has his or her prescribed role in the community, and his or her own personal place. The more unclear our own psycho-social identity, the more necessary and intense our inner search for stability. If our own inner and outer stability in life is disturbed, we become anxious. The unfulfilled expectation we had as children and young people, that we had a gift for finding our own direction in life, often causes us to be angry, resentful, aggravated or enraged. These feelings gradually edge in front of our disappointment like a shield – that can (though does not necessarily) lead to emotional poisoning. "He rages like he's been poisoned," goes the German saying. The inner drive to free ourselves becomes so great that we cannot hold back and finally snap. The power of such an outburst of rage frightens the people around a rager as much as it frightens the rager himself.

Theory 3

Timid people are not given to sudden rages. Timid people would rather just say everything, indirectly for preference, and leave others to decide how it should be understood. The timid man wants nothing more than to communicate in words his inner truth, his inner world of sensation. But his shyness prevents it. He speaks indirectly, in order not to betray the longing in his words (Walser 1999). Cowards, and people who feel inferior, suffer fits of rage. They conceal their grievance, turn their anger against themselves and then suddenly explode with rage, trying to knock the injustice out of the world. In contrast to timid people, the emotional state of ragers is confused and stubborn. Sudden rages weaken us, whilst anger and rage successfully communicated make us stronger. Fits of rage are attempts to bring our emotional life back on stream.

Theory 4

Sudden rages are an attempt to build an emotional bridge over the fissures in our lives and relationships. The cocktail of emotions before, during and after a fit of rage comprises uncertainty, injury, humiliation, inferiority, aggravation, aggression, the desire for domination, mastery, revenge and injury to others (sadism), sadness, guilt and forlornness. But, as the Desert Father Abba Hypericus is quoted as saying, "Whoever fails to master his tongue in a moment of rage will not master the other passions either" (Hell 2002). Sudden rages are goal-orientated, and directed towards rectifying an unjust situation. They are an inner surge, a feeling of brutal openness which generates fear and intimidation. Sudden rages contain moments of pre-linguistic feeling which can only be expressed animalistically. In this, they are paradoxical; the "affect-logical" aspect of sudden rage, directed towards recovery, exists in a momentary freedom from feeling, room to breathe, an equalisation of the inner and outer socio-psychological pressure ratio. A sudden rage is a momentary catharsis – but it is not a lasting release into relaxation (Ciompi 1982).

Adolf Guggenbühl-Craig (1992) believes that it's helpful for psychologists and psychotherapists to revisit one of the greatest psychological and religious texts of all time. He's referring to the Book of Job. In it, God gives no kind of explanation, excuse or reason for the terrible suffering and anguish he inflicts on Job. The book is a poetic depiction of how the Almighty torments mankind. It is not a factual report, but a metaphor. In this book the interpretation is in the story. Why doesn't Job fly into a rage? "Job was always rewarded for bravely confronting the incomprehensible nature of his suffering, because God spoke to him – admittedly without explaining anything, but still, he revealed himself. What more can a human being wish for?" (Guggenbühl-Craig 1992 p. 30) The moral of the story: without morals, life becomes a living hell. The source of the spiritual life is reflected in the face of man. The elementary power of the mind is greater than the power of human reason. We should embrace the incomprehensible nature of the powerful archetypes of Psyche and Eros. Let ourselves be bewitched by their artful stories, pictures, dances, songs and music.

As both domesticated animals and embodied souls, we can never be tamed once and for all. Try as we might (and we are constantly trying), still sometimes we shape our lives; sometimes our lives shape us. The cabaret artist Thomas Breuer showed, in his 1992 piece "Café Rage", how with the help of humour, irony and wit, rage can be effectively laughed away: comedy as therapy. Laughter at the absurdity of the banal softens the pride inherent in rage, and brings peace.

Where does rage come from?

In his book *The Forest People*, Colin Turnbull (1924–94) presents his field study of the Mbuti Pygmies in the Congo, with whom he spent three years in the 1950s. Pygmies have lived in various tribes in the rainforests of Central and West Africa for thousands of years. They are also known as the "God Dancers" because of their spiritual dances. All Pygmies recognise the forest spirit *Jengi*. To them, the forest is like a gracious personal god, who provides them with everything necessary for life. They hunt antelope, wild boar, apes and fish, and gather honey, yams, berries and various plants. All known Pygmy tribes have close contact with the farming villages along the edges of the rainforest. They trade with these settlers. Turnbull tells one of the most beautiful stories I know: of how the Pygmies deal with anger and the arguments that often come with it. The members of the tribe always sleep in close proximity to each other, constructing primitive huts from wood and leaves. When a couple argues during the night, the man calls out to all his relatives, and the woman does the same to hers. The relatives all gather in front of the couple's hut and laugh over the dispute. Each and every relative knows that next time it could be them. This is a peaceful way for a society dependent on each other for their existence to deal with potentially destructive feelings such as jealousy, rage and the wish to dominate others. The Pygmies' priority is always the immediate restoration of peace in the community, rather than establishing who is guilty or right. A commotion in the middle of the night wakes the forest spirits and disturbs the gods, which is something to be avoided at all costs (Turnbull 1976 pp. 110–14).

Rage by Numbers

"We know that when the sun was born it acquired a number of planets which began to orbit it. We know that on one of these planets there was a higher concentration of the chemical elements produced in the stars, which created life, and that this life, when it was sufficiently mature, began to contemplate how the mighty system of the galaxies came into being, what it is constituted of, and what the rules are by which it moves and develops; even today there are many questions to which it has not found the answers" (Burkert and Kippenhahn 1996).

In this book I will try to find answers to some diverse open questions concerning the phenomenon of sudden rages. Our sociological research addresses concrete, real-life problems. The investigation into rages presented here applies to all those affected by them, be they victims or perpetrators. Using this questionnaire, oriented towards qualitative social research, we made the following discoveries, amongst others:

- 24% of the population of the German areas of Switzerland are "ragers"
- 22% of the population are, or feel themselves to be, victims of sudden rages
- 36% of the people questioned come into contact with rage in a domestic situation
- 68% of the people who admitted to outbursts of rage experienced these mostly in a family setting
- 61% of ragers were aware of the things that triggered an outburst
- 65% of ragers screamed, were violent towards others, and hurled and destroyed objects
- 29% of ragers didn't suffer during an outburst
- 64% of the victims had a raging father, and 16% a raging mother.

The street survey on sudden rages took place between March and May 2006 in various towns and villages in eastern Switzerland. A total of 481 people were questioned by three men and one woman – the questions are reproduced in the appendix. A further telephone survey of 94 people, carried out in July 2006 by a woman in Bern, Basel and Zürich, was to be used as a control group. These two data sources gathered from different regions in different ways – on the street and on the phone – allowed us to make a critical comparison of the results. The emotional intensity of the personal and yet anonymous encounter on the street was clearly weakened over the phone. Knowledge of the phone numbers and names of those who took part created a false impression of closeness, and the anonymity seemed to be removed. The quantitative answers were much lower than expected. However, the qualitative answers backed up what had been said on the street. Over the phone, the number of people who identified themselves as ragers was much

Where does rage come from?

lower: just 9.57%, compared with 24.32% on the street. The difference is probably made larger by the fact that the people taking part by phone were unsure as to whether our survey was really anonymous. It might be that people who were really ragers either hung up or lied to the researcher. As we will see from the results, the phone survey – randomised with regard to age and sex – turned out quite differently from the street version. As a consequence it couldn't serve as a control group, as planned. Despite this, there were valuable answers given in the phone survey to questions about the participants' understanding of rages, their meaning, and people's engagement with them, and these will be considered as part of the qualitative analysis.

Anne-Hélia Nidecker reported her experience of conducting the phone survey as follows:

> "Over the course of six days I questioned a total of a hundred people in Bern, Basel and Zürich on the issue of rage. I had never dealt with the phenomenon of sudden rages before, nor met anyone who suffered from them. I therefore had no prior knowledge when I started the survey. It soon became clear just how many people are affected. The people I had conversations with in the course of the survey fell into three categories:
>
> 1. People who had never come into contact with rages;
> 2. People who had witnessed or experienced rages at a distance – with this group I mostly got the impression that they knew about the phenomenon from hearsay, and could only pass on a story. They were imagining what these rages were like, but didn't really know;
> 3. People with first-hand experience of rages – there were victims and perpetrators (and I'm not sure whether the perpetrators shouldn't be classified as victims too: they're the victims of their own acts).
>
> For me, being allowed to hear a lot of these – sometimes very tragic – life stories made a big impression. I found it extraordinary that most of the people I asked told these stories of their own accord. A lot of the victims said how happy they were that somebody was concerning themselves with their suffering, and

that this suffering was going to be made public. I was impressed that a small number of the victims conveyed their understanding for their tormentors' outbursts of rage. The thinking was that the perpetrators couldn't help it. This is how most of the ragers saw themselves as well. From my point of view, they're trapped in an impossible dilemma: on the one hand they feel the world doesn't understand them and they lash out – on the other hand their anger ends up hurting the people who love them most. The perpetrators are for the most part very sorry for this, but even so the outbursts continue. The most difficult thing about the survey was having to deal with these stories. I felt that when they were telling them, a few of the people I spoke to really opened up to me – and I wasn't able to offer them anything, or give anything back. All I could do was listen. Sometimes I would have liked to have chatted with the ragers for longer. But I was only there to carry out the survey, and not in a professional capacity. At the end of the survey I understood the perpetrators, and now know what rages are all about. Engaging with the issue was an enriching experience that will stay with me."

Conducting research face to face, the closeness to participants in the survey was more natural and, as we learnt from experience, more productive. In summary, it can be said that telephone surveys are less well suited to qualitative field work in the social sciences.

The empirical, socio-psychological research conducted for this book uses quantitative *and* qualitative methods. Through the medium of qualitative analysis, and with the help of "grounded theory" I have tried to quantify various sections of answers in our survey in a consistent way, using "sets" (Mayring 2002, Strauss and Corbin 1996). "Grounded theory consciously permits the building of concepts (codes and constructs) during the data survey and seeks to make them transparent" (Mayring 2002 p. 104). The goal of analysing text-based answers in this qualitative way is to make both their manifest and latent sense-structure comprehensible and statistically useful. This is done by abstracting them into sets which summarise their content. The results of our research can then be either backed up or disproved at any time by a wider study using the same system of categories and sets.

TABLE 1: Sex and age of participants

Age (years)	Number of people surveyed				
	On the street		Over the phone		
	Male	Female	Male	Female	Total
<20	30	31	1	1	63
20-29	60	59	8	8	135
30-39	37	35	7	6	85
40-49	32	59	2	4	97
50-59	34	41	10	10	95
60-69	17	24	4	5	50
>70	9	13	8	20	50
Total	219	262	40	54	575

Answers were given verbally and written up by the researchers; the hermeneutics used to extrapolate quantified statements from the qualitative content of these answers allows us to characterise them, and gives us an overview of the deeper structural connections between them. It was the unconscious and subjective meanings in their structures, content and form which were important to us.

Dimitrij Itten describes the different experiences of researchers and participants during the survey as follows:

> "Several people consented to take part in the survey. However, when they were told it concerned the issue of sudden rages, they withdrew before the first question had even been asked. Rages are pretty disreputable: oh, but I don't get into sudden rages... It's possible that for many of the people we surveyed, sudden rages are associated with violence. The question: 'Do you have outbursts of rage?' was often answered in the negative – but the person being questioned still knew a lot of people who had these outbursts, and was very knowledgeable on the subject. During the survey, I tended to feel that the person I was speaking to was repressing their own rage – hence the large number of 'no's'. The people who admitted to rages were often moved by the topic: a few times we had tears and moments of silence. A lot of people didn't understand the question, 'Why do you fly into a rage?' When couples (mostly over the age of 30) took part in the survey (only one person answered; the other was waiting for them), they never answered yes to the question, 'Do you have outbursts of rage?'"

Jan Tisato found fewer people were willing to say yes to the question, 'Do you have outbursts of rage?' I think it was important for the researchers carrying out the survey to open themselves up to people, to convey a sense of security to the participants, because rage, in my opinion, is a very personal thing. It's possible that the survey was a brief form of therapy for a few of these people. A lot was said, sometimes very quickly."

TABLE 2: Contact with rage within the family

Sex	Number (%) of the following answers to the question about rage within the family		
	Yes	No	Total
Male	87 (34)	172 (66)	259
Female	122 (39)	194 (61)	316
Total	209 (36)	366 (64)	575

The demographic breakdown of the 575 participants in the survey (259 men, 316 women), is given in Table 1. Here we can see that the participants are distributed fairly evenly across the age groups. (The group most frequently asked and prepared to give answers was the 20–29-year-olds, whose ages matched those of the survey team.)

Compared to the street survey, the percentage of people in the telephone survey over 50 was greater, and the percentage over 70 most striking. These were people who were contactable on their landlines on a summer evening. Taken together, we have here a good cross-section of the population.

In Table 2, the answers are divided by the question of experience of rage within the family. 36% of the 575 participants had come into contact with sudden rages in their family.

117 (24.3%) of the 481 people questioned on the street admitted to having fits of rage themselves. In the telephone survey this was only 9 (9.5%) of the 94 people. The much lower proportion in the phone survey was presumably due to the less anonymous situation (though, as we will see, the phone survey also yielded a markedly smaller proportion of victims of sudden rages than that found by the street survey). In total, a good fifth of the sample – 22% – identified themselves as given to outbursts of rage. The results of the street survey are divided by sex and age group in Table 3.

Most people who identify themselves as ragers are between the ages of 20–29, and 40–49. Of these self-identified "perpetrators", it was only in the 30–39 and 40–49 age groups that the women (10 and 14 respectively) outnumbered the men (6 and 12). Otherwise the men were always slightly in the majority.

TABLE 3: Self-diagnosis of sudden rage

Age (years)	Number of the following answers to the question: 'Do you have outbursts of rage?'					
	Yes			No		
	Male	Female	Total (%)	Male	Female	Total (%)
<20	11	8	19 (16)	19	23	42 (11.5)
20-29	16	8	24 (20.5)	44	51	95 (26)
30-39	6	10	16 (14)	31	25	56 (15.5)
40-49	12	14	26 (22)	20	45	65 (18)
50-59	12	9	21 (18)	22	32	54 (15)
60-69	6	4	10 (8.5)	11	20	31 (8.5)
>70	0	1	1 (1)	9	12	21 (5.5)
Total	63	54	117	156	208	364

The answers of 102 people, freely formulated in response to the question of when or how they realised they had become ragers, are summarised into sets in Table 4. 66% of these people noticed this tendency in childhood and puberty. Broken down by gender, the percentages are slightly different, since more men than women tend towards sudden rages. Men experience rages more often during conflicts and emotional arguments in relationships. People who can learn and practise regulation of their emotions by the end of puberty – to demonstrate their feelings of rage and anger to others – will probably no longer experience sudden rages.

TABLE 4: Recognising your rage

The stage of development, occasion or way in which you recognised your own tendency towards rage	Number (%) of mentions		
	Male	Female	Total
Childhood	20 (36)	21 (45)	41
Puberty	13 (24)	13 (28)	26
Young adulthood (age 20-26)	8 (14)	4 (9)	12
Adulthood	2 (4)	4 (9)	6
Conflict, anger, relationships	5 (9)	2 (4)	7
Boundaries	2 (4)	2 (4)	4
Attribution	3 (5)	0	3
No idea	2 (4)	1 (2)	3
Total	55	47	102

TABLE 5: Generations of rage in the family

Number of generations	Number (%) of mentions	
	On the street	Over the phone
1	24 (4.99)	7 (7.45)
2	46 (9.56)	2 (2.13)
3	37 (7.69)	0
4	6 (1.25)	0
5	0	0
6	1 (0.21)	0
7	1 (0.21)	0
8	1 (0.21)	0
9	0	0
10	1 (0.21)	0
No details	364 (75.68)	85 (90.43)

Let us now turn towards the victims of sudden rage. Of the 575 people we surveyed, 117 people said they had been the victim of a raging parent. In the street survey alone, this was 21.8% of 481 people. Of the 94 people who took part in the phone survey, this was only 12.7%, though taken together the figure is still about 20%. This is a lot, if we allow ourselves to extrapolate this onto the whole population. For the 7 million inhabitants of Switzerland, this would mean that 1.4 million were victims of sudden rages. I mention this as evidence for my

Where does rage come from?

statement that we are facing a veritable plague on society. According to Table 2, 36% of all the survey participants came into contact with rage in their family lives (34% of men, and 39% of women).

Prior to the survey, I made a supposition, based on my own family experiences, that sudden rage was an emotional legacy handed down through a family. Table 5 shows that a good 24% of people (in the street survey) feel that the rages in their family have endured over more than one generation.

91 people answered "yes" to the question of whether sudden rages are inherited in their family. 26 people gave us additional freely formulated answers such as "it's in my nature", "it becomes a pattern if you can't resolve it", "it's a predisposition", "I'm sure this doesn't go for everyone, but at the end of the day genetic temperaments do exist", "you have to look at social factors". These statements point in a certain direction, but would have to be verified by a wider survey.

TABLE 6: Understanding of rage in the street survey

Characteristics of sudden rage	Number (%) of mentions by:					
	Perpetrators		Victims		Not affected	
	Male	Female	Male	Female	Male	Female
Sudden rage, outburst of anger (flaring up)	20 (33)	18 (35)	14 (22)	30 (35)	17 (19)	26 (22)
Snapping, an outburst (fast, flipping out)	20 (33)	11 (21)	14 (22)	16 (19)	20 (23)	33 (29)
Loss of control	10 (17)	12 (23)	21 (33)	20 (23)	22 (25)	29 (25)
Destructive anger (aggression, vicious, violence)	4 (7)	6 (12)	7 (11)	16 (19)	22 (25)	27 (23)
Asserting power (asserting yourself, showing strength)	3 (5)	4 (8)	2 (3)	2 (2)	6 (7)	1 (1)
Jealousy, powerlessness	2 (3)	1 (2)	4 (7)	1 (1)	1 (1)	0
Other	1 (2)	0	1 (2)	1 (1)	0	0
Total	60 (100)	52 (100)	63 (100)	86 (100)	88 (100)	116 (100)

The answers concerning people's personal understanding of rages are arranged in Table 6, in seven sets corresponding to the common themes taken from the raw data. We can use these to clarify empirically what is understood on the street by "rage" (see also Table 7). It will then become apparent whether the theories I put forward before the survey are backed up by these answers. If not, what should be reformulated in view of this collection of statements? Rage is a sudden outburst, accompanied by an anger that flares up or erupts. Most people who answered this question (84 of 316: 26%) understand a rage to be a sudden unleashing or outburst of fury. 24% of those who are not affected by sudden rages see them as destructive anger manifested in violence, but only 9% of ragers can be put into this set. 3.5% of unaffected people, and a little over 6% of ragers, view it as an assertion of their own position of power and a demonstration of their strength. There is also a strong consensus between affected (19%) and unaffected (25%) men and women, that a rage is a loss of control.

TABLE 7: Understanding of rage in the phone survey

Characteristics of sudden rage	Number of mentions by:					
	Perpetrators		Victims		Not affected	
	Male	Female	Male	Female	Male	Female
Sudden rage, outburst of anger (flaring up)	1	2	1	2	12	9
Snapping, an outburst (fast, flipping out)	2	1		3	10	8
Loss of control			2	2	7	4
Destructive anger (aggression, vicious, violence)		2	2	3	3	15
Asserting power (asserting yourself, showing strength)						1
Jealousy, powerlessness						
Other		1				1
Total	3	6	5	10	32	38

The survey participants understand the loss of control of oneself and one's emotions to constitute a sudden rage. The face of rage shows its emotion, naked and visible.

Where does rage come from?

The difference between extreme anger and sudden rages is not always taken into consideration. In a collaborative study by medics from Harvard and Chicago universities (Archives of General Psychiatry, quoted in *Fokus Online*, 9/6/2006), 9,282 Americans were questioned about their potential for aggression. These psychiatrists diagnosed Intermittent Explosive Disorder in subjects who experienced a serious attack of anger as little as three times a year. On average the angry subjects had 43 outbursts in a year. For most people "it" began in puberty, at the age of 14. The symptoms of Intermittent Explosive Disorder are mostly exhibited in combination with depression, anxiety, alcohol and drug misuse, and the secondary social difficulties brought on by these moods and behaviours. In the US, only 29% of affected people have been treated to date. This tells us that more people suffer from sudden rages or severe attacks of anger than has been previously been admitted.

In his lecture "Violence in care – a taboo subject?" Norbert Matscheko, the head of the Bavarian Care Institute, addresses the risk factors associated with violence. In addition to various triggers, such as mistreatment within the family, negative role models and damaged self-esteem, he cites rage as a further risk for violent behaviour. He quotes from a study conducted by the NHS, which discovered that carers were twice as likely as other health professionals (65,000 times annually) to be consumed by these feelings.

In a study addressing the question "Can we prevent road rage?" researchers from the Centre for Addiction and Mental Health at the University of Toronto investigated how the growing concern over personal safety on the roads could be addressed (Asbridge et al 2006). They reviewed 73 scientific works which took on the issues of aggressive driving and behaviour on the road, brought together in the concept of road rage. Their operative definition of road rage is: a driver or passenger tries to kill, injure or intimidate another driver or passenger, or to damage their vehicle in a collision. A study from the UK revealed that of 60 road traffic accidents involving road rage, 20% ended with a fatality and 48% with a serious injury. Most of the really dangerous perpetrators of road rage are young men, often drunk, and with psychological problems, who drive in a reckless and aggressive manner. In a study of 2,942 drivers in Ontario, almost half had been shouted at or had rude gestures made at them by other drivers. However, only 7.2% of them had been seriously verbally threatened. These authors recommend that drivers who fail their tests for driving aggressively should be identified as potential road-ragers using a test for Intermittent Explosive Disorder. These people should then be put through an additional programme focused on non-aggressive behaviour and anger management. Further suggestions for the prevention of road rage include harsher sentences for road rage as a criminal act, mass-media campaigns like the "take it easy" motorbike safety posters placed along Switzerland's roads, court injunctions stating what type of car people who have been convicted of road rage are subsequently allowed to drive, and changes to society as a whole. What this overview of the research on road rage shows is that society is getting more violent, and road rage is just one visible symptom of this general trend. Congested roads are also a trigger. Tailbacks, according to an investigation in the US, increased by over 41% between 1990 and 2002. Most recently, air rage has also become a recognised and studied phenomenon. As with road rage, the people most often responsible for this are heavy-drinking young men (Smart and Mann 2003).

TABLE 8: Positive aspects of rage for perpetrators

Positive effects of an outburst of rage	Number (%) of mentions		
	Male	Female	Total
Letting off steam, a release	24 (39)	17 (31)	41 (35)
It does me good, staying healthy	6 (10)	8 (15)	14 (12)
Making people listen or respect me	7 (11)	5 (9)	12 (10)
Asserting myself, achieving a goal	5 (8)	5 (9)	10 (8.5)
Feeling strong	2 (3)	3 (6)	5 (4)
Letting off steam, a release and it does me good	1		1 (0.85)
Letting off steam, a release and asserting myself	1		1 (0.85)
Letting off steam, a release and feeling strong	1		1 (0.85)
Other	3 (5)	6 (11)	9 (7.5)
No positive effect	13 (21)	10 (19)	23 (19.5)
Total	63	54	117

There are gender differences in sudden rages. Women experience them differently from men. As victims, women also suffer differently from male victims. But where does this difference come from? The results given in Table 8 show the extent to which this theory is corroborated. The freely formulated answers have been grouped into seven sets and a few combinations.

In the first set, 8% more raging men than women experience a release of inner tensions and letting off steam as a positive aspect of sudden rages. In the second set, 5% more women than men felt a sudden expression of rage did them good and was healthy. Making people listen and respect them, and asserting themselves with an outburst of rage is positive in equal measure for both sexes. Roughly the same numbers of men as women were unable to see a positive side to sudden rages.

Unmasking your own masquerade – is this the meaning of emotional poison? Does a rage represent a last cry of help from a feeling of helplessness? Is that the moment when the storm arrives? The whole horror of emotional torment, emotional mistreatment of children, the humiliation of others before one's own megalomania? How do children who are victims of their parents' rage endure these violent emotional eruptions? Is the reproduction in later life of what we have ourselves been subjected to merely one possibility among many? Rage comes to the surface in order to make the unconscious conscious. I have to feel my inner injuries, whether old or new. I have to realise, through reflection and contemplation, how these injuries and the rages provoked by them govern my character. We should take note of one fact from Galen's concept of the "choleric character" personality structure in a positive sense: we can apply this power and these emotional experiences where they are needed. Cholerics and melancholics balance each other, like the sanguine and the phlegmatic. It should be our goal to relax and embrace our choleric side. Jesus was most probably enraged during the cleaning of the temple. But what do we know reliably? Most of it is buried in a heap of competing opinions.

The Reasons

First impressions shape our lives. We human beings cling to them. These initial lessons shape the rest of our emotional lives, and the first influences we experience can either help or hinder our further development. Relearning is difficult; what we *can* change is the way we live with the impressions that have engraved themselves in our minds.

The hypothesis of the basic fault is a fitting one. It's part of a useful technique for furthering the transformation that takes place in and through psychotherapy.

One of my theories, mentioned in the previous section, is the following: the fault at the core of our personhood – that is, the cause of the fault in our existence as human beings – can be found in our evolutionary passage from primates to humans. We are made up of animal and human natures. We live on the boundary between nature and culture. The culture that we, Homo sapiens, have created for ourselves over the past 100,000 years is therefore also a part of our human nature. The "basic fault" is a geological metaphor. There are faults and folds in the earth's tectonic plates, which collide and rub against each other, causing major stress. Suddenly there is a release of tension: the earth quakes because the plates are sliding further along their continental fault lines, into a new resting place. I call the result of this phenomenon in human experience the first fold. This basic fold – that is, the fold in the base of our being – is an event which marks the first fault line in our unfolding life. This initial experience brands itself on our memory. Indeed, in the vernacular we characterise ourselves as manifold, multifaceted beings. In our own emotional lives and, for the purposes of this study, especially in relation to rage, we will be confronted again and again by this primary emotional reaction, which has been socially conditioned and interpersonally acquired. Here, at this fault line, on this fault in the core of my being, my animal nature and my human nature meet. They unite in this primary fold, this basic fault in the soul.

The basic fault is what joins animal and human nature in us, and makes human culture possible. It is only if we, Homo sapiens, accept and respect our dual nature, that we can live an ethically sound, emotionally balanced, truthful life.

Temple Grandin, the author of *Animals in Translation*, was a so-called "emotionally disturbed" child. She was autistic. In primary school she was often teased and bullied by her classmates for being different. She was only able to defend herself by fighting back. As a result of her aggressive behaviour, she was sent to a special school. Fortunately for her, there were animals on the school premises. She quickly learned to live with them and to love the different animals. Yet at this school, too, when provoked into arguments with other children, she defended herself with her physical strength. Her teacher punished her every time by stopping her from horse-riding

Where does rage come from?

and looking after the animals she loved so much. One day, after losing her riding privileges, she unexpectedly began to cry. She had suddenly discovered something new. From then on, she cried instead of flying into a rage and hitting back. "I'd cry and that would take away the aggression."

Even today, whenever people treat her badly, she cries. Through this emotional exchange, swapping rage for sadness, she succeeded in bringing her feelings of rage under control for her own benefit. Feelings of rage and anger often serve as a shield against sadness. When we, like Grandin, yield to sadness and cry, aggression vanishes. By crying, I allow myself to feel vulnerable, exposed, and to show my human weakness. I thus lay my shield and spear on the ground of reality and end the warlike dance of defence. Grandin was astonished to see that the children who teased her were never punished. She observed the same pattern in the animals kept by her school. The animals, too, were badgered, beaten and poorly treated. Yet the children and adults who maltreated the animals were never punished. The animals reacted with rejection and viciousness.

Autistic spectrum disorders are in many ways similar to obsessive-compulsive disorders, which essentially come under the heading of anxiety disorders. What freed Grandin from her anxiety, her basic fault, was her relationship with animals. Whenever she was with these creatures, she found appropriate ways of calming herself. She studied ethology (animal behaviour) and psychology. Thus, as a behavioural scientist she discovered that not everything is determined by conditioned learning in the environment we inhabit. Behavioural psychologists and ethologists observe animals. General cognitive and behavioural psychologists conduct their experiments on laboratory mice, rats, cats, dogs and monkeys, whereas ethologists observe animals mostly in the wild. Back in the 1960s and 1970s both groups observed animals mostly "from the outside". Temple Grandin and, with her, a new generation of scientists, observe animals from "inside the animal mind" (Smolker 2001). She studies and deals predominantly with domesticated animals such as cows, horses, pigs, sheep, dogs and cats. Being autistic, she was able to perceive and feel the slightest variances in behaviour in her surroundings, just like the animals she studied could. This special ability also came into play when anything in her physical surroundings changed. She noticed that animals, which are strongly visual creatures, are controlled by what they see. Her gateway to a deeper and more differentiated understanding of animals was her ability to see, to experience, and to feel what animals see, experience and feel. One major difference between humans and animals is that humans have what is called "inattentional" or perceptual blindness. In a NASA flight simulator study, when experienced pilots had to land a commercial plane on a runway across which the researchers had added the image of another plane – something which would never occur in reality – not only did a quarter of the pilots not see the other plane, they also landed on top of it (Grandin 2005 p. 25).

Animals perceive details in the world that we no longer see. In this day and age humans are only consciously aware of what we expect to see. It's difficult for adults to expect something that has never been seen; we perceive significantly more as children. Everything is new, fresh and only becomes subject to perceptual habit over the course of time. Language – the familiar words and concepts we use to describe our world – enables this to happen. This reminds me of the little boy I was, who had never before seen or experienced an outburst of rage. Never before had a pitchfork been used against him as a spear. In order to gain a deeper understanding of animal nature, we must take into consideration animals' love of details and of everything new in their surroundings. In simplified terms, there are three distinct groups of animals. The first group is made up of prey, the second of predators, and the third of scavengers, animals that don't hunt themselves, but feed on carrion.

Before we evolved into Homo sapiens, by way of Homo habilis and Homo erectus, and before we became predator-like hunters thanks to our invention of weaponry, we were prey for other animals. Animals that are preyed upon are flight animals. This phenomenon can be easily observed in our domestic animals such as horses, cows and sheep. A flight animal on its own will be hunted down and devoured. Most prey animals have however evolved to the point where they can survive. As primates, and as Homo ergaster, 1.5 million years ago, we definitely fell under the category of prey. Animals that fear their natural enemies benefit from formative experiences that enable them to be watchful and capable of survival.

An experiment involving monkeys and their fear of snakes serves to illustrate this theory. We pass on our knowledge, our physical experiences and our code of behaviour from one generation to the next. The knowledge of a species is so grand and multifaceted that no single generation can bring it into being, much less invent it.

Where does rage come from?

The psychologist Susan Mineka, from Northwestern University in Chicago, Illinois, and her colleague, the ethologist Arne Öhman of Sweden, have performed some fascinating experiments on the subject of formative experiences involving fear (Mineka 1992, Öhman and Mineka 2003). Their point of departure was as follows: wild monkeys are afraid of snakes, and express their fear when confronted with them; whereas lab-reared monkeys have no fear of snakes. When the wild monkeys were shown a snake by the researchers, they exhibited a strong emotional response. They pulled faces and grimaced, flapped their ears vigorously, rattled the bars of their cages, and their hair stood on end (piloerection). In addition to this, the monkeys reared in the wild did not once look at the snakes directly. By contrast, lab-reared monkeys do not fear snakes. If you show them a snake, they exhibit no fearful behaviour. Mineka's theory is that all monkeys are born without a fear of snakes. They simply possess a natural predisposition to learn to fear them. Each monkey must have acquired this fear and anxiety from other monkeys. Through her experiment, Mineka showed how quickly, easily and efficiently a lab-reared monkey can learn to fear snakes. In the first experiment she put a wild monkey in a cage with a lab-reared monkey and showed both of them a snake. The wild monkey reacted with fear, exhibiting the expected behaviour pattern. The lab monkey experienced this eruption of fear for the first time and thus acquired a lifelong fear of snakes. This learning experience was over in a couple of minutes. The lab monkey learned exactly the same emotional behaviour as the wild monkey had expressed. As soon as the wild monkey exhibited fear of snakes, the lab monkey reacted likewise. The lab monkey could then serve as a behavioural role model for other lab monkeys.

In the second experiment, the lab monkey that had acquired a fear of snakes was put into a cage with another lab monkey that had no fear of snakes. The experiment with the snake was repeated. The first lab monkey displayed the usual signs of fear, and was just as suited to the position of "teacher" as the wild monkey had been. The other lab monkey learned to fear snakes just as efficiently. These two experiments proved Mineka's hypothesis that all monkeys have a congenital predisposition to fear when exposed to certain stimuli. Evolution has enabled baby monkeys to acquire the fear of snakes that is crucial to their survival easily and quickly. As soon as the monkeys' environment means something like this is no longer important for survival, as in the case of lab-reared monkeys, the fear isn't learned as a matter of course. In a third experiment, two lab monkeys that had never seen a snake were shown one. Together they gave in to their curiosity, without fear, and investigated the snake. Neither one of them developed its latent fear of snakes. For the fourth experiment, one of these monkeys was put in a cage with a wild monkey, and both were shown a snake. The latter immediately exhibited intensely fearful behaviour; the lab monkey on the other hand was calm, curious, and did not develop a fear of snakes. The lesson is clear: the mutual fear-free first experience with a snake immunised both lab monkeys for life against a fear of snakes. The result of the study: the first physical experience, the first lesson of this type, is the one that counts. First impressions in the realm of inherited experience and behaviour shape the rest of our lives. If we grow up with a parent who is prone to outbursts of rage, then we are shaped by this experience. We develop a fear of rages. How does modern neuroscience explain the ways in which these behaviours, crucial for survival, shape our characters? In the following section, I have simplified what is otherwise an extremely complex issue into a schematic outline, which suffices to support my argument.

The Brain

Our brain is the main component of the central nervous system. We have three brains.

- The first is the reptilian brain, our brainstem: B1.

- The second brain is the mammalian brain, our cerebellum and diencephalon – or midbrain – which consists of the thalamus and the hypothalamus: B2.

- The third brain is the cerebrum, composed of two hemispheres connected to each other through the *corpus callosum*, a thick bundle of nerve fibres: B3.

The cerebrum consists of various lobes that cover the intermediate brain. Neurologists divide the cerebrum into sections corresponding to their various functions. Our cerebrum is much larger than that of most other animals; our B1 and B2 however are comparable to other mammals'. It is primarily (but not only) our emotional and survival systems that are found here.

Where does rage come from?

The latest findings in brain- and neuroscience confirm that the more intelligent a class of animals is (as seen from the human perspective), the more developed is its B3. If we remove the B3 from a human and another mammal, we cannot discern with the naked eye any major anatomical differences between their B1s and B2s. The conclusion: the B1 and B2 of a pig and a human look very much alike. Our emotional brain is similar to that of some animals. This fact is crucial for me, and to the subject of rage. Earlier phases of evolution and their development histories can be charted through the three brains. Each of the three brains has its own sense of time and space and its own memory structure. Each evolutionary phase has created its own subjective perception of the environment. We can thus say that three disparate identities reside in our brains: B1, B2 and B3. We are reptile, mammal and human, woman or man.

B1 supports and regulates our vital bodily functions such as breathing, eating, drinking, sleeping and waking. B2 controls and enables the survival instincts represented by our emotions and our social inclinations. B3 is the seat of reason, language, communication and the many other motor functions needed for human life. All three brains are interconnected through various nerves and their synapses. We know that B3 does not dominate or even control B1 and B2. The brain creates associations; the three brains interact with each other (Edelman 1992 p. 149). The current position held by neuroscience is that we have an animal nature within us, thanks to B1 and B2, which differs from our human nature. Our human nature is in turn facilitated by the combination of B3 with B1 and B2.

As beings that have evolved from primates, we still have access to earlier evolutionary structures and substances which preserved us from extinction before we became humans, and which may continue to preserve us from extinction to this day (MacLean 1990).

Since our B3 is much larger than in other animals, our brains are able to establish more connections. In contrast to even the most highly domesticated animals like dogs, we can love and hate the same person simultaneously. We are capable of living out ambivalent emotions. Animals either love or hate another animal. Their emotions remain disconnected. At the level of our inner awareness (B2) we have direct access to our senses and to an extended mind (Rupert Sheldrake's proposition of morphogenetic fields). Humans are usually no longer aware of the raw data of our environment, which is a good thing. Our B3 arranges conscious schemata for us, and we always recognise what it presents to us. The things we perceive using B1 and B2 can't be accessed by the conscious mind. The information from these two sources is filtered and metered out – otherwise we would be subject to a constant information overload.

Information overload definitely plays a role in people who are predisposed to outbursts of rage. These people describe being suddenly inundated by emotions before an outburst. At this point, they react on the level of B1 and B2. During rages, individuals react according to fixed behavioural patterns. Ethologists call this instinctive or visceral behaviour. We register certain behaviour by another person as an assault on our integrity, and we react according to preset, deeply ingrained patterns. In both animals and humans, fear serves to curb aggression during conflicts, and regulate anger and outbursts of rage. As prey animals, we were afraid of being hunted down and devoured. Nonetheless, natural anger was and is an inner resource, used as a last resort to defend ourselves against being killed. Homo sapiens is capable of understanding quite complex issues, yet the ways in which we deal with our mixed emotions is sometimes totally incomprehensible. Precisely because we have a well developed B3, we are able to stage psychodramas, experience them, and understand them. Infants and animals, both of whose B3 structure is less dominant, do not undergo such psychological difficulties. In the interests of understanding the grand arena of emotions, psychologists and psychotherapists discern between primary emotions (pE), such as hunger, love, fear, anxiety, anger and joy, which are controlled by B1 and B2, and secondary emotions (sE), such as loyalty, ambivalence and dilemma, which originate in B1 and B2, but involve the B3 due to their complexity. Thanks to this combination, pEs become sEs, through our ability to interpret simple feelings. Feelings of shame, joy, shyness, guilt, happiness and victory emerge through this process. All of these are grounded in the pE fear and stress of separation. Each and every mammal experiences this pE.

Animals whose B3 is smaller than ours are not able to quell, suppress or negate this pE, in the way humans can, having learned to do so through the process of socialisation. Thanks to B3 we can suppress, negate, cut short, transform or even sublimate pEs. SEs emerge from these processes. Neuroscientists speculate that B3 enables us to be conscious of the existence of the unconscious.

According to this explanatory model, the unconscious would be situated on the level of B1 and B2. Many of us know from our own experience that we have a tendency to suppress emotions that appear frighteningly vivid. Thanks to the support of B3, my domesticated animal nature can develop a whole range of civilised skills such as humour, altruism, empathy and intellectualisation. This emotional sophistication often helps to stave off such pEs as fear and anxiety, which are experienced as threatening. Other domesticated animals do not have this option of suppressing or transforming their pEs into sEs at their disposal.

Emotions

Emotions are real, and a somatic experience.

Language enables us to verbalise the emotional patterns we perceive in our bodies. As the saying goes: take care of your senses and the words will take care of themselves. Thanks to our B3's capacity for sophisticated, complex communication, we can behave in a social, cultivated way. We are polite and restrained, gentle and decisive, controlled and balanced. These are all words that attest to the way we bring young people up to be socially conscious, domesticated and, for the most part, pacified. However, the mantle of civilisation is thin. At the very least we have been shown this by Auschwitz and Srebrenica, but we prefer to forget. Rage is a primary emotion, and a sudden outburst of rage is an abortive attempt to control the primary emotion. The chemistry of emotions, with its molecular feelings, is a complex field of knowledge.

Our emotions are regulated primarily in B2, by the hypothalamus. One of the most important "emotional" chemicals is the neurotransmitter dopamine. As soon as the hypothalamus is stimulated, it produces more dopamine. The hypothalamus regulates our hunger pangs and our desire to mate, amongst other things. The journey is its own reward. The unfamiliar brings us pleasure. Vasopressin and Oxytocin are hormones connected with motherhood, fatherhood and with sexual behaviour. Oxytocin is very important for our social memory. Thanks to the support of this hormone, animals are able to recognise each other. In common parlance we say that we "like to smell each other". We taste and smell good. Vasopressin enables male coyotes to be sexually possessive. The emotional regulation this hormone affords is vital in helping these animals protect their hunting territory. Vasopressin promotes aggressive behaviour among males. Once a male has mated with a female for the first time, it becomes permanently more aggressive. Prior to becoming fathers, male marmosets also experience an alteration in their brain structure. Researchers at Princeton University studied the differences in density of the nerve branches in the prefrontal cortex (B3) of childless male marmosets and males who had become fathers. The brains of the fathers had a higher nerve density and more receptors for the messenger substance Vasopressin, which plays a crucial role in the psychosocial experience and behaviour of the parents (Kozorovitskiy et al 2006). Jaak Panksepp, Professor Emeritus in Psychobiology at the Bowling Green State University in Ohio, presents a model of the regulatory circuit of rage in a mammalian brain (a cat) in his comprehensive neuro-scientific study on the affects of humans and animals (Figure 1). Perceptions, thought schemata and concepts are processed and end up in the amygdala. These are compared with patterns of arousal stored from situations experienced earlier and then evaluated. A motor reaction follows, based on this evaluation.

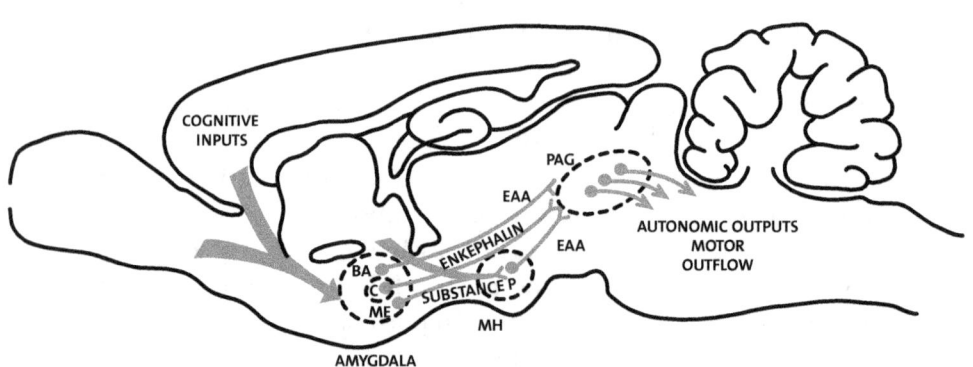

Figure 1. Rage Circuits
"Summary of the localisation of rage circuitry in a mammalian brain" (Panksepp 1998 p. 195) Perceptions, thought schemata and concepts reach the amygdala (BA, basal amygdala; C, central amygdala; ME, medial amygdala). Through changes in the concentration of Substance P in the medial hypothalamus (MH) and of encephalin and excitatory amino acids (EAA) in the periaqueductal grey (PAG), autonomous commands for motor behaviour emerge.

Where does rage come from?

The better we understand this emotional circuitry in our brain, the better we can understand the emotional foundation of our rage. We have to feel and accept the dominating force in our brains that we experience as an inner thrust of rage, and understand how this leads us to hit someone in the face. Like other researchers investigating neurodynamic processes, Panksepp sees the primary emotional systems of rage and fear as intermingled. He sees war and other destructive, aggressive human acts as triggered by B3, because social conditioning is responsible for them. He suspects that sociopathic tendencies result from a combination of genetic inheritance and the chemistry of aggression, a topic we will not pursue further in this study. According to Panksepp, anger is generated by stimuli in the social environment, whereas rage is triggered by neural circuits. As he points out, "...a human baby typically becomes enraged if its freedom of action is restricted simply by holding its arms to its sides" (p. 189). Our brains, formed by experience and evolutionary processes, have been conditioned to search for the motives of strong feelings outside ourselves. Besides the reflex that tells us to play dead, rage is our next best survival strategy, allowing us, when preyed upon, to escape our enemy's imminent deadly bite. Rage, and the sudden, violent rages which are the subject of this book, are powerful thrusts of energy that can enable us to escape from deadly dangers with our lives. Panksepp sees this fact as a basis for the future development of our emotional lives. As mature adults we can express our primitive emotional impulses in words and through language, thanks to years of socio-cognitive learning.

I interviewed brain researcher and neuroscientist Gerald M. Edelman about his work, and in particular the fact that affective neuroscience uses his research on consciousness as a basis for its view of the role that the emotional systems in the brain play in the makeup of social systems. Edelman says:

> "I can say the following: We know we have a selectional theory of the brain. The brain has an astronomical number of possible connections. The variation in its connectivity is the basis for selection after interaction with the world. But in order for the selectional system to work, other factors must come into play. The brain is embodied and the body and the brain are embedded in the world. Evolution plays a critical role by giving us value systems, diffuse ascending systems that release neurotransmitters

during our behaviour. These systems constrain selective responses. They include, for example, the *locus coeruleus* which releases norepinephrine, the cholinergic system which releases acetylcholine, and the dopaminergic system which releases dopamine for reward. These systems are deeply connected with emotional responses. They are absolutely necessary as constraints on selectional systems, which otherwise would never converge. What makes us human is a specific set of ways in which out emotional constraint systems interact with our thalamacortical system. So we need both to work. The interesting comment is this: the thalamacortical system depends very richly on interactions of an individual with the world, whereas the other systems are inherited and give you species-specificity. That is to say, we would not expect the value system of a tiger to be the same as that of a human being. We have to account for the fact that we are the only species to have true language. We have constructed a model of the value systems. What we find is that value systems without modification give rather fixed responses. But if you change the set points of these systems by learning, you get a very rich set of interactions that amplifies the capacity for learning. And the opportunity for learning is, of course, enormously enhanced by social interactions" (Itten 2006).

Edelmann's response reveals how complex the question of ethically sound emotional behaviour is.

Our neural network enables us to develop the motive-oriented power to make an impression on other people with an outburst of rage. Various impulses coming from six different sections of the brain give rise to feelings and outbursts of rage. All of these impulses are interdependent, and of course influenced by other factors, such as changes in blood pressure.

Boundaries

Territorial boundary protection is important for wolves in terms of survival, reproduction and getting enough to eat. Habitual rage is particularly helpful when other animals do not respect these boundaries. The psychologist Andrea Camperio Ciani, from the University of Padua in Italy, has conducted research comparing the evolutionary advantage of animals that experience and show rage compared to those that do not. If we consider outbursts of rage from a strategic point of view and not in terms of the process of stimulus and reaction, then rage appears to be a hugely significant adaptation: firstly, as an emotion preceding an aggressive action; and secondly, as an act of communication. Camperio Ciani investigated this type of communication with the help of game theory, in order to detect exactly when and why an individual gains a selective advantage when bluffing or simulating rage (2000). Frans de Waal (2006) confirms Camperio Ciani's results.

All domesticated animals – including Homo sapiens – have a social disposition, living in groups, clans and droves. The current hotly-debated theory of the co-evolution of wolf and man (Homo sapiens) over the last 50,000 years, and of dog and man over the last 15,000 years is very interesting.

Dogs are not mature wolves, but wolves that have been kept juvenile. Mature wolves don't bark; dogs bark to protect their territory. Various experts believe that one major reason for dogs' evolution from wolves is that human mothers breastfed orphaned wolf pups and raised them alongside their own offspring. It is thanks to this co-evolution with wolves and dogs that we became the Homo sapiens that we have been for 15,000 years. Our pets and domesticated animals share a similar emotional development with us. Neuro-psychologists have been able to observe this similarity in their research on emotions. Most of what we know today in affective neuroscience has been made possible by the domestic animals we use for research purposes. The Neanderthals, for example, did not domesticate wolves; they did not cultivate co-evolution with dogs; and they did not survive as a species.

Scientists have detected an overall decrease in the brain size of domestic animals. The size of horses' brains has diminished by 16%, dogs' by 30% and humans' by 10%. They compared the brain size of our direct ancestors, Homo heidelbergensis and the Neanderthal, with that of Homo sapiens. Our joint evolution with dogs resulted in a deterioration of our senses of smell and hearing. Our brains and those of dogs became specialised for specific functions. Early man took over planning and organisational tasks; dogs took over the duties of sensing danger, warning humans and protecting their territory. Fear and anxiety were reduced in domestic animals living with humans. With us, they are safer than those of their kind still living in the wild (Camperio Ciani 2000).

Homo sapiens learned the essentials of survival from wolves. Wolves hunted in groups, which the Homo sapiens of the time did not. Wolves had complex social structures; Homo heidelbergensis did not. Wolves had same sex friendships and friendships outside their families; our ancestors did not. Wolves are, in addition, strongly territorial creatures, which we as primates were not. The most recent genetic studies on the evolutionary divergence of dogs from wolves date this period of domestication to between 40,000 and 15,000 years ago. The dog graves recently excavated by archaeologists are up to 14,000 years old. One of these graves can be found in Bonn-Oberkassel, Germany. This proves that ever since man put down roots, he has always loved dogs and has buried them in the same way as his own relatives (Simonds 2005).

When we feel good or bad, three basic reactions, or brain systems, are always activated: firstly, the pain or pleasure reaction; secondly, the connection of this to a place; and thirdly, the necessary body temperature regulation. We are social beings with a strong need to belong. People who love each other become dependent on each other. It is not only the pleasant warmth of a social bond that has a hand in this, but the opiates of love at work in the brain. It is only natural for differences and conflicts to occur between individuals in social relationships, and one party or the other may react to this with rage. The frontal lobes (though not only these) of B3 censor, monitor and control our outbursts of rage, which are often accompanied by screams of pain. Despite being complex, socio-culturally conditioned and domesticated, in certain circumstances everyone has the capacity to blunder into the realm of primary emotions, steered by B1 and B2. This is triggered by the actions of secondary emotions: when the primary emotion of rage is inhibited and pent up by the effects of ethical, moral and religious doctrine, this can result in an outburst of rage. Regulating the expression of our primary and secondary emotions is, in this sense, a continuous cultural process, which can often also be a healing process. The great story of human evolution has been told all over the world through many shorter stories, in various creation myths.

Just as there is a doctrine of grace in the Judao-Christian tradition – "for we walk in the grace of God" (Cassian, 360–430 AD), through which our sins of pride, greed, envy, lust, sloth, gluttony and wrath are supposed to be subdued – there is a Buddhist doctrine of deliverance in the Noble Eight-fold Path: right view, right intention, right speech, right action, right livelihood, right effort, right mindfulness and right concentration. Both of these doctrines show how what we see is looked upon. I have always seen the world through my own eyes and from my own perspective. It's about observing the observer of the observers (Dürrenmatt 1986). I see you looking at me looking at you looking at me. Although we have many doctrines of the right, good and true way of living – the best known exponents of these are the three great inspirers, *de tribus impostoribus*: the shepherd Moses, the carpenter Jesus, and the camel driver Mohammed – we often live at odds with the world, finding no lasting peace of mind on earth. Now and then we find ourselves dancing on the fault line of man's emotional basic fault. Cassian sees life as full of suffering. The cause of this suffering lies for him in the hunger for meaning, in the desire, the passion for life, and the thirst for knowledge. We suffer from greed, hate, conceit, conventionality, delusions of faith and the power we exert over others. The lives of people who have nothing to eat or drink are full of suffering too, but their suffering is not caused by the hunger for meaning or the thirst for knowledge. Here dogma collides with values born of our own experience. The ancient Catholic Church invented the idea of original sin. We are all born sinners.

The Basic Fault

The Hungarian doctor Michael Balint (1896–1970) transformed the notion of original sin into the concept of the basic fault in humans in his 1968 book *The Basic Fault: Therapeutic Aspects of Regression*. Balint came to the UK as a Jewish refugee in 1939. He lived in Manchester with his first wife Alice until her death, and stayed there until 1945 before moving to London. He underwent analysis with Sándor Ferenczi (1873–1933), and subsequently became the trustee of Ferenczi's estate. In London, Balint worked in the Family Discussion Bureau of the Tavistock Clinic. He is best known for his "Balint Groups", where he taught doctors and social workers to look carefully at the psychosomatic aspects of illness, to reflect on what they were doing, and on the reactions the patient and the patient's concerns could provoke in them. He became one of the most important and influential psychoanalysts in the Independent Group of the British Psychoanalytic Society, which he headed from 1968 to 1970. As a psychotherapist, he knew that without doctors having a profound sympathy for their patients, they had no hope of alleviating their mental suffering.

In the essay published in 1923, "The Dream of the 'Clever Baby'", from which Balint developed his concept of the basic fault, Ferenczi (1980) tells of how we dream about wise babies "who are able to talk or write fluently, treat one to deep sayings [...] give learned explanations, and so on" (p. 349). He saw in this our wish to become knowledgeable. "We should not forget that the young child is in fact familiar with much knowledge, as a matter of fact, that later becomes buried by the force of repression". In a footnote he remarks: "that such dreams illustrate the *actual* knowledge of the child on sexuality" (p. 350).

My theory of the basic fault, the fault in the base of our being, is that our human and our animal natures lie in close proximity, and flow into each other. This fact is seen by most moral and ethical religious representatives as a human flaw. Kierkegaard, Nietzsche, and other thinkers who were tormented by pain, give us the insight that there is no escaping this existential pain. All the religious and esoteric lies and illusions in the world cannot convince us that we are not domesticated animals. The truth will set you free. Free to live according to the true nature that slumbers within us – and that means being able to express our feelings of rage as well as joy. A moment of sudden rage is an attempt to break free of the complications of nature and culture. It is like an attempt to escape the tightening emotional knots of our animalistic nature, and those of the reason-loving human. The shocking suddenness of an outburst of rage is a moment where "an abyss opens and closes" (Colli 1993 p. 72), a moment of deep recognition where your own beliefs cease to function and reality breaks into your world. Beneath the basic fault lies the experience of primary love, experienced in the womb. After we are born, we all need to continue our experience of this harmonious, peaceful, Edenic love. Two individuals, for the most part mother and child, are bound to each other in a harmonious mish-mash. No conflict has yet been experienced. Traumas experienced in this early stage of life can create the basic fault. In Balint's words: "...in geology and in crystallography the word fault is used to describe a sudden irregularity in the overall structure, an irregularity which in normal circumstances might lie hidden but, if strains and stress occur, may lead to a break [...] Although highly dynamic, the force originating from the basic fault has the form neither of an instinct nor of a conflict. It is a fault, something wrong in the mind, a kind of deficiency which must be put right. It is not something dammed up for which a better outlet must be found, but something missing either now, or perhaps for almost the whole of the patient's life. [...] The adjective 'basic' in my new term not only means that it relates to simpler conditions than those characterising the Oedipus complex, but also that its influence extends widely, probably over the whole psychobiological structure of the individual, involving in varying degrees both his mind and his body" (Balint 1968 pp. 32–3). The basic fault is thus experienced as an absence of this comfortable relationship between mother and child. Every person has their own fault. The basic fault can also be called a "paradise complex". Each and every soul is cracked in the process of becoming human, being incarnated.

Coming into the World

When I come into the world – the real world, shared with other people and other living things – I am limited from the start. Humans are beings with borders. "My" egg, which was already present together with all the other eggs she would ever produce, was inside my mother when she was an embryo inside my grandmother's womb. My grandmother was rooted in a community, living in a particular society, at a specific time, in a specific place. When "my" sperm left my father to meet "my" egg, it was drawn in by the dancing threads around the edge of the cell. And there, where the sperm cell slipped through, the first cell division took place. The individual unit of the egg was bisected with the unit of the sperm. Then followed the familiar pattern of cell division into 4, 8, 16, 32, 64...the two-in-one divided up to 2 to the power of 64. Only from this point on, from landing and attaching to the wall of the uterus (the endometrium), did "I" begin to grow. A magical, mysterious organic chemistry created my body out of the dual unity to the power of 64, and joined it to my mother's body by the placenta. We know, and believe we know, a great deal about how and when the growth of this embryonic life takes place. This is where the explanatory model of "embryologems" comes from. Various approaches taken from the natural sciences and humanities have been used to shape this area of speculative research, in order to achieve the optimal description of the nine months we spend in utero.

Everything influences my existence: my mother's social world, her relationship with my father, her relationship to her parents, their relationship to their parents – my great-grandparents. This is a span of four generations, which is still relatively manageable. There are, starting with me, $1 + 2 + 4 + 8 = 15$ people involved. At the next stage up, there are $16 + 32 + 64 = 112$ people. A curse on seven generations would affect 127 people. If we wanted to consider all the relationships between these people analytically, the sheer complexity of form and content would necessitate a biographical study like Sartre's Flaubert (four volumes). And then? Are we smarter than before? No: we just know more.

Just as pregnancy is divided into three trimesters, so we divide our lives into three parts: childhood and youth, adulthood, and old age. We live in the beginning, the middle and the end of life. We divide our perceived reality into inner and outer portions. And we often forget that the reality we see, experience and subjectively interpret is just a part of the whole, which we can never see clearly and distinctly. To split up an experience into subjective and objective is to divide and abstract where a whole exists. Just as we speak of different muscle groups in the body, even though the whole body has an overarching musculature, we can talk about an inner and outer life of the mind. But our experience and our behaviour always belong together: they are dependent upon each other and determine each other.

Ronald D. Laing (1927–89) divided spiritual structures and experiences into three areas: structures arising from embryology (embryologems), from the human mind (psychologems) and from myths (mythologems). In *The Voice of Experience*, his study on embryo-psychology, he tried to describe some of the structures expressed in our bodies, our minds, and our mythic rituals. – "In every case the pattern in the patterns, the common pattern, the theme within the variations, has no name of its own" (Laing 1982 p. 109). These structures can be recognised in the patterns of our own lives. They give us the formal patterns of life (our metaphors) which are reflected in our individual patterns of our own origins: intrinsically insightful content. The metaphor of the basic fault serves here as a psychologem. This is an experiential pattern in which habits are repeated. Using this we can recognise ourselves as "patterned". Sudden rage is an attempt to free ourselves from the gravity field of the basic fault. Paradoxically, by erupting from emotional stalemate, we are enacting a reaction against the basic fault which not only fails to really free us but, on the contrary, causes us to sink right back to the place we were trying to escape from.

Rage is not listed in chapter V of the ICD-10 international classification of mental and behavioural disorders. It does not appear in the index of the 15th edition of the classic work of psychiatry by Eugen and Manfred Bleuler (1983). Rage is missing from the index of most textbooks written by those psychiatrists and psychologists whose focus is largely diagnostic. I have no problem with this and hope it remains the case: the emotional release achieved through sudden rage is not a psychological "disorder" in the proper sense of the word. It is an unsuccessful engagement with the primary emotion of rage. However, people given to sudden fits of rage repeatedly hurt those around them and also, inevitably, themselves. There is of course the so-called "anger syndrome", Intermittent Explosive Disorder, extensively used by American psychiatrists. Three or more outbursts per year are necessary in order for this new diagnosis to be applied to a patient. A sudden outburst of rage brings with it a moment of mental alleviation. This is a fact substantiated by empirical science. As soon as the rage has evaporated, the sense of shame it brings with it rises up to take its place. It is mixed with an unspeakable sadness, which people cannot always articulate – sadness over having shocked, intimidated and hurt one's fellow men, not to mention the broken crockery and other objects. I myself destroyed a violin I'd inherited from my grandfather, Arnold Itten, in a fit of rage – I had to re-model it into a guitar, because my father, who at the time I considered narrow-minded, refused to buy me one. Straight away I pushed the "guilt" for this angry, destructive behaviour onto my father. He had turned me into my own victim. In my rebellious pubescent mind, I ascribed responsibility to him. His unregenerate sacrifice of his father's violin was carried out through me. This power-play by the perpetrator-as-victim is a frequently used and twisted logic for excuses, and is born of a bad conscience. We have spent more than 2,000 years living in a "guilt culture" shaped by Christianity, which in terms of ethics and mental hygiene cannot hold a candle to the ancient Greek "shame culture".

Jesus (the Hebrew Yeshua), who was oriented towards cultural and psychological change, tried to free our souls from the culture of guilt. "Come to me, all you who are weary and weighed down. And I will refresh you. Lay all your burden of sins and guilt on me, the sacrificial lamb of the Almighty, so that you may live free of them." To live free of the basic fault. To have the choice to live in another way, if you have the ability and the inclination. The question of guilt belongs in the domain of social justice. There it must be decided who is guilty of what and must therefore make amends. The psychological apportioning of blame is futile and never leads to an emotional release. It is hollow and empty, and only has temporary meaning. Ascribing guilt to somebody does not solve any of life's difficulties. On the contrary, this sort of emotional manipulation creates problems where there were none before. This problem-oriented power-play forces us to look for solutions where there aren't any. A socio-psychological habit like this can only be changed by adopting a new art of living. This way I can take responsibility for the way I am suddenly gripped or possessed by rage. The "point of no return" in a fit of rage can be seen just before it is reached. After every attack, a fresh possibility exists not to carry on being this false self, but to liberate yourself by reflecting on what you've experienced. The metaphor of the basic fault can be helpful, like a raft taking me from one bank of my life to the other. In this way every theory, together with its models, is a raft on the ocean of life.

Creation Myths

Following on from these reflections on the basic fault in human life, here is another variation of the creation story from our Greek ancestors.

> There were once three brothers. They were called:
> Zeus   who lived above   on Mount Olympus
> Poseidon who lived in the middle in the sea
> Hades   who lived below   in the underworld

All three regions of life are represented and occupied by these roles. These three gods are the sons of Chronos and Rhea. Rhea hid Poseidon safely in the middle of a herd of sheep, so that Chronos could not find him and eat him: the father as predator, hunting the son as prey. It all went well; Poseidon grew up and married Theophane, whose name means "she who appears as a goddess". However, a wild, powerful god like Poseidon is very highly sexed, and also lusted after his sister, Demeter. This goddess of fertility,

Where does rage come from?

described as clever, wise and cunning, changed into a mare to protect herself. Poseidon noticed her deception and coupled with Demeter in the form of a stallion. His sister was so incensed by this act that she changed into Erinys, the goddess of rage. Then there was no more horse-play.

This story, a myth, is what the Greeks told their children when they wanted to know why it was they got angry. But why is there a goddess of rage? If a feeling is given a name, we can play with it. Understandably, Demeter did not want to linger unnecessarily as Erinys. She took herself to the river Ladon, let herself sink into its waters, and magically washed herself clean of her rage. After her bath, her love of life returned – but she was pregnant by Poseidon. She bore a daughter, the nymph Despoena, and the black-maned horse-god Arion. Demeter's anger at this experience was so fierce that in some places she is still honoured as Demeter the Fury (Graves 1969 p 61). Demeter is the earth-mother, mother earth. She is ever-changing, so that she can mix with other living creatures. If she is caught out, as she was by Poseidon, she flies into a rage. Poseidon believed she was playing a trick on him, though Demeter's only thought was to protect herself from his lust. If one person wants something that another doesn't, it can lead to a power struggle over who can and must do what. Do we rage when, like Demeter, somebody sees through our masquerade? The minute my false self ceases to afford me protection and I can't deceive myself and others about my true feelings, an outburst of rage precedes a phase of disappointment. I am exposed. I am simply myself. Why should I be someone else, when I can just be myself? Being disappointed or disillusioned is like being discovered, uncovered. There is no illusion any more – I am not fooling anyone. Sudden rage is an acknowledgement of the latent feeling of rage within me. This is the beginning of something new. When Perseus, the wanderer, had cut off the head of the Medusa (one of the faces of Erinys), the magical horse Pegasus leapt out of her neck (Kerényi 1972 p. 114). Another story about the creation of the first horse in Greece tells of a contest between Poseidon and Athena. In a rage, Poseidon struck his trident against the rocks of the Attic Plain, and the horse came forth out of the bedrock. Another story about fits of rage in the eclectic mythology of ancient Greece is that of the snow-white raven. It was Apollo's favourite bird, and Apollo asked it to watch over his beloved, the princess Coronis, whilst he saw to his affairs in Delphi. When the bird brought news of Coronis's marriage to Ischys, Apollo's rage was focused on the messenger. He cursed the raven for not pecking out Ischys's eyes – and from then on all ravens were black. Thus jealous rage as well as sudden, violent rage is deployed in Greek myths for the spontaneous punishment of another creature.

Apollo complained to his sister Artemis of his unhappiness in love, and she drew one arrow after another and let them rain down on Coronis to avenge her brother. Meanwhile Zeus, the proud father of the gods, punished Ischys with a bolt of lightning. Coronis had been pregnant by Apollo before the wedding. Her spirit was already in Tartarus, and her body was laid out on a funeral pyre, when Apollo came to his senses. He was distraught by Coronis's death and tried to bring her back to life, but failed. Hermes intervened. By the light of the flames he cut the baby, Asclepius, from the body. Apollo took his son to the cave of the centaur Chiron. This teacher of the healing arts and proverbs cared for and taught the boy, who was to become the leader and demigod of Epidaurus, the most famous therapeutic centre of the ancient world. When Asclepius brought three dead people back to life, he annoyed Hades, who complained of him to Zeus and stoked his rage to such a point that he killed the divine doctor on the spot with a bolt of lightning (Graves 1969 p. 175; Kerényi 1972 p. 146).

The famous symbol of the healing god, the snake around the staff, still adorns the signs of pharmacies in many countries, and the logo of the World Health Organisation. In these brief fragments of myth, we can sense the dangerous, sometimes deadly nature of sudden rage. When I feel secure in my own cunning, when I think that I have fooled everyone, but they then see through my ruse and fool me in turn, nothing can stand in the way of an attack of rage. This fearful emotion, and the things that result when it is released, can be bathed away as Demeter demonstrated. And so I give myself over to the cult of Hygieia, the goddess of health.

In the Tanakh or Hebrew Bible, which comprises the books of the Old Testament, there are four stories about the wrath of God.

> And the people cried unto Moses; and Moses prayed unto the LORD, and the fire abated. (4. Moses, 11.2)

Yes, how often we complain, and wish aloud that we'd never been born. Hearing this, the Almighty and Eternal God, the creator, is gripped by a fiery rage. And then we feel threatened when because of our existential lamentations, the boundaries and protective walls of our nomadic encampments are breached by fire, which we interpret as the fire of the Almighty. Fire drives the lions away.

> And Israel joined himself unto the Baal of Peor; and the anger of the LORD was kindled against Israel. And the LORD said unto Moses: "Take all the chiefs of the people, and hang them up unto the LORD in face of the sun, that the fierce anger of the LORD may turn away from Israel." (4. Moses, 25.3–4)

> For a fire is kindled in My nostril, and burneth unto the depths of the nether-world, and devoureth the earth with her produce, and setteth ablaze the foundations of the mountains. (5. Moses, 32.22)

The fiery rage of the Almighty will burn up everything, raze it to the ground, and so threaten the basis of our existence. The foundations of my emotional and personal habitus are shaken. I realise it can't go on like this; the basic fault and the story of our fall from grace, seen as a social morality tale. How can I free myself from the things I've learnt and acquired? Either we change our way of life or become religious? The answer lies in conversion – *Teschuwa* (Hebrew), *Metanoia* (Greek).

In human society, in being with each other, we need to experience the truth of our feelings again and again. This is the life-affirming justice necessary for "you and I", "them and us": live and let live. The end never, ever justifies the means.

Psychotherapy can always provide an oasis of peace in our everyday lives.

The soul, hardened and stiffened by the blows life deals us, can be made soft and porous again. True psychotherapy as a caring treatment for body and soul leads to a *Metanoia*. There is then a "before" and "after", bound together by a continuity which is at first imperceptible. The insight into this new continuity is the ethos of therapy: in his "you", every "I" finds his own being. The therapeutic duet, the conversation of souls, is the foundation of being together in human society that we can all experience.

Rage in Animals

Temple Grandin notes with interest how dominant domesticated dogs have to be kept down physically, low to the ground. Once a dog experiences the killer instinct of hunting again, it can't be put back in its place. Grandin also recognises that human stress factors, and mistreatment of animals, can fuel the animals' rage. She gives the example of how Springer Spaniels have been over-bred so that they are in a constant state of alertness and tension. What has happened now is that there is a specific Springer "sudden rage syndrome" which comes over the animals as suddenly as an epileptic fit. The aggression released as a result of this can be a cause for concern.

Grandin differentiates between two sorts of animal aggression: the hunting aggression of the predator and emotional, affective aggression.

In administering a killer bite, predators exhibit a fixed sequence of behaviour that never changes. The prey is held down until it suffocates. For all predators, a sudden movement provides a trigger for pursuit and attack. Police officers who have to operate in dangerous, potentially fatal situations, experience something similar. If a suspect moves quickly and unexpectedly, officers are liable to open fire. This is why they usually shout: Stop! Stay where you are! Don't move! A situation like this can lead to a discharge of both emotion and ammunition – and there are often deaths.

When a predator makes a kill, the rage-zone in its brain is never activated. Anyone who has observed cats will know that predators always kill silently.

Things are different when it comes to affective aggression. During fights over territory, whether the goal is defence of a hunting area or supremacy within the herd, rage can be activated. An enraged animal makes a lot of noise, stands erect and makes itself look bigger, aiming to strike fear into its opponents and to defend itself. But sudden rage is a painful emotion. Humans and animals alike, according to Grandin (2005 p. 139), "do not enjoy having their rage circuits turned on, and will avoid it if they can". Affective aggression is so-called "hot", driven aggression. Cats are a good example of this, as their hair visibly stands on end (piloerection) and their backs arch into a bridge as they puff themselves up. They are electrified, totally alert, and their hearts beat much faster than normal – the adrenalin system is fully activated.

This is similar in humans: when we fly into a rage our affective-aggressive animal nature is activated. A fascinating experiment was conducted by Raleigh and others, in which dominant aggressive pets were given Prozac (fluctine) (quoted in Grandin 2005 p. 144). This antidepressant, intended for humans, caused an increase in the animals' serotonin levels: the lower the serotonin, the more aggressive the animal. This should be kept in mind for when we come to the issue of depression and rage. Is an affective aggression, suppressed and directed inwards, in fact an aspect of depression (when we view depression as chronic fragmentation, filled with old grief, and the unacknowledged feeling of living a lie)? Taking this into consideration, a few things become clearer about why we, as Homo sapiens and former primates, have this propensity for sudden rage. What is the rage switch in our brains for? Sudden, violent rage is our primitive last resort, a final attempt to assert power and stay safe from the deadly bite of a predator with us in its sights. In the wild, when a lion attacks a buffalo, the buffalo still has a chance to save itself with the help of rage. This also goes for primates and our predecessors, Homo erectus, before we were able to protect ourselves in other ways. The theory arising from this would be: rage is the final mode of defence for an animal whose life is in danger. Prey animals are much more fearful than predators. Humans are familiar with this feeling, when we are manoeuvred into a corner or pressed up against a wall. Rage sets in at this point, and makes its presence felt through a powerful inner strength that can be used in our defence. After every outburst of rage, it is important for us to note whether it came from the urge for dominance or defence.

Aggression

Grandin (2005 p. 143), lists the following sorts of animal aggression:

1. Assertive aggression. This category includes dominance aggression and territorial aggression.

2. Fear-driven aggression. This includes maternal aggression to protect young.

3. Pain-based aggression.

4. Intermale aggression. Intermale aggression is influenced by testosterone levels.

5. Irritable or stress-induced aggression. This includes redirected aggression, such as when a cat gets agitated by the sight of another cat outside but can't get to it so attacks another cat or person inside the house instead.

6. Mixed aggression. For instance, fear combined with assertive aggression.

7. Pathological aggression.

Grandin comes to the extraordinary conclusion that animals with the most complex brains, like humans, are the self-same creatures that are capable of the cruellest and worst behaviours. Is this the price we pay as a species for this grandiose complexity: that there is so much more, organically speaking, to go wrong? Still, we have the greatest flexibility in our feelings and behaviour: good, bad and everything in between. Lonely animals and humans tend more towards rage than those who live in communities that function well emotionally and socially. In children who have been emotionally neglected and so tend towards oppositional behaviour, we note that they react aggressively to ambiguous, unclear situations rather than recoiling from them in fear as most children do. At such moments, a fit of rage can mask emotional pain. Although these children also feel fear, they direct attention away from it. In this case, a sudden bout of rage is an escape from an unbearable situation. This becomes fascinating when we differentiate between fear and anxiety.

Fear is an emotional reaction to an outside threat: I tread on a snake. Anxiety is an emotional reaction to an inner threat: I think I'm treading on a snake.

Fear gives rise to the familiar concept of "fight or flight". When I'm afraid, I know exactly what is really happening. In these moments it becomes clear to us why we are emotional beings: thanks to our feelings, we are able to survive, and to know that nothing is neutral. For the most part, emotions are unconscious and require us to pay attention to what we *sense*, not what we think.

Philosophers' Rage

Our logic is determined by our emotions and not vice-versa. The following story is a little anecdote which illustrates this. Edmonds and Edinow (2005) recount how, on Friday 25th October 1946, the incumbent Professor of Philosophy at Cambridge, Ludwig Wittgenstein, threatened Karl Popper, Reader in Logic and Scientific Method at the London School of Economics and a guest lecturer at the Moral Science Club, with a poker. Bertrand Russell, the third great philosopher at this evening session, was himself shocked by the violent exchange of words between Wittgenstein and Popper, which began shortly after the start of Popper's lecture. It is a fascinating fact that there are so many different and often conflicting recollections of this emotional event. Popper claimed that real philosophical problems existed, but Wittgenstein interrupted him and said that there were only "puzzles" determined by language, which could be solved by various linguistic games. Whereof we cannot speak, thereof we must be silent, and simply live out the experience. Popper and Wittgenstein had their sights set on each other before this, their first and only personal contact. From the very beginning the situation was emotionally laden. When Wittgenstein interrupted the lecture: "Wrong, Popper – what you're saying is wrong," Russell, who was sitting between the two antagonists, sternly accused Wittgenstein of never being able to listen to what other thinkers had to say. "You misunderstand me, Russell, you always misunderstand me" (Edmonds and Edinow 2005 p. 144). Wittgenstein played with or brandished the poker (depending on which report you believe), trying to make his position clear, which he didn't succeed in doing because he was fast becoming angry. On being challenged by Wittgenstein over the validity of moral rules, and asked to give one as an example, Popper answered: "Not to threaten visiting lecturers with pokers". That was too much for Wittgenstein. He laid/threw/flung the cold/hot/glowing poker (again, depending on who you believe) down on the floor and stormed out of the seminar room in King's College, slamming the door behind him. Rage even has power over loud, stubborn logicians.

Neurologists

It is only thanks to emotion that we can guess and foretell the future. It is the instinctive aspect of our nature. Many people who suffer from rage are often cut off from their other feelings. Antonio Damasio (2000), a neurologist and brain scientist, says that our higher cognitive facilities would break down if the underlying emotional system was destroyed. If he had to choose between the cognitive and the emotional system, he would choose the emotional. Feelings give us a feeling for what is going to happen, so we can make the right decision. The process usually takes milliseconds: first the feeling is there, then I accept the feeling, which is intentionally directed, and finally I reach a decision: all in the blink of an eye. The qualities which are particular to human consciousness: pain, rage, colours, heat, audible tones etc. are a subjective experience of "qualia". Gerald M. Edelman's hypothesis of a "dynamic core" shows how every conscious experience which can be distinguished from others constitutes a "quale". This can be a primary perception, an idea, a thought, or a mood. When viewed retrospectively, qualia appear by themselves, and then as part of a composition. Thus sudden rage would be a quale of suppressed rage that can't be held back any longer and so erupts (Edelman and Tononi 2001).

In Klaus Grawe's book on neuro-psychotherapy (2004), aggression, anger, rage and other primary emotions don't appear in the index. Given we know that aggressiveness is linked to the rage-circuits in our brains, this omission is astounding.

Joseph LeDoux asks whether we rule our emotions or whether they rule us. For him, rage in all its forms belongs to the primary emotions in man and beast. As a successor to Charles Darwin, who linked the two emotions of fear and rage and saw the expression of these as an involuntary action, LeDoux regards a sudden fit of rage as rage which has not become cortically conscious and therefore controlled. Sudden rage is usually activated by sensory impressions directly via the hypothalamus, without first passing through the sensory cortex.

As a result we can say that sudden rage is mostly triggered unconsciously – that is, outside of conscious perception. I believe it was LeDoux (1996 p. 82), who proposed a fascinating experiment on this theme. We find a narrow alleyway that lies in almost complete darkness, and put a piece of wood that looks like a snake on the ground. Then we let our subjects walk into this alley. As soon as they notice the object on the ground, they quickly run back. At a safe distance they stop, think about it, and wonder if it might have been a branch. And so they walk back slowly, led by their curiosity. LeDoux calls this the fast and the slow pathway of knowledge.

Sudden outbursts of rage are fast; simmering rage is slow.

Perhaps sudden rage, as described in the earlier stories from myth and religion, is a leftover from our early human ancestors. Homos sapiens were hunted, and were perhaps food for other animals. In this period of our history, it could have been a life-saving action for an enraged man to give a lion as good as he got, to tear open its throat or beat its skull in with a stone held in the right hand. The archaeologist S. Mithen (1996 p. 290) writes: "There is clear evidence that early hominids were hunted and killed by carnivores." Fits of rage may have been a last resort at moments where the survival instinct kicked in, and a man was attempting to avoid being killed and eaten. Most of us who experience sudden rage would say that the main trigger is not being respected, accepted – not being seen and heard for what we are. In our prehistory, rage and the feat of killing another animal would be purely oriented towards survival. In the inner cosmos of the emotions, we have the feeling of being preyed upon and devoured. You hold your breath; eternity becomes the here and now. If nothing happens now, it will be because of me. Does the fear of death come just before the Point of No Return: fear and trembling? Abraham and Isaac – are they acting out God's fit of rage, a heated outburst from the so-called All-mighty? Is the act of sacrifice a collective discharge of sudden rage? Is war the politics of this rage, and how do politicians utilise fits of rage to stay in power? What about rage as a survival strategy for your inner self?

During an outburst of rage, do we sense how humans are connected to the omnipotence of creation?

In an evolutionary phase where groups of Homo sapiens were defenceless, these outbursts created a barrier of rage against the forces of nature, and a power which sought to control them. Just as hedges, enclosures, ramparts and later walls protected us, so sudden rage could be deployed productively to some extent. Moses's rage and his destruction of the stone tablets because the people danced around the golden calf is a metaphor for the regulation of a community. Sudden rage can thus have ethical outcomes.

In a dream, the Almighty came down from the mountain and smashed to pieces the thing I had created: it was a scripture containing rules for communal living. Does sudden rage exist in the dream world? Had I had a rage-dream? When our natural enemies – animals and the spirits imagined by our ancestors – disappear, inner enemies increase: from inner to outer, from social to personal. In my sleep, I was a red-cross worker, and shot concentration camp officials who had reported sick to me, but that was more revenge and justice than rage. I could already see the headline that would be printed in the newspaper, so this cannot count as a rage dream. Do animals – elephants, tigers, horses, cows, dogs, bulls etc. suffer from sudden rage? Where do we reach the limits of our tolerance, where does rage wreak mental and social destruction in the family, to be inherited through the generations? How is rage inherited: emotionally? Why is it "in the family"? Are there more people affected by it in the country than in the city? Do more people in western civilisations suffer from it that in Africa, Asia and Latin America? Has sudden rage increased since these regions were colonised? Who can find answers to these questions? In this study, I am going in search of them.

Calming the Heart

Here is a soothing thought: in ancient Babylon, the word *shappatum* (connected to the modern Sabbath), was used for specific days of the year which were also known as "calming the heart" – more specifically, days of atonement and so the soothing of God's rage: the day in the middle of the month, probably identical to the night of the full moon, has a similar name. "In addition to this, of the "evil days" or "days of rage" in a month, four fall on the seventh, fourteenth, twenty-first and twenty-eighth.

> "In some societies seven is a holy number. The concept of a comprehensive totality of space and time is apparently linked to this; it may be that therefore underlying these critical days may have been the idea of the restoration of a violated integrity, the idea of bringing injustice ... social and personal injustice can serve as roots for sudden rages. Moshe ... throwing down the tablets in a rage which had flared up suddenly, so that they shattered on God's mountain" (Buber 1952 p. 164).

> It happened, as soon as he came near to the camp, that he saw the calf and the dancing: and Moshe's anger grew hot, and he threw the tablets out of his hands, and broke them beneath the mountain. He took the calf which they had made, and burnt it with fire, ground it to powder, and scattered it on the water, and made the children of Yisra'el drink of it (Exodus 32:19–20, Hebrew Names Version).

Where does rage come from?

In the Authorised Version of the King James Bible, the passage reads:

> And it came to pass, as soon as he came nigh unto the camp, that he saw the calf, and the dancing: and Moses' anger waxed hot, and he cast the tables out of his hands, and brake them beneath the mount. And he took the calf which they had made, and burnt [it] in the fire, and ground [it] to powder, and strawed [it] upon the water, and made the children of Israel drink [of it]. (Exodus 32:19–20)

Prior to this, the following conversation had taken place:

> And the LORD said unto Moses, I have seen this people, and, behold, it [is] a stiffnecked people: Now therefore let me alone, that my wrath may wax hot against them, and that I may consume them: and I will make of thee a great nation. And Moses besought the LORD his God, and said, LORD, why doth thy wrath wax hot against thy people, which thou hast brought forth out of the land of Egypt with great power, and with a mighty hand? (Exodus 32:9–11)

These biblical reports show how sudden rage can form a part of everyday communication between the worlds of God and man.

In the most common genealogy of the Greek gods, Uranus and Gaia are the parents of Chronos and Rhea. Their grandchildren – Hestia, Demeter, Hera, Hades, Poseidon and Zeus – play out their dramas as adult gods on Mount Olympus. Zeus received thunder and lightening, the symbols and tools of his power, as a gift from the one-eyed giants (Cyclops) after he had freed them from the pit of Tartarus where Uranus had imprisoned them. As far back as the Greek myths of creation, sudden rage is seen as the emotion of shock and resentment at being tricked by the cunning of others, who you had wanted to outsmart with your own cunning. Cunning is a word that stands for cleverness, slyness, deviousness, and craftiness. And in the Promised Land, God's singers sang of the rage of the Almighty.

> Forty years long was I grieved with [this] generation, and said, It [is] a people that do err in their heart, and they have not known

my ways: Unto whom I sware in my wrath that they should not
enter into my rest. (Psalms 95:10–11)

The Lord at thy right hand shall strike through kings in the day
of his wrath.(Psalms 110:5)

I am constantly astounded by the ferocity of the divine rage ascribed to the Almighty by psalm singers. Is this where the fear of God comes from?

In their book on Borderline Personalities – which are actually split or distributed personalities – Kreisman and Straus (1992) describe cases of sudden rage as part of this condition. Borderline Personality Disorder has been defined in DSM III (1980), with a more sophisticated definition in the 1987 DSM III-R, as an inability to bear life's contradictions. People with BPD are described as trapped inside their inner dilemmas. Their lifestyle, philosophy of life, strategies and beliefs are not consistent. "Millions of individuals with BPD are provoked into attacks of rage, directed against the people they love most." They often feel helpless, empty and bored. Boredom is seen here as a defence against their own anger at life. They use it to suppress their feelings of rage, and sudden rage becomes a latent power within them. People with BPD have no real ontological security. Their lives aren't anchored to the middle point of their true selves. Their struggle for a self-sufficient identity is so exhausting that they use sex, drugs and rock'n'roll to try and reach some sort of resolution. This is an attempt to escape from the pain they inflict on themselves and others, through their own emotional injuries. This nightmare that drains their vitality, coupled with dominating behaviour, is only perceptible again when their deep sadness is admitted as a fresh sign that they are really alive. This is when they are really able to feel how the protective armour put on in their childhood now threatens their own existence. "Sudden rage can flood into the workplace and actually destroy a career." Kreisman and Straus cite the following triggers for this: Borderline personalities can be emotionally unsettled by highly structured or unstructured jobs. An over-critical boss who makes certain personal remarks, in combination with their uncertainty over their own professional competence, their over-sensitivity and anxiety, can make these people feel rejected. Someone who feels they have been pushed away like this will often work themselves into an uncontrollable anger, which is expressed in a sudden attack of rage. Kreisman and Straus's clinical picture is made up of eight categories: the fourth they describe as "Raging Bull" (1992 p. 57). This is an unjustified, intensive rage and a lack of anger management. People diagnosed with this often air their grievances, suffer from ongoing (chronic) anger and regularly get into fights. Outbursts of rage by Borderline personalities are almost always unpredictable and naturally cause anxiety in the people concerned. Each individual outburst bears no direct relation to the trigger that is experienced and observed. In people with BPD, triggers act upon their underlying fear of disappointment. Both authors describe scenes familiar to all of us. The enraged person throws plates and other objects around. Or they chase another person with a kitchen knife. In moments like these, sudden rage can be seen as a cry for help. They are testing the devotion and reliability of their partner: "Do you love me, do you like me, even when I hate you, hit you, throw plates at you?" Their deep anxiety around closeness and commitment can be briefly dulled by sudden rage. An attack like this is really a cunning strategy to make this longed-for and at the same time feared intimacy impossible. Individuals with BPD first create distance, then look for intimacy again from the partner they have distanced with their rage. They complain: "*I* always have to try to get close to *you.*" This is how the paradox of suffering is lived out. Kreisman and Straus describe (1992 p. 175) how Borderline personalities have fits of rage during psychotherapy sessions, in order to test their therapist. Is he or she *really* there for me? For them to give up their own resistance, these people require honest communication, support and sympathy. Before I can become healthy, I want to be accepted as a patient together with my sickness, my injuries and my resistance to the therapist. In one example, rage through innocence, Pat attacks her husband Jack with an outburst of rage because he was too busy at work to come and meet her for lunch. She oversteps his boundaries and produces a renewed distance from him. Pat herself is causing the thing she complains about. In her rage, she is completely and fully intimate with Jack. With her clamouring and screaming, she brings her rage at Jack into the here and now. He has to take more than one step back in order to re-establish his mental space. Pat runs around but makes no headway. Keeping quiet at moments of heightened emotion can allow you to move forward. I will discuss this at greater length in the third part of this book. The fear of loss visible on the faces of those who suffer from sudden rage reflects the continual loss of their human dignity caused by their own rage. This is the mental catastrophe inherent in this gruelling method of regulating one's emotions.

How does rage manifest itself?

The Triggers

When asked, "Are you aware of the triggers for your sudden rages?" 61% of people questioned answered yes (Table 9). It's only when we feel the triggers for rage in our bodies that we can begin to do something about them. This proportion is therefore a positive sign of the potential for change in an emotional life ruled by rage. The different types of perceived triggers are summarised in Table 10. Among the freely formulated answers appeared the following: feeling under attack, verbally or bodily; being ignored or misunderstood; disappointed expectations; when the system we live in treats you unfairly; being betrayed by others; people pushing your buttons; being rubbed up the wrong way; getting nervous and stressed when somebody does something that doesn't meet my expectations; feeling injured deep inside; it comes out of the blue; breathing more deeply, and a louder heartbeat.

The people surveyed on the street who suffered from outbursts of rage described these as screaming, flaring up, raving, exploding, violent, injurious, destructive and erupting like a volcano. If we look at the percentages in Table 11, we can see that 18% more women than men are more likely to bottle up their feelings and then explode.

TABLE 9: Awareness of the triggers of sudden rages

Answer to the question: 'Are you aware of the triggers for your sudden rages?'	Number (%) of perpetrators		
	Male	Female	Total
Yes	37 (59)	35 (65)	72 (61)
No	26 (41)	19 (35)	45 (39)
Total	63 (100)	54 (100)	117 (100)

TABLE 10: Types of trigger

Trigger for rage	Number of mentions by perpetrators	
	On the street	On the phone
Powerful feelings (impotence, disappointment)	10	2
Conflicts	9	1
People	8	1
Physical perception	5	2
Banal things	3	
Other	13	
Total	48	6

TABLE 11: The experience of sudden rages

Usual way an outburst of rage starts/what happens during an outburst of rage	Number (%) of mentions by perpetrators		
	Male	Female	Total
Build-up or event, then explosion	18 (43)	26 (52)	44
From nought to sixty, explosive, volcanic	20 (38)	12 (24)	32
Explosion, then a feeling of calm	6 (11)	4 (8)	10
Build-up or event, then explosion, then a feeling of calm	3 (6)	2 (4)	5
Other	6 (11)	6 (12)	12
Total	53 (100)	50 (100)	103

Conversely, 14% more men than women describe their experience of rage as volcanic, and describe the speed of the attack using the metaphor "from nought to sixty".

In the phone survey, seven out of the nine self-declared ragers gave comments: the answers from three male and two female respondents come under the "nought to sixty" set; two women said

How does rage manifest itself?

they experienced an explosion, and then felt calm. Unfortunately these data have no value as a control group.

When we look at the answers to the question about the meaning or point of rage, divided into age groups, we can see that of 117 people given to fits of rage, 21 people did not answer. All the same, Table 12 gives us a good overview of how rages manifest themselves in men and women of different ages.

TABLE 12: The point of rages for perpetrators

Sex and age	Number of the following answers to 'what is the point of a sudden rage?'							
	Letting off steam	Asserting myself	Protection	Attracting attention	It's just human nature	Other	It's pointless	Total
Male								
<20	3		2	1	1		1	8
20-29	3	3	1	1	1	3	3	15
30-39		1					1	2
40-49	1	1	2	1	1	1	4	11
50-59	6			2		1	1	10
60-69	4		1				1	6
Female								
<20	4				1	1	2	8
20-29	3	1			2		2	8
30-39	3	2					4	9
40-49	3	2					3	8
50-59	5	2					2	9
60-69	1	1						2
Total	36	13	6	5	6	6	24	96

Where Does Rage Manifest Itself?

Sudden rage occurs most often in our family lives. Many children are victims of these ferocious outbursts, which they often don't understand. The family sphere is where most of us show the dark side of our personalities. This is the way it's meant to be: at these moments we need the protection a family affords. Our family life today has shrunk from the extended family in which at least three generations lived together, to single-parent households. In this form, the family is far and away less capable of absorbing and controlling the dark sides of all its members. We live in a fragment of a fragment which, in an act of self-deception, we still call family. Noticeably more women (85%) than men (54%) become enraged in a family setting (Table 13). Sudden rage in the business world balances this out in terms of both absolute and relative numbers. The result is that 22% more men than women have fits of rage in various different places.

The phone survey revealed a trend similar to the street survey (Table 13): most people succumbed to rage with their families.

TABLE 13: Locations for attacks of rage

Location	Number (%) of mentions by perpetrators					
	On the street			On the phone		
	Male	Female	Total	Male	Female	Total
At home (in the family)	26 (54)	38 (85)	64	2	1	3
At work	7 (14)	6 (13)	13		1	1
In leisure time	5 (10)		5		1	1
Various places	11 (22)	1 (2)	12		1	1
Total	49 (100)	45 (100)	94	2	4	6

Emotional Repression

In an attack of rage, one or more triggers finally bring a powerful emotion that has been repressed to a point of no return. This moment of violent, uncontrollable emotion, as with all other constricted feelings, passes through what is called an "emotional wave".

At the start of this, the emotion rises through your body into your conscious mind. It's like a stream that suddenly has to carry more water. A sudden tidal wave breaks into it. The movement of emotion becomes staccato, chaotic, and quickly gets out of control. The emotional release of this chaos allows calm to descend again. This holds true for the usual ebb and flow of the emotions. But when somebody has a fit of rage, they have made a psychosomatic effort to quell an overwhelming flood of emotion. In this case, when their emotion shifts into chaos, it requires a massive act of strength to hold back something that is ultimately ungovernable, unbelievable, and untameable. And when they finally have to let go of the reins, their inner savage is released.

How does rage manifest itself?

People whose mental and social traumas cannot be accepted and integrated into their everyday lives can often be argumentative and arrogant as a result. This is a character trait displayed by people who often feel indecisive and inferior. When a man or a woman finds themselves being pulled down into this negative spiral, they can be really incapable of doing anything but having a fit of rage in an attempt to get themselves out of the dead end they have ended up in.

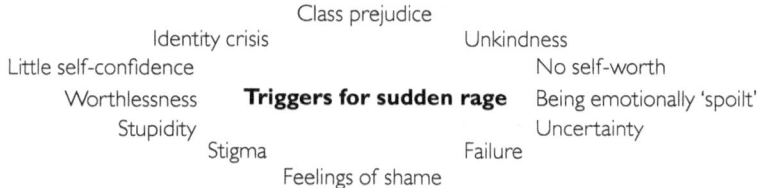

```
                    Class prejudice
        Identity crisis              Unkindness
Little self-confidence               No self-worth
    Worthlessness    Triggers for sudden rage    Being emotionally 'spoilt'
        Stupidity                    Uncertainty
              Stigma           Failure
                  Feelings of shame
```

"*Alpine Fire* blazes the competition away. Film buffs choose Fredi M. Murer's incest drama as the best Swiss film of all time." This was how the Swiss Sunday broadsheet, the *SonntagsZeitung*, brought us this extraordinary news on 6th August 2006. Murer's film was released in cinemas in 1985, and won the Golden Leopard at the Locarno film festival the same year. It's an innocent love story of an elder sister and her younger, deaf brother who is on the verge of becoming a young man. The children live with their parents, and their pigs and cows, on one of the Swiss Alps. Their tension-laden family life ends in a sudden blaze of rage. The father, whose rage is unleashed by jealousy and his feeling of powerlessness, tries to shoot his son for sharing his awakening sexuality with his sister. In a staggering inter-generational struggle, the aggressor loses his life. The important themes in this film, which has now been crowned the best Swiss movie of all time, are the social and mental tension between traditional (the mountain) and modern (the valley), between patriarchy and youth, between the apparent power of the father and the powerlessness of the mother. The father is intent on having only the minimum necessary contact with civilisation in the valley. There are just a few groceries that have to be brought from there up to the mountain: the essentials of civilisation. The father determines the hows, whys and wherefores of their life. He demands complete power. The paradox of an idyllic life lived in the lap of nature on the Urner Alp, and the taboo placed on a natural, youthful, physical expression of joy (eroticism) is shown in the blazing of the alpine fire and in the dreadful sin of the father that burns within it. Incest, rage and tragedy are the strong thematic roots of this deeply moving piece of art.

<table>
<tr><td></td><td>Normal inhumanity</td><td></td></tr>
<tr><td>Overestimating your own abilities</td><td></td><td>Smart-aleckiness</td></tr>
<tr><td>Desire to be all-powerful false self</td><td>Phenomena in an</td><td>Craving for recognition</td></tr>
<tr><td>Hate</td><td>outburst of rage</td><td>Raving madness</td></tr>
<tr><td>Jealousy</td><td></td><td>Tantrums</td></tr>
<tr><td>Self-preservation</td><td></td><td>Domineering behaviour</td></tr>
<tr><td></td><td>Inconsiderate behaviour</td><td></td></tr>
</table>

Shakespeare's Othello is another depiction of a character with an unstable personality, who is torn apart inside. Othello, often rightly, feels he is constantly driven or manoeuvred into social constrictions. His inclination towards the rage that erupts from him at various points contributes to the catastrophe which crashes down upon him and Desdemona, his passionately adoring bride, like a giant, deadly wave. The phenomenon of the torn or broken heart (schizo-phrenos, from the Greek *skhizein*: to split, and *phren*: mind) often conceals a buried "Othello complex". This has recently been investigated by a team of Swedish psychiatrists for its propensity to trigger violent offences. Only 5% of the acts recorded in the criminal register were in fact carried out by people suffering from a broken heart. The researchers compared 98,000 personal files on schizophrenics and other psychotics, who had been treated at a Swedish hospital over a period of 13 years (Fazel & Grann 2006). Sudden rage in the workplace is not without its dangers. An attack of rage can lead to a warning, and a repeat attack to an employer justifiably giving the perpetrator their notice. This is demonstrated by an employment tribunal in Frankfurt, in a case between a book-keeper and a hospital. The bookkeeper had apparently long been irritated by her colleague's "arrogant and snippy" behaviour. When the colleague came into the bookkeeper's office one day, the latter lost control. She yelled, "Get out of my room!" and slammed the door shut with a loud bang. The hospital gave the bookkeeper a warning. As the tribunal chair outlined, workers have a duty to conduct themselves with restraint in the workplace. If somebody is irritated by a colleague's disrespectful behaviour, they can take their grievance to their manager. In no circumstances does this justify shouting and slamming doors (www.jobber.de/studenten/iptc-zin-20020927-30-dpa p.1). Sudden rage, together with terror, is the original form of force. Rage as an activist, making the world a better place: an agent for change. But rage can be a trapdoor, a crack through which people can fall into destructive anger. Sudden rage is not inherently murderous. But it can be a lifelong task for some people to subdue their rage so that it doesn't become violent and murderous. The rage they experience is then no longer sudden. But wanting to behave sensibly when faced with complete nonsense is so ridiculous as to be impossible. This is how most utopias start: a little refuge in the woods; a commune perhaps, subtly advocating a design for life, a fresh start for mankind; a welcome oasis in the world's turbulent history. This will protect you effectively against rage, and from any needling feelings of grief, sorrow and anger, for a while. But what works for one person – this method of "finding inner peace" – doesn't work for everyone. This loneliness is as sterile as that of Siva. It means holding back the life that is in you. Life no longer germinates and sprouts: it withers. You don't appreciate it as the holy thing it is for those people who practise it. And you're back to square one, having to start all over again. Then once more we encounter sudden rages, as experienced by monks, priests, mullahs, nuns, and other holy people who have fallen from grace. *Oh nameless shame!*

The Olive Garden

Up he went under the grey leaves
quite grey and worn out in the olive-lands
and laid his dusty forehead deep
into the dustiness of his hot hands.

This, after all. And after this, the end.
And now, should I go there while I go blind,
and why do You require me to say
You are? For it is You I cannot find.

I can find You no longer. Not in me.
Not in the others. And not in this stone.
I can find You no longer. I'm alone.

I am alone with all of mankind's grief
to which, through You, I tried to bring relief,
Alas, You are not he. Oh nameless shame.

Later, so they said, an angel came –.

But why an angel? Ah, then came the night
and leafed with careless fingers through the trees.
Disciples, restless, stirring in their dreams,
But why an angel? Ah, then came the night.

The night that came was not unusual,
a hundred others pass in such a way.
Its dogs sleep there, and there its stones are lying.
Ah, a sad night, ah, just one of those
that waits until the coming of the day.

For angels will not answer such a prayer;
from such as these great nights are never hewn.
Those who have lost themselves are lost in turn,
and so they are abandoned by the fathers
and barred forever from the mothers' womb.

(Rilke 1919)

The Destruction of a Culture

Films – the visual narration of life – can be one way of engaging with the destruction of our culture of coexistence.

The film version of Jonathan Safran Foer's novel *Everything is Illuminated* provides this sort of enlightenment. It is a story of life in hard times, in Second World War Ukraine. Trachimbrod, a small village, is destroyed like so many others by the German Wehrmacht. The reason: Jews and other people had been living there together peacefully. At the start of the story, there is the search. The search comes first. It starts with a collection, which makes a proper search possible and necessary. In the beginning is a burning longing for illumination. At first there was the journey. Later came the rest. From the final resting-place by the river, which Trachim B. had previously had to cross, and in the middle of which an axle broke, drowning him, there finally came a dwelling – a hamlet, and later a village, called Trachimbrod. When the German soldiers flattened the village and the synagogues, they tried to make the Jewish men spit on

How does rage manifest itself?

the Torah, lying tattered on the ground. Augustine (the collector)'s father was the only man who refused to spit on the Torah. The soldiers carried out their threat, to shoot into the vagina of his pregnant daughter. She survived because the bullet killed the foetus. She crawled to safety. Nobody was allowed to help her. Jonathan's grandfather was born in 1925, and his saviour Augustine in 1927. When their lives were destroyed by terrorists and war criminals, they were 18 and 15 years old, and it was 1943. Grandfather Safran came to the United States as a refugee, and lives there still. His grandson, Jonathan, receives an old photo from his grandmother on her deathbed, and this arouses his curiosity. He begins to research, looking for the woman whose picture appears on the photo, next to the man who would become his grandfather. He reaches back into the past, ending up in Odessa in the Ukraine, and there he meets Alexander. Alex's father and grandfather are the owners of "Heritage Tours". The grandfather suffers from outbursts of rage. The father, caught in the transgenerational wave, beats him. His cowed, subservient mother says nothing. The family owns a snappy, frightened dog. Alex's grandfather is often anti-Semitic. He no longer wants to see or hear anything, and so claims to be blind as a form of self-defence. In 1943, when the Wehrmacht destroyed Trachimbrod, they killed all the men. Alex's grandfather was the only man to survive the slaughter, although he was injured. He threw his coat with its yellow Star of David back onto the heap of bodies. Believed to be dead, and now resurrected, he escaped. In Odessa he walked into a new life. The woman who would become the guardian of Trachimbrod saw this departure. She collected everything from the ashes of the village's life, everything remaining from the murdered men, and kept it in her house. From then on, Trachimbrod existed only in cardboard-box archives and the memories of refugees. The woman in Jonathan's photo was the collector's sister. During the story of Jonathan's search, Alex's grandfather regains access to his own repressed past. His rage dies down the more of his life he is able to see and accept. That was me. Through this insight he also gets back the eyesight he has given up. He has passed the violence that had been dealt to him on to his son and his grandson, until he finally realises who he is, was and will be. The mental fissure, unconsciously caused by the terror of the Wehrmacht soldiers, could be repaired. He sees that his past lives on, through him, in his son and his grandson, and that it cannot be extinguished.

The ring that Jonathan has been waiting for is the engagement ring of the pregnant daughter whose father refused to spit on the Torah, Jonathan's grandfather's first wife, the ring which she wore and buried. She knew that one day someone would come looking for it – one day the collector would hand it over to Jonathan. She said:

> "The ring does not exist for you, you exist for the ring. The ring is not in case of you. You are in case of the ring. It only is."

Destruction – a cracked, broken society – the Basic Fault. The only thing more painful than actively forgetting, thinks Jonathan, is being lazy about remembering.

Being familiar – overly familiar – with terror, identifying with the aggressors, is one, temporary, survival strategy. Life is a temporary situation, an eternal here and now.

Rage in a Cultural and Religious Context

Many artists have reflected on the issue of sudden rage. They write about experiencing it themselves, or through other people.

Bachmann and Frisch

In his fiction, the writer Max Frisch (1911–91) constantly thematised the rage ignited in him by his jealousy – the jealousy, for example, that he felt towards his then partner Ingeborg Bachmann (1926–73). When she flirted with other people, it was an expression of her development as an individual, though it also acted as a trigger for Frisch's sudden, ferocious rages, and a blind anger against what was happening to him (Waleczek 2001). "The thematic centre of Frisch's work is the identity crisis. The self which falls apart, which doesn't find its purpose and form, which suffers, doubts, gets lost in a false image of itself – there are many variations on the theme" (Bircher 2000 p. 97). Frisch met Bachmann in Paris in 1958. At first they lived together in Zurich then, from 1960, in Rome. Frisch got a divorce from his first wife, Trudi von Meyenburg, and asked Bachmann for her hand. She said no. Following this, a dance of jealousy unfolded between the two lovers, making their life together impossible. Bachmann broke it off. Frisch went to Zurich; came back again. Bachmann took him back. This wild, chaotic dance of love lasted until 1963. "The brilliant, drug- and alcohol-dependent, uncompromising Bachmann and the wordsmith Frisch, a careful, slow, and dogged worker, were too different in their characters. But at the same time they were bound by a series of common interests – for example, the creation of a literary cosmos from the cosmography of their own selves; the passionate search for a language that could express the reality of experience in an fresh, unsullied and truthful way; their interest in sounding out the rifts and depths of individual identity; finding new narrative modes that would adequately reflect the problems and fractures of the self, and the experience of a fragmented world" (Bircher 2000 p. 58). Both were mistrustful of each other, and secretly read the other's diaries (Bachmann) and letters (Frisch). This rekindled and fuelled the jealousy anew, and gnawed away at their sense of self-worth. Bachmann wanted to savour her freedom to the full: she even pursued a programme to build a new morality based on her own experiences, for a society that, following the two great wars, was striving to create a new order using old models. It would be a new Bachmann-morality that would be applicable to everyone. She wanted to dissolve all forms of convention then create something new from all the fragments of being. Here we see megalomania at work, played out through Bachmann as a moral apostle. Her mental breakdown following the split from Frisch eventually led to her horrific death by fire as a result of an accidental blaze in her bedroom (caused by a cigarette that had fallen from her hand whilst she was asleep). Eros and Thanatos, the love and death drives, overcame her. Both Bachmann and Frisch depicted their love-hate relationship in their books. In the course of this therapeutic act they argued with themselves and each other. Bachmann in *Malina* and *The Franza Case*; Frisch, early on in *Gantenbein*, then in *Montauk* and finally in *Bluebeard*. Frisch's relationship with Bachmann was the most important of his life, and the one that caused him to confront his sudden rage head-on. Bachmann was enraged and indignant when she recognised herself in Gantenbein's wife Lila. She felt she had been used as an object of study by Frisch. Friedrich Dürrenmatt once mentioned in passing that, in contrast to him, Frisch took his personal issues and made them universal. Dürrenmatt said: "My experiences are very strong in the moment I experience them, then they fall away, I forget them, and later they surface, transformed [...] For me, Frisch consisted of an abundance of observations, experiences, of life, and I admired – I still admire – the boldness in the way he works from an entirely subjective viewpoint. Frisch is always the subject, his subject is the subject. That is his honesty. Seen against that, everything in my world seems filtered. Everything I experience, every thought, sinks back as if into darkness, and comes back changed, in a completely different form, in which I recognise myself only later" (Frisch and Dürrenmatt 1998 p. 16). Once again, you can't have the best of both worlds. Frisch could let his experience of sudden rage be distilled and vaporised in his writing. With the benefit of this hindsight, he was also able to release himself from his own fragmentation. Through making himself and his experiences the subject-matter, he may have been able to experience himself as a whole, brought together in and through various characters in his novels.

Kafka's father and the Pink Panther

In his *Letter to My Father* (translated by Karen Reppin 1998), Franz Kafka describes his father's strengths and advantages, but ends up talking about his mistakes and weaknesses, "into which your temperament and sometimes your violent temper drove you" (p. 12). The son describes his father as at bottom a kind and tender man. "You can only treat a child as you yourself are constituted with strength, noise and violent temper, and what is more, in this case it seemed to you extremely suitable because you wanted me to be a strong, brave boy" (p. 16). The damage to the child had already been done. "What was always incomprehensible to me was your utter lack of sensitivity to the kind of suffering and shame you could inflict on me with your words and judgements; it was as if you had no notion of your power. I, too, must surely have often hurt you with words, but then I always knew it, it pained me, but I could not control myself, I could not hold the word back, I regretted it even as I was saying it. But you lashed out with your words without hesitation, you felt sorry for no one, neither during nor afterwards, one was absolutely defenceless against you" (pp. 18–19).

Many children who find themselves at the mercy of their raging fathers feel what Kafka describes here. These are fathers who live by the motto: do as I say, not as I do. Kafka was oppressed by

How does rage manifest itself?

the fact that his father, "you, the toweringly authoritative person for me, never held yourself to the commandments you imposed upon me" (p. 20). The world of Kafka's boyhood was divided into three parts. The first was his role as a slave, the second his father as the reigning monarch, and in the third, everybody else, who lived perfectly happily without being ordered about. A child has no choice but to suffer his father's rage, and Kafka's torment led him to take refuge in a safer, imaginary world. His father ranted and raved about other people, but forbade other people in the family from doing the same and condemned them when they did so. Thus the young Kafka lost faith in his own abilities and actions. As a tool for child-rearing, rage is a blunt and ineffectual instrument. "I think it was because the expenditure of rage and malice did not seem to be in proper relation to the matter itself, one did not have the feeling that this rage was generated by this trifling matter of sitting far from the table, but that it had existed in all its dimensions from the beginning and only by chance used in this manner as a pretext for breaking out. [...] One became a sullen, inattentive, disobedient child, always on the run, mainly within myself" (p. 32). There were moments when his father not only screamed and went red in the face, but actually became insensible in his rage. This was also liable to happen in his shop, with customers and employees. Kafka describes his mother as worried and worn down, because she endured her husband's tyrannical, hate-filled attacks out of love for her family. Kafka had lost his self-esteem. He felt a boundless sense of guilt towards his father. The raging tyrant made his slave feel guilty for having been responsible for his ruler's outbursts. In this way, the perpetrator becomes his victim's victim. This is a particularly unhappy relationship. As a young adult, Franz Kafka made his own attempt to be independent, beginning primarily with him writing his experiences down. Kafka was 36 in 1919 when he wrote the letter; he died five years later. Kafka's letter to his tyrannical father, along with the rest of his oeuvre, lifts a veil of lies and dishonesty which had influenced not only his father's life, but his own. In his writing, Kafka could breathe again, and create a space for himself that was free of fear. According to the physics of sudden rages, society holds the lid on the rage of the individual, who like a pressure cooker will eventually explode. But the physics is false: the lid is not held but slammed, with a violence which is inherent in our institutional structures.

In the biographical film *The Life and Death of Peter Sellers* (2005), Sellers's life story reveals the contradictory nature of rage, and its dark side: his violent temper tantrums, and his inability to love. Geoffrey Rush plays Sellers, the chameleon-like quick-change artist, to perfection. Britt Ekland is played by Charlize Theron. Peter Sellers is best known as the comedian in the film *The Pink Panther*, and as a brilliant actor. But the same man who got under the skin of almost every role he was offered was unable to deal with his everyday life. He fell in love with women who didn't want him, and left women who did want him when he no longer wanted them. He was prone to deep depressions. Sellers made his name with the Pink Panther, but the longer he played the part of Inspector Clouseau, the more he hated it.

Ah, how we love to personify elemental forces. Let us draw a parallel with a Greek myth. To borrow a phrase from my teacher, Francis Huxley (1976 p. 35): rule 4: "To change the subject, draw a parallel." This is what I will now do, as we turn towards a myth that is central to European culture.

Psyche and Eros

In the grand narrative of Psyche and Eros, we encounter the sudden rage of Aphrodite (Venus), the mother of Eros (Amor). Following the legend recounted by Apuleius in *The Metamorphosis* (or *The Golden Ass*, translated by Thomas Taylor, 1997), we will pick up the story at the part where Psyche is looking for her lover Eros amongst all the peoples of the world. The reason she can't find him is that, following his flight from their love-nest, he is lying in his mother's room with a burned shoulder and a terrible stomach ache. Meanwhile his mother is bathing in the ocean, amusing herself by swimming about, being the most beautiful love-goddess – and then she listens to a seagull which tells her that her son, Eros, has burned himself and is laid low with a fever from his wound.

"What?" cries Venus in a loud voice, suddenly filled with rage. "So, then, this hopeful son of mine has got a mistress! Come tell me [...] the name of her who has solicited the ingenuous and naked boy". "I am not certain," counters the chatty seagull, "though, if I well remember, he is said to have been vehemently in love with a girl, whose name is Psyche" (Apuleius p. 96).

"Psyche?" cries Venus, increasingly furious. "Does he then love her who is the rival of my beauty, and who is emulous of my name?

How does rage manifest itself?

And does he mean to make me, who first brought him to the knowledge of her, act the part of a bawd?" (pp. 96–7). She finds Eros in his room and gives him a thorough scolding, threatens to take his wings, his bow and arrows and his torch, and disown him as her only son. She is not yet too old to have another child. His father, Hephaestus, and his stepfather Ares, the god of war, are brought into it. Eros should be afraid of them and show them the proper respect due to a father by his son. She wants to prune his hair and wings. Full of intent and bitter gall, Aphrodite leaves the palace. There she meets Demeter, the goddess of agriculture and civilisation, in the company of Hera, Zeus's queen and the goddess of marriage. Both of them see the rage in Aphrodite's eyes. What is the matter cousin? My heart burns; help me to gather my strength for revenge, and find the fugitive Psyche. Both goddesses already know about what Psyche and Eros have done, and try to soothe Aphrodite's rage a little using friendly persuasion. They attempt to demonstrate to the love-goddess that her beautiful son has fallen in love. Thus he is practising his mother's art, which is all about furthering his own happiness. They even go so far as to say, "Which god or man will from henceforth tolerate the way you spread your love around, when you punish the self-same love in your son so harshly? When you forbid him contact with alluring beauties, and exercise your rage against a girl whose gift of feminine beauty, given to her by you, has brought her happiness? Practise what you preach."

Meanwhile Psyche hopes for the support of both these goddesses, Hera and Demeter, in her search for Eros. Although both look kindly on Psyche's passion and her search, their family ties prevent them from coming to her aid. Resigned, Psyche senses that there is no helping her. She decides to throw herself on Aphrodite's mercy in the hope that this will lessen her rage. It is a gesture of abasement. On her way to the goddess's heavenly gates, Psyche meets "Habit", who greets her mockingly, "Ha, you wretch you." She grabs Psyche by her beautiful thick hair and drags her triumphantly in front of Aphrodite. Aphrodite, enraged, bursts into loud laughter, shakes her head, makes a scornful gesture and says to Psyche: "So now you're finally paying tribute to me and greeting me as your mother-in-law. Or is this visit more about your lordly husband, who took the burning oil you anointed him with so badly?" She calls for "Fear" and "Longing" and tells them: "I give this guest over to you." The two take Psyche away and torment her. Psyche is beaten, and when she is brought before the goddess of love again, Aphrodite flies in her face, "rent her garments in many places, tore her hair, beat her on the head, and severely chastised her in various ways" (p. 103); a sudden attack of pure rage.

After this, Aphrodite gives Psyche a series of labours to perform as punishment. First, she must sort a huge heap of wheat, barley, millet, poppy seeds, peas, lentils and beans into separate piles. Ants help her complete the task. During this night, Psyche and Eros are both under the same roof in Aphrodite's palace, Eros kept under close guard in a special room in the heart of the building; a torment of love. Then Psyche must fetch the golden fleece from the sheep with the golden wool, a cup of water from the river Styx in the underworld (the Styx is the river the gods swear by and Kokytos is the river of sorrow) ... and although she manages this with the help of an eagle, the vengeful Aphrodite is not appeased. On the contrary, she is even more fixated on destroying Psyche. Aphrodite gives her a box to take to the underworld, into Orcus's gloomy mountain, and give to Proserpine with the message: "Aphrodite asks you to give her as much of your beauty as she needs for a day." Her own beauty had faded in caring for her sick son; a truth and an untruth in one. Psyche knows that in sending her to Tartarus, it was undoubtedly the goddess's cruel intention to rid the world of her. She goes to the nearest high tower, to throw herself off. The tower speaks to her, giving her tips on how to complete her lethal task. First she needs two honey-cakes, one in each hand. In her mouth she takes two coins. The far-sighted tower makes it possible for her to go into the blackest darkness, and come back into the starlight. He warns Psyche not to open the box. The goddess of hell, Proserpine, fulfils Aphrodite's wish and fills the box with "desire". Psyche returns happily but her curiosity overcomes her reason. Yielding to her youthful desire to see just a tiny bit of divine beauty, she opens the box. Inside is hellish sleep, which grips her in a trice, laying her out on the ground like a corpse. Eros, his strength regained, escapes out of his window and flies to Psyche, takes the sleep from her, locks it back in the box and wakes her with the point of one of his harmless darts. He speaks to her mischievous nature and encourages her to take the box straight back to his mother. "And I will take care of us", says the god of love. Eros flies to father Zeus, explains their unfortunate situation, and asks for his support. Zeus first rebukes him for his cunning and his jokes, but still grants him

How does rage manifest itself?

the prettiest girl on earth. As a punishment he has to live with his jealousy and paranoia about his rivals for her affections. On Zeus's order, Mercury calls all the gods and goddesses to the wedding, where he will bind Eros in the chains of marriage. Zeus marries Psyche and Eros with the words "He has chosen and courted a girl for himself. Let us as one give her to him! He marries her in this moment. From now on he will enjoy the eternal fullness of love in Psyche's embrace!" The daughter born to Psyche after this, so the gods tell each other, is called "Pleasure" in the language of mortals.

According to a different genealogy of the gods, Eros is a child of Chaos and a brother to Gaia, Tartarus, Darkness and Night. Gaia and Uranus (the sky) are parents to Aphrodite, who marries Hephaestus, the son of Hera. Gaia is also the mother of Chronos – who, with Rhea, begets Zeus, Poseidon, Hades, Hera and Demeter (Grigson 1978 p. 82).

In the love story of Psyche and Eros, Aphrodite's sudden rage is depicted as the dark side of the goddess of love. Although her cousins try to pacify her Aphrodite, driven by jealousy and a need to control others, feels justified in humiliating her future daughter-in-law. This version of the love myth tells us that even on Mount Olympus Aphrodite's fits of rage triumphed temporarily. Another of the grand narratives which influence our understanding of the human mind concerns unwitting family relationships.

Jocasta, Laius and their son Oedipus

In the following story of Laius, Jocasta and their son Oedipus, practically all the characters are controlled by feelings of rage. The goddess Hera is enraged by Laius, who has abducted and raped his friend's young son, Chrysippus, and neglected his wife Jocasta's sexual needs. She therefore sends Barrenness and the Sphinx to Laius's kingdom, Thebes. In her rage the goddess of marriage and fertility punishes the people of Thebes as a whole. To try and find a way out of this mess, Laius sets off to consult Pythia, the Oracle of Delphi. She prophesies that Jocasta will become pregnant with a son, who will grow up to kill his father. Laius's course of action is clear to him: there must be no pregnancy. This means there can be no fertility for his people either. Queen Jocasta tricks Laius into bed with alcohol and sweet nothings, and finds herself pregnant. After the birth, Laius stabs his baby son through the feet in anger, and abandons him in the mountains. The king hands his helpless son over to the elements, and leaves him to die. We all know a variation of this story. A shepherd in the service of the neighbouring king (Polybus of Corinth) saves the little boy, Oedipus – whose name means "swollen foot". He grows up in Corinth's royal palace as a welcome son to the childless ruler. The fact of his adoption is kept a secret from him. Like all pubescent children, he grows thirsty for knowledge, asking himself: who am I? Where do I come from? Who and what will I become? Are my parents really my parents? Who were my ancestors? He sets off to Delphi, to question the Oracle himself. When Oedipus enters the priestess's shrine, she is full of rage and forbids him entry. Nothing like this has ever happened in Delphi. "Get away, you miserable wretch," the Oracle rages, "you will kill your father and marry your mother! A terrible curse has been placed on you. Away with you!" Oedipus is seriously shaken by this harsh treatment, and despairs over the curse that hangs over his young life. The knowledge that he thinks he has fills him with shame – although he is not yet guilty of anything. He thinks: Right. Then I will never go back to Corinth. His solution is to avoid the people he believes are his parents. He takes his fate into his own hands. No harm shall be done to his "father" Polybus by Oedipus's hand. Sometimes we shape our lives; sometimes our lives shape us.

Oedipus tries to escape his curse through conscious action. What he cannot imagine is that in doing this, he is heading directly towards the fulfilment of Hera's rage-curse. This ancient play demonstrates to us the fact that our lives happen consciously and unconsciously, openly and hidden, really and truly. What will be will be. The worst possible thing comes to pass: the young wanderer, who has grown up as a king's son with a healthy sense of what is right and just, who can hold his own as an equal among equals at court, meets a coach in which an aristocratic older man is sitting. The crossroads is narrow, as is sometimes the case. Who is higher born and therefore has right of way? Oedipus is used to asserting himself. If anyone should insult him, and feel himself to be better and more important, he is perfectly able to defend himself. The old man – the audience knows this, but Oedipus doesn't, yet – is his birth father, Laius. King Laius orders him abruptly to step aside. He has no idea that this wanderer is a king's son – the son he conceived and then abandoned – who has no intention of taking orders from a stranger. Oedipus refuses to take orders. He only listens to the gods and his

How does rage manifest itself?

royal parents. The logical consequence: a power struggle. And so it comes to a short, sharp exchange of blows. "In the fight, rage flared up in him," (Köhlmeier 1998 p. 51).

Both opponents are burning with rage. Oedipus hits Laius so hard on the head that he causes fatal bleeding on the brain. Thus Oedipus has fulfilled the first part of the Oracle's prophecy. Excited and self-satisfied with his war-like nature, he walks on and comes to the gates of Thebes. At the entrance to the city sits the Sphinx. She keeps the citizens on the edge of starvation and poverty. Because of her, many tradesmen avoid this dying kingdom. Everyone who wants to enter the city is confronted by the Sphinx's riddle. She devours all those who cannot answer it. This is the way it has to be for Oedipus's curse to be fulfilled. The Sphinx is a personality type like the one we are investigating: defensive on the outside, she keeps a close watch on the inside, and life becomes a prison without us realising it. Oedipus meets the Sphinx, she asks him the riddle, and he knows the answer. The riddle is: "What creature, which has only one voice, walks on four legs in the morning, and on two at midday, and is strongest when it walks on two?" Man, answers the strong young man. The Sphinx disappears, and Thebes is freed. Since the king has fled the country, the saviour of the Thebes is invited to marry the queen. And so the second part of the curse is fulfilled. Oedipus marries Jocasta, raises children, and lives the high life. He has arrived. After a period of peace, another famine is arranged for Thebes – the gods are still at play. King Oedipus consults the seer Tiresius (who has his own long story, which we will not go into here). He says, when Oedipus finds the murderer of the old king, Thebes will be freed from hunger. This is how the best of all whodunits begins: detective, judge and executioner are unwittingly united in the figure of the wanted criminal. In sudden rages, the same actor plays all these roles. A person who flies into a rage feels himself to be a judge over other people who are different from him and who therefore, precisely because of this difference, have done something wrong in his eyes by going their own way instead of following him. When King Oedipus finds out that it is he who has killed the old king, that the queen is his lovely mother, and that he has thus fulfilled his prophesied fate, he puts out his own eyes in a "holy" rage with the pin of Jocasta's brooch. Blinded, he sees the tragedy of his life. Blind in life; insight in blindness. He takes himself off to where everyday life and the consciousness it brings with it cannot reach him. His mother/wife kills herself. A shock wave hits the next generation, his half-siblings and children. Be wary of being blinded by rage.

The poet

Horst Kurnitzky (1981) depicts Oedipus as one of the heroes of the western world. This is a story about the destructive foundations of western civilisation.

In his book on Oedipus the Tyrant, Kurnitzky draws on Friedrich Hölderlin (1770–1843), who adapted Sophocles's play. Hölderlin had a choleric personality himself, and often flared up into sudden rages. To give an example, one outburst of rage led to a separation from the house of his beloved Susette Gontard. Her father was jealous that Hölderlin spent so much time reciting poetry to his wife and daughter. "...this man is always sitting with my wife! He rushed into the room and towards Hölderlin. A sudden rage unmanned the young poet, who knew himself to be innocent, and an ugly scene would have followed if a look of shock from the lady of the house had not given him his control back. He quickly left the room, packed his suitcase, and turned his back on the house that same night" (Bertaux 1981 p. 292). Rage has an important place in Hölderlin's work. As a primary choleric, he uses the powerful emotion of rage in a positive way. Nevertheless, he still sees sudden rage as "blind anger". The myth of Oedipus I have just recounted has been adapted by many dramatists. Aeschylus, Euripides, Sophocles, Seneca and Voltaire have all written "their" Oedipus. More recently, Cocteau and Gide amongst others have adapted the story for a modern audience. Sigmund Freud's theory of the Oedipus complex is probably the most widely known version. This is the deep and complex depiction of a mental and social conflict, which concerns society as a whole, but also communities and the individuals who live in them. It involves the "primary scenario" of the family, the goddess's curse, the family at war, mating and sexuality, trauma and the punishment of paedosexuality. It sees the institution of marriage as a royal palace, and it concerns fertility – and sudden rage.

The Sphinx (whose name means "the strangler") was a man-eating monster with a woman's head and breasts, the body of a winged lion and the tail of a snake. As the (incestuous) child of the snake-woman Echidna and her son Typhon, she honoured her mother and father. Typhon, a monster, was seen as the personification of volcanic fire. The Greeks believed he dwelt in Etna, and caused its volcanic eruptions.

"Wherever we come into contact with history, the circumstances are such that they presuppose earlier stages of existence: nowhere is there a beginning, everywhere a continuation, never a simple cause, always already consequences" (Bachofen 1975 p. 13). At the start of our civilisation – when we stopped wandering through our natural surroundings as children of nature and began to settle as farmers – there was a transformation (a metamorphosis) of nature into culture. We transformed from animals into god-like beings, into gods, which had the power to transform humans and animals, even to make plants out of humans. The Oedipus myth has a pre-history: the story of how Cadmus, the founder of Thebes, searched for his sister Europa, couldn't find her, but at the place where he had slain a monster (a snake or a dragon; Typhon), sowed the dragon's teeth in the ground and grew a "new race of men", the Sportoi. The stories in the stories are so tangled together that it is impossible to grasp them directly. In them, we recognise the achievements of the process of civilisation; we rely on abstraction to allow us to understand the reasons behind what has gone before. Cadmus, the hero, is rewarded with marriage to Harmonia, the daughter of Ares, the god of war, and Aphrodite, the goddess of love. Cadmus and Harmonia are Oedipus's great-great-grandparents. Jocasta comes from the race of the Spartans, the dragon-people. Sudden rages can be seen as expressions of a competitive emotion, vying for the attention and favour of the gods in man's war against his own nature and the nature of the world around him. And so we find ourselves in the middle of the maelstrom that is the struggle for survival, with its rules of power-play: points scored for achievements – and defeat, domination and subjugation, as in the modern fairytale of the "ideal" couple.

Simone de Beauvoir and Jean-Paul Sartre

In her book *Tête-à-tête: Simone de Beauvoir and Jean-Paul Sartre*, Hazel Rowley (2005) presents the lives and love of these two highly gifted writers and philosophers. Sartre (1905–80) and de Beauvoir (1908–86) were a couple until 1941. When Sartre was 36 and de Beauvoir 33, they ended their sexual relationship. Despite this, jealousy, sudden rages, anger and "the rage of a sick man", as Sartre called this overwhelming emotion, still had their place in their relationship, which was at once highly orchestrated, intense, open and familial. They both lied to themselves and others. Both joined forces to lie to third parties. They deceived themselves and others with the "pact" they lived by. It was a marriage neither of them wanted to live in; it was an existential attempt to turn their relationship into a work of art. And somehow they succeeded in this. They had a "family" who they both supported – particularly de Beauvoir – and who they thus made financially dependent upon them. The couple, along with de Beauvoir's lover Jacques-Laurent Bost, went on a six-week holiday to Greece in the summer of 1937. Sartre refused to go on the walks de Beauvoir had planned, which he found exhausting. De Beauvoir confessed that at moments like this she was capable of shedding tears of pure rage. When Sartre did join her on a hike on the island of Santorini, they walked to the ruins of Thera in a merciless heat: when they got there, they were both completely exhausted. To reach a bus back, they had to tramp across half the island, and when they got lost, Sartre worked himself into a short, sharp fit of rage. He was capable of driving his partner to her wits' end at times like these, and then playing the victim afterwards. De Beauvoir relates how her young friend Sarahin wanted to do more than just hold hands: she wanted to sleep with her. De Beauvoir let her, as she could find no faults in Sarahin, only limitations, as she wrote to Sartre: "she asks me to explain the obscenities [in Sartre's work] – but only in my room, with her face turned to the wall. I call her a frightened doe, which drives her into a rage" (Rowley 2005 p. 106). In her letters, she told Sartre every detail of her lesbian affairs, making him into her voyeur. Sartre's girlfriend, Wanda Kosakiewcz, sometimes surprised him with the frothing fits of rage he provoked in her. At such moments Sartre – a double-crossing, cheating liar – considered whether he wouldn't be better off living an honest, upright life. In these shameful situations, he redressed the balance of respect by showing his own rage. He felt obscene in doing this. But again it was a sign of life: sudden rages are Sartre's volcanic expressions of an existential separation – isolation – from his fellow man. In the summer of 1944, Wanda had an affair in Paris with Albert Camus, whilst they were rehearsing Sartre's play *The Flies* together. Sartre was hurt, and it proved to be a turning point in his relationship with Wanda. He was tired of her insane rages, even though he was well aware that he had provoked them with his own behaviour. They split up. Despite this, Sartre supported Wanda financially for the rest of her life, and wrote six plays for her. In so doing, he gave her the only roles she could ever have as an actress. In 1965 he even bought her a flat, and went on holiday with her for two or three weeks every year. His connection to her was deeply fraternal, but also paternal. Once the relationship had taken this form, it calmed both his and her rage.

Sartre hated jealousy. He thought individuals should be able to control their feelings rather than getting carried away by them. He always saw his violent outbursts of emotion as hidden protestations of love. It was important to him to have the freedom to play his own emotions like a hand of cards, and not to be played by them. Sartre's idea of a "temporary moral code" seems to me to be like an umbrella that he could unfurl to protect himself from the storm of emotional outrage he created. How did Sartre deal with the dishonest state of affairs he had lied himself into? He vacillated between temporary reality and temporary morality (Cau 1985). In the real world, the French were waging the Algerian war (1958) – and Sartre was almost beside himself with political rage. He wrote intensively all day long, drank a lot, and took up to six tablets of corydrane (a mixture of aspirin and amphetamine) a day. By the evening he was wired, and de Beauvoir said: you've had enough to drink now. But "enough" was never good enough for Sartre. Against her will, as she put it, de Beauvoir gave him another glass. After this game had been played out two or three times, she reached her limits and threw a fit of rage, smashing her glass on the kitchen floor. But mostly she found it exhausting to quarrel with Sartre. She knew he needed a drink to relax – but at the same time he was gradually destroying himself. It was a collision of destructive anger. De Beauvoir felt her outbursts of rage to be a fait accompli, caused by Sartre. For example, he and another woman decided together, without telling de Beauvoir, to extend their joint trip to the USSR for another ten days. She however was adamant that she wanted to go back to Paris. When she confronted him, he told her that they had already agreed they would extend the trip. De Beauvoir felt the red mist descend into her head, she saw red, and the words that she screamed were blue: "you don't give a damn about me." He was silent. Sartre lied to de Beauvoir about his drinking, and the doctor's appointments he had missed. When she caught him out, he laughed and said, "It would have taken far too long for me to explain myself to you, so

I took a shortcut." Lying as a shortcut. At times like this she could hardly hold back or bury her rage.

How great is the distance from repressed rage to paranoia? The fear of the moment makes eternity into an obsession. The fear of eternity makes the moment into an abstraction.

Martin Walser tells another story in *Fink's War*, a tale which bears the motto: a person who is fighting for his life cannot stop fighting for his life (1996 p. 192). The story of the government official Fink and his struggle for justice is written playfully in his inner voice, which gives Fink sage advice and encourages him to be more economical. It reminds me of Friedrich Dürrenmatt's monster lecture "Justice and Law". I dreamt about Dürrenmatt last night: he had got fatter, heavier and more ponderous. In spite of his bodyweight, he was agile and witty. He came to visit my practice in St Gallen. He had something or other to tell me – he always had something fascinating to say. I reminded him of a story about his father, who pushed him up against a wall in anger, and asked him to please just leave him in peace. Both were extremely angry, although I suspect Father Dürrenmatt was not in the grip of a sudden rage. All the same, this power struggle led to the regulation and control of the violence that had flared up during it. His father's rage was caused in part by Dürrenmatt provoking him in front of a friend. Dürrenmatt was 17 when this happened. *Fink's War*, according to Walser, is a book about preventing injustice and power (1996 p. 164): "Unless they have lost the ability to feel emotion, a person can't do anything with power. And a power that you don't exercise, you don't have. So you have to exercise it just to prove you've still got it." An outburst of rage is an orgy of power-proving, in which a person can sense whether, even after all the injustice they have swallowed and the injuries they have suffered, they still have power. They are taken from a vulnerability they nurture in secret, to a hurtful but intoxicating display of power, through the destructive force of an attack of rage. An attack creates an unconscious bridge to my inner vulnerability which, if I happen to be the public servant Fink, or Hitler for example, I don't want to show to the outside world. I need adequate protection for my vulnerability in order to show the world my strength of character; power over myself. The old phrases of parental discipline echo in our ears: pull yourself together! Get a hold of yourself! Sadly the old ones are not the best ones. Even so, like Martin Walser and other writers, we can experience language as a healer in our mental processes. We feel the truth rise up in us again and again, allowing us to hold our own in the world and find our bearings.

Roth and Bloom

She is a successful British actress; he is a well-known American writer. In their relationship, each was confronted with the other's outbursts of rage. Both saw themselves as victim and perpetrator. The protagonists in this story are Claire Bloom, the English actress who was married to the New York writer Philip Roth for three years, and was with him for a total of 18. They shuttled between London, Connecticut and New York. In her memoirs, *Leaving a Doll's House* (1996), Bloom describes a nervous, commitment-phobic Philip Roth: traits the writer kept hidden beneath his impeccably behaved, serious exterior. Both partners took pains to control their relationship with the other, out of a need to feel secure. The transitions of power, when one ruled over the other, were fluid. "The power Philip had over me," writes Bloom, "wouldn't have existed without his ability to be a tender, thoughtful and understanding man" (p. 173). But the "other" Philip, the one she was afraid of; the one she used the art of love in an effort to avoid, was always there. She was plagued by the fear of his leaving her as much as of provoking the "other" Philip into being. When Roth disintegrated into depression at the end of the 1980s, Bloom was no longer able to prevent his mental breakdown with her love for him. In *Operation Shylock*, which appeared in 1993, Philip Roth describes this experience of temporary madness, partly brought on by a combination of Halcion and Xanax, which were supposed to be protecting him from a complete, suicidal breakdown. He describes how Halcion intensified his suicidal tendencies. It was his psychoanalyst and psychiatrist who prescribed him this medication. The real reason for his depression was buried deep within him: his fear of abandonment, which had the effect that he never really let himself into relationships, and couldn't give himself completely to a woman. If he were to open himself up and give himself to her, she could leave him. And then he would be lost. This is a commonly heard idea from people who view the world from the dire straits of anxiety. Bloom describes one of her own episodes of sudden rage as follows: Roth gave her the manuscript of *Deception*, his latest book, which was almost complete. Unusually, it had already been lying on his desk for three weeks at this point. He gave it to her early one morning before he left for his writing studio. Full of excitement, she opened the manuscript, and found "her" personal story and that of her family, portrayed as self-hating Jews. Roth described "Claire" – the name of "his" actress in the book – as an uninteresting middle-aged woman who was constantly crying about something. The things she read there about his adventures with younger women, who "she" was jealous of, rendered her speechless. When Philip came home earlier than usual, bearing an exquisite Bulgari snake ring with an emerald head, she flew into an almighty rage. Trembling with rage, she told him just how shabbily he had treated her. She wanted their names removed without further discussion. Philip tried to explain his standpoint. Because the protagonist was called Philip, the name of his wife – i.e. Claire – would enrich the text. No, she said, definitely not. Like him, she too was a public figure. She made him recognise that she had the legal wherewithal to prevent the book's publication. Hesitantly, Philip gave in and agreed to delete her name. Afterwards Claire, reassured, accepted his "guilt offering" as she called it, and wore it still when her memoirs were published. After their wedding (she had proposed to Philip), they had a wonderful first year of marriage. In the second year, Claire sensed that Philip was distancing himself from her emotionally. She points to an unspoken something as the reason for a rip that began to form in the harmonious mesh of their relationship. When she asked Philip what he was afraid of, he replied he was tormented by the thought that she might leave him. In the summer of 1993 Philip was suffering from depression again, and his mood swings were so extreme that Claire couldn't make sense of him any more. He showed her his hate, the poisonous side of his emotions, and he demonised her. At the other extreme he went for walks in the park at the Silver Hill Psychiatric Hospital (where he had admitted himself) without mentioning the hate-filled conversation they had just experienced in couples' therapy. A lie developed on both sides of the relationship: Claire was no longer able to speak openly about her daughter Anna, who Philip didn't like because she made demands on Claire's time; Philip had an affair with "Erda", a mutual friend. Claire was blind and Philip was manipulative. This secret did their marriage no good at all.

She felt increasingly abandoned by him, and he felt increasingly overwhelmed by her neediness. Both could see their own confusion,

How does rage manifest itself?

but still couldn't understand the other's. During her last night at the hospital, before Philip was released, Claire sat at his bedside and said: "We have been apart for over two months. Take another two months to complete your recovery and then, please, let me come home." A long silence ensued. Philip looked up at her, his eyes filled with hate, for at least fifteen minutes. She begged him to say something. "We went down to the dining room," Claire goes on, "and I tried to make conversation. Philip was shaking with fury by now. Halfway through the meal, he asked if I had finished, and made a move to go back to his room" (pp. 231–2). In the room, he accused her of trying to poison and destroy him. He would never be able to be normal again. Claire ran screaming from the room, and called a doctor. She wanted help for herself and Philip straight away. She told the night nurse on duty what had happened. At this point, she wanted to die more than anything. The life she had built with Philip had become unbearable. For a night, Claire became a patient in the hospital herself. The following morning she spoke to Dr Bloch, Philip's doctor, and was astounded to find him sympathetic towards her, even after all the negative things Philip had said about her in their couples' therapy. Bloch told her that what Philip said didn't sound truthful. Was another woman involved, asked Claire. He could neither confirm nor deny this. She was left to read whatever she liked into his silence. Bloom's friend John, summoned from Toronto, took her home. "The more I told him that I loved him, the more cold and rejecting he became. The more cold and rejecting he became, the more I felt motivated to tell him that I loved him" (Bloom 1996 p. 215). They performed the traditional emotional dance of abandonment and smothering. The crack between words, feelings, and the deeds that accompanied them became an unbridgeable chasm.

In his novel *I Married a Communist* (1999), Philip Roth got his own back on Claire Bloom for her kiss-and-tell treatment of their marriage. His main protagonist is the narrator's former English teacher. Murray describes the experiences and the tragedy of his older brother Ira, who was given to sudden fits of rage. "But when the canary died, everybody at the funeral was laughing away except Ira [...] When *I* started to laugh – because it *was* funny, Nathan, *very* funny – Ira lost control completely. That was the first time I saw that happen to Ira. He started swinging his fists and screaming at me. [...] He broke my nose at the bridge, a seven-year-old. [...] From then on he was in fights all the time. That's when his extremism began." (Roth 1999 pp. 65–6) "Anger is to make you effective. That's its survival function. That's why it's given to you. If it makes you ineffective, drop it like a hot potato" (p. 77).

"Think of the tragedies. What brings on the melancholy, the raving, the bloodshed? Othello – betrayed. Hamlet – betrayed. Lear – betrayed. You might even claim that Macbeth is betrayed – by himself – though that's not the same thing" (p. 86). *Similar* is not *the same*. Coincidentally, another of Philip Roth's former lovers, Janet Hobhouse (1948–91) titled her autobiographical novel *The Furies*.

In an extremely tender narrative, full of *joie de vivre*, she describes her affair with Jack Vronsky (Roth), a man who lives a Spartan life and is plagued by depression (pp. 194–204). The "furies" don't appear here, but in the boarding schools she grew up in, in her relationship with her single mother, and in her own frustration at not daring to explore her true feelings more. Sudden rage was a part of her life and her mother's, and their tortured relationship stands at the centre of the novel, like wind on the waves of the sea. In a comment on the book jacket, Philip Roth praises the author for her honesty.

Religion

"The book of Exodus, which is the second book of the Hebrew Bible, contains the following story: Moses and his wife Zipporah were on their way somewhere – where they were going, the report does not reveal – and looked for a place to stay with their young son. There the God Yahweh came to them, seemingly irate, with the intention of killing Moses. But Zipporah, making a snap decision, took a sharp stone and used it to cut away the foreskin of her son's sexual organ. With this she touched her husband's penis and uttered the peculiar sentence: "Surely you are a bridegroom of blood to me". This tactic worked: Yahweh curbed his rage, and left Moses alone" (Holl 2003 pp. 69–70).

What is the purpose of this divine rage? Is Yahweh merely feigning his intention to kill in this story to trigger the scene in which Zipporah circumcises her son? What we can take from the passage, quoted here as a motto for this part of the book, is that Yahweh is able to curb his rage. All that is necessary is a little red blood on the penis of his intended victim. Zipporah's presence of mind and her ability to act fast also shows us that a ritual is necessary to

How does rage manifest itself?

calm Yahweh's rage. Holl, representing the many voices of ethnologists and theologians through the ages, explains the moral of this story of religious militancy: "One thing there can be no doubt about: whenever a tribe, a people, a state, a religious community, a secret society etc. labours on an impossible problem, it requires a ritual that establishes a common bond. Then people have to shout, dance, sing, drum and march. Then they must venerate flags, pictures and statues. And when the usual rituals are not enough, then people have to be cut, and killed. This is the way it was for the Neanderthals, and this is the way it was for Adolf Hitler" (Holl 2003 p. 73). Counting the entries for "rage" in the concordances to the Hebrew Bible (HB) and Christian Bible (CB), I can find 31 in the HB and 20 in the CB. "Raging" is mentioned eight times in the HB and five in the CB.

It's fitting that two of cinema's greats, Werner Herzog and Klaus Kinski, collaborated on the film *Aguirre, Wrath of God* (1972). The film's central theme is an obsession with power. Who has the power to determine what, how, when, why, what for, from whom and for whom things are done? Who possesses symbolic power, and the power of symbols? For the most part, the basis of power is the possibility of enforcing it. Dictators regularly play god, determining who lives and who dies. Terrorists kill themselves through a megalomaniac desire for power. This film is about the misery suffered by the Incas of Peru, whose way of life – whose very lives – are threatened by the Spanish Conquistadors. Some of the tribal elders invent the myth of El Dorado, as a survival strategy. Using this idea, they can tempt their power-hungry, gold-obsessed conquerors and occupiers further inland. In other words, the made-up story of a glittering utopia provides a ray of hope for both sides. The leader of the Spanish, Gonzalo Pizarro, together with a few hundred battle-ready soldiers in armour, strike out to find El Dorado. They are accompanied by nobles, clergy, and of course Indian slaves. The reality of the thick rainforest hinders the search party's progress. After much deliberation, it is decided to send out a vanguard of 40 men on rafts. Don Pedro de Ursua is appointed to lead this group. Various obstacles such as rapids, hostile Indians, tensions within the group, accidents and deaths decimate the troop. In despair, de Ursua orders them to turn back and rejoin the main party at base camp. There is a mutiny, led by Corporal Don Lope de Aguirre, played by Klaus Kinski, arrogant and defiant, who persuades the remaining clerics and soldiers not to give up on the dream of El Dorado but to pursue it further, beguiling them with a vision of incredible power and wealth. De Ursua and a few loyal followers are put in chains and left behind. Power passes from one ruler to another, leaving the first downgraded to the status of a mere man. He becomes a prisoner of his thwarted power. The power-play continues: in a rebellion against the Spanish crown, the greedy nobleman Don Fernando de Guzman is crowned as de Aguirre's puppet-king of El Dorado. Marching orders are given in the direction of the Promised Land. They press deeper and deeper into the jungle; deeper and deeper into the madness that will undo them all.

The film's symbolism is centred on power, megalomania and the desire for fame. We all know – even if we don't want to acknowledge it – how useless this attitude is for society, when it is used purely as an end in itself. The rebel de Aguirre celebrates his rage as an end in itself: a well-honed ritual of power. His gripping monologues are a part of this, in which he defines himself as the "wrath of God" who, if he really wanted to, could make the birds fall dead from the trees. The pairing of megalomania and rage portrayed here results in idiotic behaviour. It is the same insatiable hunger for power that we find in the Grimm fairytale "The Fisherman and His Wife". The man and the woman both fail cruelly when they try to use divine power on earth. Kinski played Aguirre so authentically that his own madness threatened to break down the dividing line between the character and reality. This often brought Werner Herzog, who was then a 28-year-old rookie director, and his team to the brink of despair. Kinski who, like his character, was given to outbursts of extreme rage, deployed his power in the same cunning and ruthless way as Aguirre, in order to keep getting his own way, seizing ever more power through continual, forceful intimidation of his peers. If I, Aguirre, want the birds to drop dead from the trees... then the birds will drop dead from the trees... I am the wrath of God. The earth I pass will see me and tremble." It is said that Herzog "hustled his crew through the thick rainforest in inhuman conditions, sparing nobody". He even threatened to shoot his egomaniacal star Kinski if he left the set. By the end of filming, the two "leaders" were estranged, and disparaged each other in public. The one enraged, the other possessed. The diabolical megalomaniac caught in the web of a lust for power (www.filmzentrale.com/rezis/aguirre.htm www.filmstarts.de/bilder/kritiken/Aguirre).

How does rage manifest itself?

Even the much-extolled "great Russian soul" is a comparatively late "invention", formed around the end of the 19th century, when Dostoyevsky was first translated. The prototypes of this soul are contradictory in the extreme: the emotional spectrum ranges from rage to sentimentality and from workaholic to madman.

Rage as a Deadly Sin

J. Werner's book *The Seven Deadly Sins* (1999), presents a sober discussion of the diabolical temptations the monks wrestled with: wrath, greed, sloth, pride, envy, gluttony and lust. For Adolf Holl (2006 p. 48), this is the list originating in old Christian monasticism "from which all wicked and false attitudes are derived". I am particularly interested in what Werner has to say about the deadly sin or "wicked attitude" of rage. He believes that in weak people, the "fire in your belly" of anger becomes the rage in your head. Anger and rage have no face of their own, but contort our faces into grimaces.

"The man who is enraged knows his enemy: he knows who has hurt him; the angry man knows only himself." Sudden rages storm straight towards their intended goal. They are intentionally directed, since "a person's rage is provoked when his honour is dented or even taken from him". The shame which usually follows a sudden attack of rage is the secret weakest link. Werner looks at Heinrich von Kleist's book *Michael Kohlhaas,* which describes senseless revenge, fanatical hatred and excessive rage. Rage sets clear and visible boundaries. Shame cries in the silence: don't go too far! And, oh nameless shame, I have already gone too far, crossing my own boundaries and other people's. At the same time it is our goal to shame our opposite number, at that moment seen as our opposition, with our rage. A rage is an attempt to hide your own true self, your true being, behind the mask of your false self. But a tiny rip in the fabric of your reason, caused by this uncontrollable emotion, is sufficient to let the split nature of your own identity escape suddenly into the public domain. Sudden rages used for self-preservation serve to isolate your true self. We can keep others away from us with an attack of rage. Someone in the grip of rage is providing a forceful rejoinder to a perceived attack on his authority, which ultimately puts him in the right. According to Werner, the deadly sin of wrath (rage) "exposes power that has no foundation in any authority, power that has not been ratified by anyone, as impotence". An attack of rage pushes the boundaries of reason. A sudden attack can't be understood whilst it is happening. It has something "non-conscious" about it. In a rage, we generally express a judgement about other people that we think is the only fair one. Only when we start listening to the voice of reason again can we finally discover a balance between rage and the logic that calms it. The composure practised by monks and nuns overrules the rage in them, which would otherwise express the tragedy of endlessly loving Almighty God, a being whose creations anger him with their way of life. And so we have thrown a few enlightening reflections into the darkness of the second deadly sin. Our topic however is *sudden* rages. These are an emotional turmoil, a demonic possession, a susceptibility that goes far beyond the usual everyday form of rage.

Is God invulnerable? No. Is His righteous wrath, as it is depicted in the Hebrew and Christian Bibles, tolerable for humans? In any case holy rage excites our tempers, and we sense a lesson about when retribution is necessary. Sometimes, when I read these texts, I sense the author's desire to embellish the divine lust for rage with crass examples. What is the voice of the Almighty used for here? Unjust rage makes a racket, brings disquiet and provokes rage in return.

Sudden rages. The wrath of God is the movement of the human mind, exalting itself to a position where it can punish sin (Laktanz 1919 p. 4).

To triumph over "ira", it is necessary to lead a life of quiet contemplation, which looks beyond the material world. The wise man can't be affected either subjectively or objectively by injustice.

He is elevated above the subjective feelings of indignation and pain. The monks tried to tame their rage by practising inner peace. In this way they could break the vicious circle of pain and revenge. If you cause somebody no further pain, he will not have to avenge himself with a just punishment, which will cause new pain. With peace we can end the duty to injure on both sides, putting our wisdom into practice. Yeshua (Jesus), the mediator, appeases the Almighty; as a human being he knows the effect that holy wrath can have. On Good Friday he experiences this first-hand. *Eloi, Eloi, lama sabachtani* – "My God, my God, why have you forsaken me?" (Lapide 1996 p. 88). Paul writes his epistles to the early Christian communities as if he were Jesus's chief secretary: "Now that

He has died for us, and we have become acceptable to God as righteous people, we will remain protected from the wrathful judgements of God through Jesus's mediation. God is allowed to display his wrath and his power to those he has created. In His anger He created imperfect vessels, which are designed to break, but still He tolerates them in His magnanimity. Keep the peace with everyone, where possible. Do not take revenge into your own hands, but leave rage, judgement and revenge to God." "Much more then, being now justified by his blood, we shall be saved from wrath through Him." (Berger and Nord 1999 p. 148; Romans 5:9). As Paul had never met Jesus of Nazareth, and saw himself as a missionary of Judaic reform, he felt pressured to justify himself. This may in hindsight have led to a degree of self-righteous fantasising when he preached. Like most missionaries, Paul wanted to lead the heathen world to the God of Israel (Romans 9:22, 12:9; Lapide 1994 pp. 86–9).

According to Paul, rage is a positive, natural impulse coming from our animal nature. Those who cannot exercise their rage in the normal way will succumb to the passionate embrace of sudden rages. These rages are the root of self-righteousness, since the destruction of my mind and the disturbed state in which I live must be taken into account. From now on my rages are legitimised as "understandable" reactions to an injurious attack. I feel that the shocking pronouncements I make in my rages are "just".

The texts quoted here give us an insight into the emotional behaviour of the Almighty. He rages against His creations, and yet still reaches out to them. This seems positive. It looks to us as though God is "striking us down" in His rage. But He is also a father-figure, who immediately lets mercy prevail and takes pity on us. The bitterness of His rage can be curbed if humans regret what they have done.

> "O LORD, according to all thy righteousness, I beseech thee, let thine anger and thy fury be turned away from thy city Jerusalem, thy holy mountain: because for our sins, and for the iniquities of our fathers, Jerusalem and thy people are become a reproach to all that are about us" (Daniel 9:16).

> "O Israel, thou hast destroyed thyself; but in me is thine help. I will be thy king: where is any other that may save thee in all thy

> cities? and thy judges of whom thou saidst, Give me a king and princes? I gave thee a king in mine anger, and took him away in my wrath" (Hosea 13:9–11).

> "...we all had our conversation in times past in the lusts of our flesh, fulfilling the desires of the flesh and of the mind; and were by nature the children of wrath, even as others" (Ephesians 2:3).

> "And, ye fathers, provoke not your children to wrath: but bring them up in the nurture and admonition of the Lord" (Ephesians 6:4).

Now and then Paul the prayer leader gives out a decent tip. From now on, Yeshua will intercept the wrath of his Abba. He stands between Him and us. "I will therefore that men pray every where, lifting up holy hands, without wrath and doubting" (Timothy 2:8). Amen and carry on praying; a defiant prayer in silent rage. We have all seen what can come of spiritual leaders making grandiose promises. Enraged supplicants fly planes into towers to fight for their god.

However, other supplicants say:

> "For the wrath of man worketh not the righteousness of God. Wherefore lay apart all filthiness and superfluity of naughtiness, and receive with meekness the engrafted word, which is able to save your souls. But be ye doers of the word, and not hearers only, deceiving your own selves" (James 1:20-22).

And might the revelatory voice of John contain something of a divine spark as well? It is hardly to be believed that when the Day of Judgement, so longed for by Christians, finally arrives, nothing other than an outburst of holy rage should come to pass.

> "[Evil doers] shall drink of the wine of the wrath of God, which is poured out without mixture into the cup of his indignation; and he shall be tormented with fire and brimstone in the presence of the holy angels, and in the presence of the Lamb" (Revelations 14:10).

How does rage manifest itself?

> "And I heard a great voice out of the temple saying to the seven angels, Go your ways, and pour out the vials of the wrath of God upon the earth" (Revelations 16:1).

As cruel as these dramatic, fearful ideas are, they warn of the consequences of a godless life. They are only true when counterbalanced with their opposites. The old-school prophets spoke more kindly: "And in that day thou shalt say, O LORD, I will praise thee: though thou wast angry with me, thine anger is turned away, and thou comfortedst me" (Isaiah 12:1), than the quick-tempered know-it-alls of Revelations.

But we certainly don't need to wait for the end of days: the story of Herod has already shown us what happens when a king succumbs to rage. When the three wise men fail to report back to Herod on the birth of Jesus:

> "Then Herod, when he saw that he was mocked of the wise men, was exceeding wroth, and sent forth, and slew all the children that were in Bethlehem, and in all the coasts thereof, from two years old and under, according to the time which he had diligently inquired of the wise men" (Matthew 2:16).

Everything that came later was mere imitation, from Hitler to Stalin to Mao. Torturers gripped by rage, all of them.

In Yeshua's parable of the feast, the host is unexpectedly let down when all his guests decline his dinner invitation. "I pray thee have me excused," say the guests to the servant who has been sent to invite them. A servant is somebody who cannot express his own opinions. And what happened? "So that servant came, and shewed his lord these things. Then the master of the house being angry said to his servant, Go out quickly into the streets and lanes of the city..." (Luke 14:21).

We are all familiar with this. Even Yeshua understands the feeling of rage that arises from the disappointment in this story. And if the Almighty speaks to you, what then?

> "And Moses said unto God, Behold, when I come unto the children of Israel, and shall say unto them, The God of your fathers hath sent me unto you; and they shall say to me, what is his name? What shall I say unto them? And God said unto Moses, I AM THAT I AM" – *Ehie Ascher Ehie* – *Elohim* (Exodus 3:13-14).

Moses's Rage

In his study *Moses: History and Legend*, Eckart Otto (2006) describes Sigmund Freud's view of Michelangelo's Moses. This figure is depicted in the tomb of Pope Julius II in Rome, and Freud saw in it a man of God who, although he looked upon the sins of his people, had overcome the rage that welled up in him. Moses carries God's stone tablets with the Ten Commandments in his right hand, and they are not broken as they are in many other images. According to Freud, Michelangelo was trying to depict a Moses who, unlike the biblical version, didn't destroy the Commandments in a fit of rage. Here is a Moses who sits down, breathes a sigh and watches what is happening in front of him. He exercises control over his rage. Michelangelo's Moses thus becomes a peculiar symbolic figure. If you have seen the statue, you will know how many possibilities for psychological projection it invites. Otto's theory is that Michelangelo's Moses – and thus also Freud's – is the Moses who came down from Mount Sinai the second time, after being given the replacement stone tablets by Elohim. This would mean that Moses had experienced something that helped him to sate his rage. Moses changed "I have no choice" into "I can choose". Like him (at least, like Michelangelo's version), every one of us has the possibility of regulating our rage. I can take a break; start to notice what's going on in the here and now. Then I can sense the mighty forces at work in me; I can turn my attention inwards and dig down to the reason for my agitation. I can regulate the force of sudden rage in my whole body using my latent ability to disperse and distribute this force. We open ourselves up to the heavens and give ourselves some more mental space.

> "How can the knowledge about 'Moses' the man have been passed on orally for 500 years, before the first Moses story appeared in written form? The answer is the Passover celebration, which still lies at the heart of the Jewish religion today. What began as a shepherds' ritual to keep evil demons – the 'destroyer' (Exodus 12:23) – away from the men and their animals, changed over time to become a memory of the exodus from Egypt, which remains at the centre of Passover – the Haggadah – today" (Otto 2006 p. 34).

How does rage manifest itself?

> "[...] O my LORD, send, I pray thee, by the hand of him whom thou wilt send. And the anger of the LORD was kindled against Moses, and he said, Is not Aaron the Levite thy brother?" (Exodus 4:13-14).

> "Also the LORD was angry with me for your sakes, saying, Thou also shalt not go in thither" (Deuteronomy 1:37).

The account of the exodus from Egypt is the originating story of Israel. Moses is depicted as the iconic founder of the Passover in Egypt. Moses as leader of the exodus, Moses as mediator for the commandments on Mount Sinai, Moses having first sight of the Holy Land, which he was no longer allowed to enter. Moses: the punisher punished, the enraged man and the pacified. So many hidden and manifest narratives contained in one symbolic character. Knowledge of Moses as a historical figure is little more than speculation: he was possibly a tribal leader, "who lost his life in the attempt to bring his tribe across the river Jordan. Moses is not mentioned in any sources of the time outside the Bible. So our picture of Moses is a literary one, contained in a long story in the Pentateuch" (Otto 2006). Moses was the founder of a religion. He played a large role in establishing Yahweh, the God of the desert, of storms and war, in Palestine. The historical Moses was supposed to have lived in the 12th century BC. The written story of the Pentateuch (the first five books of the Bible) only begins in the seventh century BC. But whatever the facts, we still have the story of Moses, which shows us our human limitations. This is the illustration of a metaphor with Yahweh – or Elohim – which can help us to recognise how limited our ability to command men and nature is.

> "Before the exile, honouring Yahweh was largely a partisan affair, and the honouring of one God in Judah, which did not call into question the gods of other peoples..." (Otto 2006 p. 69).

> Hear, O Israel: The LORD our God, the LORD is one (Deuteronomy 6:4)

I can't go into the extent to which this centralisation towards a single God served the kings of Israel and Judah's understanding of belief and power around 1000 BC. But the writers in exile following the catastrophe of 586 BC attempted to balance out the tension, indeed often the dilemma, between Yahweh's rage and His love in their stories. Elohim needed the people to cast a golden calf – and to dance circles around it in a religious ecstasy of their own making. This was the situation that was necessary for Moses, as a mediator in the service of Yahweh, to step in and vent his rage, to great effect. This laid the groundwork for the show of forgiveness by Yahweh which followed. Yahweh or Yahu (according to the stories in Deuteronomy 5:9-14) is above all unforgiving in his rage. It casts a shadow over several generations before Yahweh is satisfied with an apology. Only then can he stop blaming and forgive the descendents of those who hated him for his outbursts. For me as a psychologist, this means that outbursts of rage can be traced back at least four generations. Only when I, as the great-grandson of my ancestor Johannes Itten (1853–1947) turn away from rage, will Yahweh look kindly upon my meekness. By so doing, I can dissipate Yahweh's rage in my own mind. Outbursts of rage are a plague on society, the emotional consequences of which echo down four generations. A person in the grip of rage takes on the role of "god" or "goddess", who will permit no other gods but them. I alone rule. These tyrants will always sink despairing into the deep quagmire of their delusion, because there are ever more of their own kind. This is Otto again (2006, p. 70):

> "In the Decalogue (the Ten Commandments), there is a prohibition on people worshipping other gods. The reasoning for this is that the devotion of God to his people totally transcends His rage, so there is always the hope that after His rage, God will turn His heart again towards His people."

The Apostle's Rage

The apostle Paul was "called" by Yeshua, and this experience triggered a fundamental spiritual change in him. Either we find a new route, or we turn to religion. Paul was born in Tarsus, in Asia Minor, studied the Torah with Rabbi Gamaliel himself, and was an observant Pharisee. In this period, Pharisees aspired towards a particular kind of holiness. They cherished the "raising of the dead – hope", and imagined that this would make them pure and angelic, and free of sin. Then, and only then, they (and only they) could stand with the real angels by God's throne and have Him for themselves.

How does rage manifest itself?

"Here," says Klaus Berger (2005 p. 13) "lies the origin of the Christian hope of entering heaven." Paul suffered from outbursts of rage. He pursued and fought the Hellenic Jewish Christians, verbally and physically. Amongst these was Stephen, the first Christian martyr, whose death by stoning Paul witnessed. Stephen's crime was that he and his companions were "filled with the holy spirit". They were ecstatic in the way modern Dervishes are. Paul – jealous, hungry for power and full of righteous indignation – disagreed with their chosen spiritual path and therefore pursued them; one religious orientation and belief system against another; an uncertain religious certainty against a certain religious uncertainty. Following a so-called "conversion", Paul too became filled with the holy spirit (*ruach*, which in Hebrew is a feminine noun). His "conversion" occurred between 34 and 36 AD. We have only his statement: the Almighty revealed his son Yeshua to him. The story which he made of it was: during his appearance, Yeshua had asked him, "Why do you pursue me?" – although Paul was not actually pursuing Yeshua, but the Hellenic Jewish Christians. Did Paul fabricate this version of events, or is he relating a dream to us, in order to identify himself with his "victims"? We will never know. A person in the grip of rage makes himself into his own victim. Because of you I must suffer, and now I suffer with you, who must suffer because of me. He became a Jewish missionary, led by Barnabas, who introduced him to the inhabitants of Jerusalem (48/49 AD). There Paul met the young Peter for the first time, and James, Yeshua's brother. Paul, like many of us, was a city-dweller. There, a moral pluralism exists without a definitive measure of what should really be "right and/or wrong". In ancient cities, as in the modern world, an attempt was always being made by the universities to motivate citizens into living peacefully together, using the art of reason and the philosophy of life that went with it. The country dwellers of that period were referred to as *pagani* (country folk), who as "heathens" were more deeply embedded in their traditional culture and religious practices. Paul preached to the population of the city. Unlike Yeshua, he had no organic, rural metaphors and parables to draw upon. Yeshua did not justify himself; Paul did. Our various psycho-geographic experiences shape our different mental characteristics. Be your own metaphor! This means the possibility of conveying yourself indirectly in your own verbal images. Paul requires the metaphor of *iostes* (equality) for his new ethics. "Paul applies the principle of strict equality as much to the connection between man and wife as to that between rich and poor, strong and weak" (Berger 2005 p. 24). He wanted to be of equal worth. Paul was short, restricted by his epilepsy, had bandy legs, and earned his living as a manufacturer of rough cloth (2 Corinthians 12:7). I suspect that Paul felt just as inferior after his conversion as he did before it. He used his trurnaround, for perfectly understandable reasons to do with his own survival strategy, to transform himself into the "long arm of the Lord". He portrayed himself as Yeshua's witness, who suffered in his stead. 2 Corinthians 4:10: "Always bearing about in the body the dying of the Lord Jesus, that the life also of Jesus might be made manifest in our body". And Berger (2005 p. 24): "Paul did not shrink from likening his own fate to God's resurrection of Jesus" – just as hundreds of thousands of leaders of religious sects in Europe, the US, Asia and Africa still do today. And what is he trying to conjure up with this? For the members of the Christian community, Yeshua as Christ could be experienced *through Paul*; a masterstroke. Berger writes: "It was precisely because Paul so often emphasised his weaknesses (I have nothing impressive to offer), that he sounded legitimate". Paul felt himself to be accepted by God in his "humble" subservience, and celebrated himself in this negative, psychopompous way as Christ's "best man" – whose role was to marry Him to his congregations. He was a charismatic advertiser of the Christian heaven to come. He "encountered" the risen Christ in a vision, and this gave wings to his hopes for the future. Thus the here and now became more bearable for him. He felt the resurrection of Yeshua within himself, his body transformed, and assimilated with Elohim. "This is the main Pharisaic issue. All life has no other purpose than this: to become god-like by the power of God's mercy. The resurrection as a transformation is the most important step towards this" (Berger 2005 p. 62).

Adolf Holl's lecture on how our hopes of salvation are crushed sees him describe Christianity as a disappointment; Heil-Hitler – another disappointment; Protestantism – a disappointment; Islam – a disappointment; Communism – a disappointment; the Enlightenment – a disappointment – and so on. This feeling that life is one disappointment after another generates a great deal of despondency, against which we must defend our minds in order to be able to live without bursting into fits of rage (Holl 2005). In spite of everything, after an attack of rage there is often a green shoot of hope: things could be different. But how different do they have to be to ensure more of the same doesn't happen? The director of the Abba or Yahu drama could have arranged things so that in Paradise, the tree of knowledge wasn't so clearly identified. A snake would not have happened upon the idea of speaking to the naked Eve (because after all, the snake's creator is also the director of this piece), and tempting her with the vain hope that more knowledge would bring her freedom, independence and deliverance. Julian Huxley's book *Religion without Revelation* (1960) offers us the religion of modern humanism. Without revelation there is no disappointment. The three great revolutionary seducers of mankind unintentionally created a lot of positions of power for men – usually the ones wearing the priests' robes (Schröder 1992).

And the moral of the story is? "All knowledge leads to disappointment" (Lessing 1983 p. 211).

Social Psychology and Society

The further we distance ourselves from what we class as religious, the more we search for the answers to life's important questions in the area of the social sciences. The word *Jähzorn* – sudden rage – is seldom to be found in the index of a textbook. But in *Psychiatry and Psychotherapy* by H. J. Möller et al (2001), I hit the jackpot. Under *Jähzorn* I found: "Sudden rages and outbursts of emotion without a meaningful connection to the stimulus form the foreground of explosive personality disorder. Emotions cannot be arrested and dealt with adequately – instead they are discharged quickly and violently" (Möller et al 2001 p. 364). This means that when I'm enraged, I can't hold my feelings inside and integrate them into my self. If I was trained in a particular way as a child, and had to form a certain kind of personality in order to please my parents and conform to their cultural and religious values, then this mental disturbance might be an attempt to change this. A dream about this: the captain sat quietly and calmly in his carpentry workshop. I was very agitated and said: Come on, when is our train going to leave? The train was open at the front, where the locomotive was, like the prow of a ship. I had been travelling on it from Finsbury Park to Stroud Green, but it had reached an elevation that fell precipitously away into the depths, and was apparently going no further. The train stood still. The mood was tense. I and my fellow travellers were being attacked by a mob. I defended myself by throwing tools from the captain's workshop in the direction of the mob. I searched for the mayor so that I could make a complaint. At the same time, one of the mob who was terrorising the passengers came in. He was as old as me, but looked older. He was holding out a pitchfork like a lance in my direction, and came towards me with quick steps, like a member of the peasants' revolt. The stage manager of this dream had also left me a pitchfork close at hand, standing in a corner to my left. I fought this ruthless attacker: it was like fencing. I could immediately tell that my opponent was a better, more experienced pitchfork fighter, and I gave up. He stopped. That was the extent of my dream. Where the inner struggle ends, peacefulness can begin. Here is a hint from within, on how I can try to change this pattern, change the way I react in certain situations. This, as we all know from experience, is no easy task. However, it is always possible to change the way we live out the patterns created in childhood. For this we need the possibility of choice. The choice to be satisfied with ourselves – as the people we are and will be. To accept our own abilities and limitations. When I awoke from this dream, of course I thought about the incident by the well, and the pitchfork flying towards me, which I spoke about at the start of this book. The moment the echo of an old hurt, which has never really healed, is triggered by something in the here-and-now, you can be gripped by a fit of rage. But this doesn't have to happen. When I fought defensively in my dream, I was contending with my own emotional history, and that of others. I was caught up in the inner force, the inner struggle, the inner malfunctions of an entire family tree, which passed on the feeling of "not being good enough" from one generation to the next. Somebody or other would always be getting into a rage, going off the deep end, and taking up the struggle against somebody more powerful. If we are to believe some of the findings of modern neuroscience, it is no longer my own free choice if I then do something bad as well. In a TV programme entitled *The Seat of Evil* (2005), the brain scientist G. Roth asked: what would be so wrong about taking people who were likely to commit crimes, and locking them up in advance? The root of evil is to be found in the brain. "I don't believe people have the power of free will as it's commonly defined", says the German psychologist Hans-Joachim Moskowitsch. The logical consequence of this argument is that we should be locking up those who have the potential to commit violent crimes: nobody stands a chance against his own brain (*Süddeutsche Zeitung* No. 171, 2005

p. 35). The man who this theory was tested on kept pointing out the way he was socialised as a child, which included being spoilt by his grandmother, who had brought him up. He described his continual alcohol consumption, which sometimes rose to incredibly high levels, as the main trigger for his violent acts. The flat, one-dimensional view this programme presented, pinned down by the beliefs of the scientists and the person they were treating, is clear: everything is already programmed into the brain. A person's initial socialisation makes tendencies in the brain into fixed patterns and then, as with this man – diagnosed as a psychopath – it's impossible to change anything. Psychotherapy, according to Roth, is a wasted effort. In his opinion, if we lock people away who have dangerous infectious diseases, why not do the same with psychopaths?

A conclusion like this rests on egoistic-logical foundations. Thus modern neurological psychiatry lets itself be exploited, in order to win favour briefly with those in power. So from my point of view, Dürrenmatt's essay "The Brain" (1998), about a brain which thinks itself into being, is a welcome addition to the philosophy of neuropsychology. "Attend to limbic imperatives." This sees a human being as a construct of the brain, which thinks itself into a human body. This is a visually paradoxical image, like the hammer which hammers the nails into its own handle. Our emotions go back at least 100 million years, whilst human perception is only a few hundred thousand years old. This means our limbic system is covered by the neocortex. When we use our neocortical reason, we must always remain in contact with the resonance of our limbic system. We should cultivate the connections called for by our mammalian limbic brain. Thinking with our hearts slows our rage down. Sudden rages are impulsive moments where we are disconnected from our own feelings. As mammals, we need a healthy "relatedness", a relationship structure, so that the strands of our neurophysiology can be interwoven correctly. Most of the things that make up an individual who functions well socially come from his/her experiences of being connected to others. This happens first and foremost through his/her network of relationships with parents, siblings, uncles and aunts, grandparents and so on. Love is the formative, creative power at work here. It is always a somatic experience. Children who receive minimal care and devotion go on to become disruptive members of society. Those who have been neglected in turn neglect their community and society. The brain has a complex structure, with its web of neuronal barriers to acts of violence, and this doesn't form by itself. If the brain remains limbically uncultivated, this can ultimately prove fatal. Neglect of the limbic system can result in a brain which, in its combination of reptilian brain stem and cunning neocortex, has no inhibition when it comes to attacking other human beings. Neurological research into the emotions shows that billions of neurons – neuronal connections – are missing from the brains of neglected children. There is something missing from the synaptic self. These missing cellular connections and synapses in turn have social consequences. The proof lies in the children suffering from this today who tend towards acts of violence. Youth violence is rising rapidly. In Hamburg for example, between 2004 and 2005, the number of serious or dangerous acts of violence grew from 1626 to 2040 in the space of a year – a rise of 25% (*Hamburger Abendblatt*, 3/11/05 p. 1). These children's quick rage, their blindly destructive anger, surprises parents, social workers and educational psychologists. Their violent acts are often committed for trivial reasons. The triggers in no way correspond to the violence committed in outbursts of rage. The brain is a social organ. Emotional bonding, and bonding with a community, is also neurophysiology. If the first bond between child and primary carer is good enough, the child will usually make it out into the world in one piece. All good psychotherapists know from their own teaching experience what is necessary for the therapeutic relationship to have a healing effect. It's primarily a corrective experience, showing the patient what it means to have a relationship. The so called "limbic emptiness" (the therapist is not really engaging in a relationship with the patient) inherent in our modern medicinal and psychiatric practices is perceived by an increasing number of people. In many places, people who have been disappointed by it look for their healing from new-age healers, shamans and conjurers. Hitler and his party knew exactly how to get people who felt disconnected, and existentially lost, under their mad spell, using the suggestive magic words *Heil Hitler*. (*Heil* means "well-being" or "salvation" in German, as well as being the greeting, "hail"). They promised a "healing constellation". When everything revolves around us, your healers, then you will be healthy. Their goal was to win power over the massed peoples of Europe, which for at least 12 years they succeeded in doing. This socio-psychological and religious bonding always has fatal side effects. In outbursts of rage we experience a double force – the mental paired with the physical. We sense brutality's struggle to assert itself in the world – inwards and outwards, in the family, in relationships, in the community, in the tribe, in society. Violence is tempting – in fact it exerts an uncanny pull on us, via the TV news, films and crime novels. Who wasn't fascinated by Hitler, Stalin, Mao, Milosevic, Amin? Intellectuals, psychologists, highly educated people – and even the leftist revolutionaries of 1968, myself included, went to anti-Vietnam demonstrations and sang "Ho Ho Ho Chi Minh". But then we also sang "make love not war", and still read Che Guevara, and Mao's little red book. There are paradoxes in every generation. Brutal lust; lust for the brutal. The whole of nature, everything we call "creation", repeatedly becomes the scene of violence. In nature there are forces that have a transformative effect, and we call them destructive for our world.

Sacred Violence

"We must expect what belongs intrinsically to human nature, to the human being as an animal, to be violent – and we find this deeply unsettling", writes Guggenbühl-Craig (1992 p. 89). C. G. Jung called what is completely destructive in us the archetype of the shadow, the destroyer – murderer and suicide. Freud called this the death-drive – *Thanatos* – which seeks to destroy all life and vitality in us. Whether conscious and/or unconscious, this ultimately plays no decisive role in an individual's life, as we have seen in soldiers and murderers. Both together are uncanny, ungovernable, and destructive to the mind. Most of the famous dictators, like Hitler, Stalin, Hussein and Napoleon, are psychopaths and sociopaths. They are all pathologically fascinated, even at times delighted by the violence they can command through their armies and police corps. They become ever more unrestrained, more brutal, more senseless, until a fatal bullet brings their reign of destruction to an end. What we must do in order to fully develop our minds, is to accept the whole of our human nature. For most of us, it will be difficult to accept the archetypal shadow of evil, the murderer and suicide. If you can feel the No to creation within you, you are able to say Yes more deeply and truly. "The archetypal shadow forces us to confront ourselves – for psychological and religious reasons we must keep seeing and experiencing what is terrible in us, in the world and in God, even when we start to find it sinister" (Guggenbühl-Craig 1992 p. 101).

Individuation leads to the integration of the physical, mental and spiritual aspects of living, vital Eros, and Thanatos (the death drive), which pushes us on to the end. The rager's search for a scapegoat is a well-known phenomenon. Their megalomania is the trap they are caught in like an animal destined to be sacrificed. They sacrifice themselves again in every attack. In so doing they also make those around them into sacrifices at the altar of their mania. The original trauma was the trauma of our ape-man ancestors: that of being hunted and devoured by animals. For a long period of time this was our reality as a species. This could be where the reason lies for our habit of clearing a sacred space for violence. Barbara Ehrenreich (1999) puts forward her theory of the sanctification of violence as follows: when our primate ancestors were faced with the terror of death, in the shape of the predators who want to eat them, they became aware of the feeling of rage which is so important for survival. This triggers a more altruistic desire in every individual to fight for the survival of the group, and these two things combined lead to a moment of total reverie. Ehrenreich sees a qualitative leap into becoming human in the point at which we made the transition from being creatures always on the lookout for food, to being hunters who would finally dominate the entire earth. After we had killed off our predators or decimated them to non-threatening numbers, so that they stopped being a problem for us, the hunters were freed up to pick fights with their own kind in other tribes.

Today wars are what predators once were: life-threatening and lethal. In his impressive book, *On Killing*, Lt. Col. Dave Grossman (1996) describes the cruelty of modern warfare. As a former soldier in Vietnam, the moral of the story is clear to him: war is hell on earth. The psychological damage done when one soldier shoots another in plain sight is that two souls die: that of the dead man and that of the living. In the old tribal communities, there was a god of the rule of war, a god of revenge and a god of violence. In the various wars of modern history, not all soldiers have shot at the "enemy", even when they could have done. In the Second World War it was a mere 15–20%; in the Korean war it was 55%, and in Vietnam 90–95% of soldiers who shot at an enemy they could see. Grossman shows convincingly how young American soldiers in

How does rage manifest itself?

Vietnam received a "more effective" form of training in killing, in order to overcome the natural inhibition to killing another human being. This result was achieved by the operative mental conditioning of recruits. Shoot-em-up video games are targeted in the same direction. The modern tragedy of the soldier is far greater than it used to be. Today the warrior can no longer attach himself to a strong, emotionally supportive group. He experiences a progressive loss of emotional security within the group. Following a battle, the contemporary soldier doesn't get to enjoy the important cleansing rituals of a tribal warrior. Unfortunately these things are no longer practised. Many soldiers find themselves returned to civilian life too soon after an intensive and brutal battle. This transition involves none of the various healing rituals of earlier times, and the result is that from this point on, many soldiers carry on living in civil society with Post-traumatic Stress Disorder (PTSD). Fortunately, according to Grossman, very few soldiers have a "killer rage" in them. They are only the most aggressive psychopaths and sociopaths. Statistically, it's only 2% of the male population of a country at any one time, who are able to kill without regret or remorse. The reports of a massacre of civilians in Iraq perpetrated by US soldiers illustrate this. A US marine infantryman spoke of his comrades' "blind hate". Following a bombardment in November 2005, and the death of a marine, several soldiers from the same company went crazy. Their rage-fuelled rampage killed 24 Iraqis, including women and children, according to the reports (*St. Galler Tagblatt*, 1/6/2006, p. 5; 20 Minuten.ch Zürich, p. 12). At the same time, this example illustrates and backs up research by Grossman and Ehrenreich. In a soldier, a fit of rage can break through all the civilised emotions that usually prevent him committing murder. These emotionally damaged soldiers went berserk. They were attacking the damage done to the cohesion of their group, caused by the killing of one of their comrades – a cohesion which afforded them emotional protection from the horrors of the theatre of war. This group killed 24 people in their revenge attack. Shortly afterwards, they made a desperate attempt to cover it up. Their own inner wounds, torn open by having taken part in such a brutal, tactically senseless attack, remain as a dark hole in their hearts forever. It destroyed their worlds. If you take a life, you destroy two souls: the victim's, and your own. This story clearly shows the transition from being the trigger of somebody's rage to becoming the victim of the deeds they then commit in blind hate.

A Meditation on Rage

The New York psychoanalyst Michael Eigen wrote the only book I know of on the phenomenon of sudden rages, in 2002. He describes the book as meditation on rage, pain and the self. For Eigen, one of the worst aspects of rage is the affinity between this powerful emotion and the claim of self-righteousness. Rage knows no boundaries – whether in politics, religion or art. Rage for Eigen is an alternative to growing mentally as an individual. Rage is an attempt to fill the inner void, which is doomed to failure, and which masks an inability to truly recognise one's own emotional life and show one's feelings. As a psychoanalyst, Eigen is concerned with addressing our capacity for acts of explosive violence. When it bursts out, rage is an attempt to bring something that doesn't fit, something experienced as unharmonious, back into line. This attempt at self-healing for the most part ends in re-traumatising the self. How many children of raging parents are familiar with this: their father or mother was emotionally disturbed as a child and still suffers from this early wound; in their rages, they pass this on rather than stopping it. They open up new wounds. They pass on the responsibility for ending this destructive pattern by dealing with emotions properly. Our survey shows that, paradoxically, seven out of 100 people who suffer from sudden rage don't want to be cured of it. My suspicion is that they are afraid of the emotional scars. In such people, self-hatred spreads insidiously. After each attack they find it more difficult to live with themselves. Letting go of their own emotional baggage – the stories we tell ourselves to legitimate our actions – is not something they want. So they obstruct the possibility of beginning something new. This kind of existential freedom makes most of us, as creatures of habit, anxious. Eigen (2002 p. 44) observes how various combinations of rage and dependency, rage and weakness in his patients are mixed with sexual pleasure. When a patient opens up emotionally, without using rage to do it, when he or she feels more and feels more deeply, and thus can breathe more easily, he/she is already taking the first step on the path that leads away from the fear of his/her own life and vitality. As patients, we come to realise it's not others who have to change (or the state, or the economy), but that we ourselves need to awaken the power to change that slumbers within us. As soon as we are ready to let go of what has happened to us in the past, it lets us go too. The inner opponent in the dream I narrated earlier stopped fighting me. The emotional protection I have erected around my old, hurt childhood feelings is worn away word by word, as I tell my life story, during psychoanalytic psychotherapy. According to Eigen the new contact with these feelings is made possible by our own recognition: "Oh my God, I *am* there." The new experience of expressing our own rage passionately and directly, without it being sudden and destructive, is proof of our mental and social maturity. We have finally become adult and wise. "When rage strikes, feel it – that is the message of this book. Feel feelings, feel the raging through and through, pulsing through muscles, bones, glands, every particle of being. Feel the surge and keep on feeling it. Feel it more" (Eigen 2002 p. 168). That helps. According to Eigen, there is no cure for human nature as it is. We ourselves are the misery and suffering that we are trying to overcome.

In his study on the "rage economy" of world politics, *Rage and Time* (2006), the philosopher Peter Sloterdijk considers various withdrawals from the world bank of rage. He begins with the ancient Greek stories of Homer's *Iliad*. Its heroes act as warrior-vessels, always ready to receive the energy of rage that streams suddenly into their bodies, and this is counted as a virtue. As soon as this rage fills a war hero like Achilles or Nestor, flaring up and filling them from within, then thanks to the gods, the directors of this drama, they become frenzied warriors. Their rage is employed in every successful slaughter. "The domestication of rage affords the ancient form of it a new masculinity." Now the politician, working for the state (*polis*), is filled with righteous rage and uses this power to achieve what he sees as the only correct thing to do. In the modern age this means achieving what most serves your own interests and advantages. The recognition of others as equal players in the game of Polis lays a moral foundation for the calming of this rage. Not being recognised by others as another player can trigger a rage in both parties (justified on both sides), in order to redress the balance of moral recognition. In domesticated moral rage, a lot of energy lies idle, which can and must be prepared for use in each transaction necessary in the rage economy. The bearer of the rage can then profit from this energy transfer. The great cycle of rage, oriented towards the explosion stage where there is a final, sudden flare-up, has proved useful to revolutionaries for its transformative energy. The fanatical fight against barbarity, according to revolutionaries of every colour, must not shy away from the use of barbaric methods itself. One barbarous act of rage drives out another. "The little circle of rage and abreaction belongs to the basic facts of processes involving emotional energy." There is nothing to be done about this, as the people who need the sort of energy rage gives them have no desire to change themselves. "God", the almighty, the just and loving, is used as a force of auto-aggression by all kinds of religions and their adherents, mostly of the male sex. "In truth the title of God in these discourses can be understood simply as the deposit box where rage is saved, and where a frozen desire for revenge is stored. A wrathful God is nothing other than the asset manager of earthly resentments, which are retained in Him, or in His diabolical junior executive, and kept ready for withdrawal later on." These missionary zealots, who feel they have been treated unjustly, have a reserve of divinely-managed assets of resentment. These are linked to the erroneous principle of appropriate punishment: the unbelievers have earned the day of wrath. Whatever is used as a self-justifying argument – religious, communist, capitalist, anarchist, moralist – reflects the despotic megalomania of these fanatics in the name of virtue.

Perpetrators

I know from my own therapeutic practice, that men and women who suffer from sudden rage actually do *suffer* when they let go of their pent-up rage in this way. We therefore included a question on this in our survey. For Table 14, the answers to the question "How do you suffer from your own rage?" are reduced to whether the people who admitted to attacks of rage suffered as a result of it. Of the 117 ragers the survey uncovered, 66 said that they suffered in one way or another, and 27 said they didn't.

For this majority of ragers, if the pressure of suffering becomes so great that friends and acquaintances start to draw away from them, he or she may go down the route of psychotherapy.

TABLE 14: Suffering from your own rage

Suffering from your own rage	Number of perpetrators		
	Male	Female	Total
I suffer	32	34	66
I don't suffer	14	13	27
Total	46	47	93

There is no difference between the sexes in their answer to this question. What I do find astounding however is that nearly a third of the people who answered this question claimed not to suffer from this explosive method of regulating their rage. Maybe this is an important aspect of why sudden rages have become a veritable plague to society. For this sizeable group, having rages doesn't mean they feel they have to change their lifestyle. The newspaper *Welt Kompakt* entitled their article about the supermodel Naomi Campbell (36) "Madam Rage", after she had smashed up a room on her new boyfriend's yacht. Campbell's rage keeps making the headlines. This time, according to the papers, she had a row with the ship's cook, whose antipasti and choice of wine were not exactly to her taste. She went berserk: crystal glasses and Chinese porcelain plates were thrown to the floor; she attacked the expensive antique furnishings. The damage caused by this outburst was reportedly £45,000. The chef, hauled over the coals by Campbell, apparently fought back – but her megalomania didn't allow for backchat. Another aspect of her imperious behaviour is her refusal to respect any boundaries, her own or other people's. One of her ex-assistants claimed that Naomi had attacked her at least four times. The model was arrested in March 2006, and "admitted hitting her housekeeper with a jewel-encrusted mobile phone, causing an injury to the head that required several stitches" (*The Observer*, 4/7/10). In 2000, Campbell pleaded guilty in Canada to hitting an assistant on the head with a phone. As punishment she was made to attend an anger-management course (*guardian.co.uk*, 16/1/07). But in the long term, she hasn't profited from this sort of behaviour training. No structural change has taken place in her personality. This can usually only be achieved through lengthy psychotherapy.

TABLE 15: Perpetrators' descriptions of their own behaviour during rages

Behaviour	Number of mentions by perpetrators		
	Male	Female	Total
Shouting	15	6	21
Using force against other people	5	2	7
Destroying or smashing things	9	7	16
Going berserk	3	1	4
Insulting others or laying blame	3		3
Becoming withdrawn	1	1	2
Injuring myself	1		1
Other	1	5	6
Shouting and using force against others	5	8	13
Shouting and destroying or smashing things	2	9	11
Shouting and going berserk	4	2	6
Shouting, insulting others or laying blame	1	3	4
Shouting and becoming withdrawn	1	2	3
Shouting, using force against others and destroying or smashing things		2	2
Shouting, using force against others and going berserk	1	1	2
Shouting, destroying or smashing things, and going berserk	1	2	3
Using force against others and destroying or smashing things	1		1
Destroying or smashing things and going berserk		1	2
Destroying or smashing things and insulting others or laying blame		1	1
Becoming withdrawn and injuring myself		1	1
Total	55	54	109

In our survey, we wanted to know from each person we asked what they or their relatives did during an attack of rage. Tables 15 and 16 classify the answers of the ragers and the victims of rage by gender.

What do female perpetrators do during rages? Of the 54 women who answered the question, 13% destroy or smash objects, 11% shout and scream, 4% use force against others, 2% go completely berserk, and 9% do various other things.

How does rage manifest itself?

What do male perpetrators do? Of the 55 men who answered, 27% shout and scream, 16% destroy or smash objects, 9% use force against others, 5% lay blame or insult people, 5% go completely berserk, and 2% injure themselves, withdraw or do various other things.

TABLE 16: Victims' descriptions of perpetrators' behaviour during rages

Behaviour	Number of mentions by perpetrators		
	Male	Female	Total
Shouting	8	12	20
Using force against other people	7	9	16
Destroying or smashing things	2	5	7
Going berserk	5	2	7
Insulting others or laying blame	1		1
Becoming withdrawn			
Injuring themselves			
Other	2	3	5
Shouting and using force against others	9	11	20
Shouting and destroying or smashing things	5	5	10
Shouting and going berserk	2	8	10
Shouting, insulting others or laying blame		1	1
Shouting, using force against others and destroying or smashing things	1	5	6
Shouting, using force against others, destroying or smashing things and going berserk	1	1	2
Shouting, using force against others and going berserk	2	4	6
Shouting, using force against others and insulting others or laying blame	1		1
Shouting, destroying or smashing things and going berserk		1	1
Using force against others and destroying or smashing things		3	3
Using force against others, destroying or smashing things and going berserk		1	1
Using force against others and going berserk		1	1
Destroying or smashing things and going berserk		1	1
Destroying or smashing things and insulting others or laying blame		1	1
Total	46	74	120

What do female victims experience during an attack of rage? Of the 74 female victims who answered the question, 16% were shouted at, 12% experienced force used either against them or others, 3% said perpetrators went completely berserk, and 4% had various other experiences.

TABLE 17: Reasons given for repeated rages

Reasons for rage	Number (%) of answers from perpetrators
Frustration and problems, dissatisfaction	26 (24)
Altercations with other people	24 (22)
I can't control myself	19 (17)
It's a natural tendency	14 (13)
I don't think it's an issue	7 (6)
Other	12 (11)
No idea	7 (6)
Total	109

What do male victims experience during an attack of rage? Of the 46 male victims who answered this question, 17% were shouted at, 15% experienced force used against them or others, 11% said the perpetrator went completely berserk, 4% saw objects being thrown around or destroyed, 2% were blamed or insulted, and 4% had various other experiences.

The question about specific types of behaviour during outbursts of rage was answered by almost everyone, regardless of whether they identified themselves as perpetrators. We have provided eight sets of answers or areas of behaviour here. 42 perpetrators told us that they entered into at least two overlapping areas of behaviour during an attack of rage, and seven people said they entered at least three. In the victims' answers there were 47 combinations of two areas, 15 combinations of three and two of four. This difference may come from the fact that more victims answered the question, and the victims of rages are experiencing them as the behaviour of another person. Their perception is multifaceted, more direct and more differentiated than that of the person who is the grip of rage themselves. 65% of ragers scream, use force against other people, destroy or smash objects around them, or combine two, or all three, of these types of behaviour.

How does rage manifest itself?

When we asked the perpetrators why their outbursts of rage kept happening, we received the answers summarised into sets in Table 17. It's obvious that there are difficulties and areas of people's lives here in which something could be done to change their emotional responses (rage). Madam Rage would belong to the 6% who are not willing to engage with their outbursts and the suffering they cause to others. Their narcissism causes them to take personal offence at what, from their point of view, is a momentarily hostile environment. They don't suffer from a confusion of their own feelings and the regulation of these, but confuse various categories of social concomitance. The Campbells of this world feel they are victim-perpetrators. Just because a stupid, incompetent cook couldn't put a sensible menu together, Campbell is made into a victim who now, unfortunately, will have to vent the rage inside her. She is forced to become the perpetrator of sudden rages by the cook, or in other cases the cleaning lady. So the maxim is brought to bear on her: "all our righteousnesses are as filthy rags" (Isaiah 64:6).

Our gender influences our decisions and our fate. This is something that becomes especially apparent in extreme or emotional situations. When a person, be they male or female, falls into a depressive mood following an outburst of rage, and resorts to claiming they are the victim here, I see this as an attempt to relativise their own responsibility and the feelings of shame that come with it, as they look back on their outburst.

One example that serves to illustrate this situation is that of a heavy plant operator who owed rent of £1,000 on a plot in a caravan site, which was being demanded by his landlord. He destroyed the site-owners' house, causing hundreds of thousands of pounds' worth of damage.

"[T]he man also wrecked the couple's two cars standing in the drive of their detached home and then brought the bucket down on a marked police patrol car as it arrived at the scene. Janice Gledhill, 52, who co-owns the caravan park in Bradwell-on-Sea, Essex, was in bed shortly after 7am yesterday when she awoke to find the man charging the six-year-old house with the digger" (http://www.telegraph.co.uk/news/uknews/1522522/How-tenant-answered-landlords-rent-demand.html). By the time the police were able to stop him – he had demolished their patrol car – he had already almost completely destroyed both the couple's cars and their house. He was not only charged with damage to property, but also attempted murder, as the landlady was still in bed when he began to destroy the house. He was annoyed by their demand for him to settle his debts. His sense of self-righteousness made him feel he'd been treated badly, and he blew a fuse. This is an example of the lack of feeling in sudden outbursts of rage. The man completely lost his self-control. In his megalomania, which was reinforced by the mechanical power of his digger, he acted like a tyrant. His hatred for the landlords and his feeling of self-righteousness triggered his outburst of rage. His destructive anger took his pattern of behaviour from that of an adult male back to that of a little boy. He was unable to contain the emotional impulse "rage", and express it in an age-appropriate manner. The feeling of rage gripped him suddenly and broke out of him. A fit of rage is generally a brief, sadistic desire for the power to destroy others. A desire to cause them pain. The force of the digger, and the momentum of the bucket, express movements that the enraged man is unable to accept within himself and live out in a respectable way. Because I don't know the details of his life, I am unable to give a reliable social diagnosis. A diagnosis is always social, if we see it "in the context of the original social situation where it belongs" (Laing 1974 p. 42). Obtaining a perspective in this way is a process that must be constantly repeated. I repeatedly see and hear what plays out in a situation where I am present as a psychotherapist. If the plant operator had had the possibility of sharing his huge, pent-up emotional impulse with somebody, I suspect it would not have come to this compulsive act. He wanted to reveal himself – to express how bad things looked inside him. Without a doubt, he wanted to be seen. And in a negative way, he certainly achieved this. The papers didn't show a picture of him, but of the results of his destructive anger. It is a proven fact that sudden rages are mostly expressed through destructive anger. The perpetrator is trying to draw attention to his/herself through this. Now, finally, they will be seen and recognised. For the most part a man like this is deeply confused, and has low self-esteem, which he hides behind the façade of his false self. In this masquerade he divorces himself from his true human self. He uses this detachment to protect his true feelings, and try to isolate them. This is only partially successful. Defending yourself by being perfect, and thus giving no cause for possible criticism, always fails. So this plant operator is at the same time separated from and related to his fellow man. In his outburst of rage, he literally goes "through the roof", and breaks into the lives of his landlords. He destroys their boundaries. He destroys their home, their shelter

How does rage manifest itself?

from the cold, water, wind, and the other forces of nature. If he were to come to me for psychotherapy, this overstepping of boundaries would be the first issue he would need to engage with. How is he in harmony with himself? How does he experience his relatedness to others? Psychotherapy is a special social activity between human beings, in which our subjective being and our "relatedness to others is used for therapeutic ends" (Laing 1974 p. 26). There are countless cases of men inflicting damage on other people's property during an attack of rage, with the help of their cars. The triggers for these acts are many and various. What I get to hear about in my consultations are feelings of powerlessness in combination with periods of involuntary long-term unemployment. Under the influence of alcohol, a feeling develops: I've had enough, somebody has to sort things out for me right now. I call this psychic begging.

At the start of a course of therapy it is therefore always necessary to work directly with the patient's perception of their own body. First I ask questions to clarify what the distance between the patient and me should be. Is it ok? Is he or she too near or too far away? Is the distance good enough for the here and now? If not, what can he or she do to make it right? If so, do they feel in their bodies that the distance between us they have chosen is good enough? After this has been clarified, and the patient's feelings reported, we take ten deep, full breaths. By doing this we can travel inwards, and become aware of ourselves from the inside out. More breath, more vitality. During this breathing exercise it is important to be as open as possible to the things around me, the visible world of the consulting room. This clarification of distance and boundaries, and creating breathing space for the emotions in the here and now, are all preparation for therapeutic treatment. It's like going to the station, in order to get on a train to travel somewhere. Where the journey begins, we begin. When I don't know where I'm going to any more, I have arrived at myself, said Brian Keenan (1993). Then a patient's symptoms, pain, questions and problems help to signpost the way forward. They point out where I'm going to. The German saying "The path always leads towards fear" contains a deep wisdom. Thus we want the innermost core of our being to be our point of departure, the middle point of our senses, we want to feel our own vitality and, in the way we express ourselves, share our time with other people. In psychotherapy, I will become aware of the rhythm of my life, embedded in my former way of being. We begin with where we want to get to in psychotherapy. We must travel nowhere. We will be allowed, if we want and are able to, to arrive at our true selves. The metaphor of the journey is widespread in psychotherapy literature. Two examples of this can be found in Jesse Watkins's "Ten Day Voyage" in Laing's *Politics of Experience* (1969) and Mary Barnes's *Two Accounts of a Journey through Madness* (1988). Psychotherapy – a ritual in which movement can be practised as a journey towards the true self, and a process of dissociation from the false self, our old survival strategy. During psychotherapy we are inside and outside at the same time. The place where transition from one to the other takes place, our skin, is also where the mind resides. All the various concepts – the professional vocabulary – for our injured, ruptured, interrupted relationships with the life in, through, over and around us supports our new orientation. All organic, natural life is endlessly complex, complicated, and only fleetingly comprehensible. Sudden rages, like other emotional phenomena, can only be understood in relation to our lives as a whole. Someone who is in a rage is moralistic, because he has a temporary desire to humiliate and lecture his fellow men. There are generally a lot of projections in play here – and recognising these as such is another important step at the start of psychotherapy. Those of us who are ragers must learn to recognise the negative sides of our rage. Table 18 shows what the ragers in our survey experienced as bad, troublesome and negative.

TABLE 18: The negative side of rages for perpetrators

Negative effects of an outburst of rage	Number of answers from perpetrators
People around me suffer and are afraid, it destroys relationships	34
Bad conscience and feelings of guilt following rage	21
Loss of control	17
Senseless	17
I become more unpopular	10
I have insulted people	6
Objects have been destroyed	5
Other	14
No negative side	7
Total	131

How does rage manifest itself?

Just as in the above story about the man and his digger, 26% of ragers who answered the question about the negative side of their outbursts recognised that the people around them suffered from their sudden bouts of rage. Their extreme emotions made their nearest and dearest afraid, and destroyed their relationships with each other. At least 16% had a bad conscience and suffered from feelings of shame. Around 12.5% cited the senselessness of their outbursts and their personal loss of control. A minority of roughly 5% did not see their outbursts as negative. The category of "other" comprises 14 answers including loneliness after an attack, mental damage inflicted on others, and the rage not achieving its aim. This insight into the negative side of rages is necessary for the perpetrator to be able to do something to escape the vicious circle of rage.

As I have mentioned, the emotional history of sudden rage in an individual or a family usually stretches back over several generations. The following section looks at part of a family history which produced one of the most destructive ragers of the last century.

The Hüdler Family

One family provides an excellent example of the way that outbursts of rage are propagated from one generation to the next: the Hitlers (formerly the Hüdlers).

In the Hüdler or Hüttler family, it was common practice for those in positions of power to control others with discipline and fear when they felt their power was threatened (Zdral 2005). An unmarried lady by the name of Maria Anna Schicklgruber (1795–1847) had a child out of wedlock: Alois Schicklgruber (1837–1903). She was probably impregnated by Johann Nepomuk Hüttler, who was 12 years younger than her. Nepomuk was 30 and Maria 42 when Alois was born. Five years later, Maria Anna married Nepomuk's brother, Johann Georg Hiedler. Each brother wrote his surname differently – this was their search for their own identity. Both surnames mean the same in German: "cottager", a peasant farmer who occupied a small cottage and worked a portion of the fields belonging to the county or duchy. Nepomuk was married to Eva-Maria Decker (1792–1873), who was 15 years older than him. They had a daughter, Johanna (1830–1906), who later married Johann Baptist Pölzl (1828–1902). This half-sister of Alois Schicklgruber-Hüttler had 11 children. Maria Anna gave her son Alois, whose father she neglected to name on his baptismal certificate, over to her husband's brother – the child's natural father. He grew up in the same household as his half-sister Johanna. She was seven years older than Alois, a fact used in the literature as evidence that her father, Nepomuk, was unfaithful with Maria Anna. At the age of eight, Alois became a member of the household of a wealthy farmer, his "father" Nepomuk. Two years later his mother died. Nepomuk, who lived in the village of Spital in the Waldviertel of Lower Austria, looked after his "son" well after this. Through his contacts, he got the boy apprenticed to a shoemaker in Vienna. The conventional thinking of this period shackled everyone into their own social class. Social mobility from one class to another was possible, but very seldom happened. For a social climber, this meant there was a stigma around their ancestry which, as in the case of Adolf, Nepomuk's grandson, had to be obsessively concealed. Alois grasped the chance to further his education and became a customs official in various rural areas. Despite being the illegitimate son of a farmer, with only a humble primary school education, Alois had made it. The former shoemaker was a customs inspector for 40 years. In 1895, when he was 58, he was pensioned off. His son from his third marriage, Adolf, was six years old. Alois is depicted as a repeatedly violent father and husband. At 36 the social climber and customs official married an official's daughter, who was sickly and 14 years older than him. In marrying a woman who was clearly older than him, we can see him engaging in a transgenerational repetition of his parents' situation. At 39, Alois Schicklgruber applied and was officially granted leave to change his name to Alois Hitler. The name was a middle way between Hüttler and Hiedler. At 30, he had already been recognised as the father of an illegitimate child – a little girl called Theresa.

When he began an affair with Franziska Matzelberger, a girl in the Streif guesthouse in Braunnau where he lived, she was just 17 and legally underage. At the same time the equally underage Klara Pölzl, the eldest daughter of Alois' half-sister, was employed in the Hitler household to look after Alois's wife Anna. Officially, Alois was Klara's cousin, older than her by 23 years. In fact he was her mother's half-brother, and had grown up with Klara's mother from the age of eight. He was therefore Klara's uncle, and in a gesture of submission, she even called him uncle! His sick wife got to hear of the affair between Alois and Franzi. She spoke to him about it and asked for a divorce in 1880. Three years later, when his ex-wife died, with the earth still fresh on her coffin, he married his lover Franzi. Following her instincts as a young woman, Franzi asked Klara the housekeeper to leave her house. Before her marriage to Alois, at the age of 21, she gave birth to Alois Junior. A year later, their daughter Angela came into the world as a legitimate heir. Franzi then fell ill with tuberculosis, and her husband fetched his niece Klara back to the household. He began a relationship with her while his 23-year-old second wife lay dying. He had another child with 23-year-old Klara, who was still the housekeeper. After his second wife's death, Alois wanted to marry Klara. By now he was 47 and Klara was 24. Officially they were cousins once removed. They sought a dispensation at the local Catholic church. If it had been public knowledge that Klara's grandfather, Johann Nepomuk Hüttler, was Alois's father, they would never have been allowed to marry. Now however the beloved niece became a housewife. Klara was mother and stepmother to two small children. Gustav, her first-born, was already five months old when they married. The marriage service took place at six o'clock in the morning, and at seven the bridegroom, entirely unromantically, went to work. Something secret, hidden, lay in this wedding ceremony. There was no joyful celebration, nothing lovely or dignified, no meal worthy of the occasion, taken with friends. This was the wedding of the couple who would become parents to the future, unborn dictator Adolf, born as their fourth child (third son) in 1889. His mother was 28 and his father 51. All three children born before Adolf – Gustav (1885–7), Ida (1886–8) and Otto (1887–7) were already dead. Whether incest has a role to play in this fact, we can only guess. His brother Edmund, born in 1894, died in 1900 when Adolf was 11. These deaths caused numerous, gruelling, psychosomatic periods of grief for his mother, Klara, and huge disappointment for his father Alois. In a professional context, he was a compliant official, but at home he was given to physically violent rages; a man with a well-functioning official mask, who in his own home beat his wife and committed marital rape. In 1895 Klara fell pregnant with her second daughter, Paula (1896–1960). If we look at the surviving photographs of Alois, we can see an insecure man with a desire to rule others (Zdral 2005 pp. 15 and 28). A civil servant of the second class, Alois had an outwardly good social position. Inside however, I suspect he was mentally torn, and suffered from the stigma of his parentage. This was in spite of the fact that his father, Nepomuk, had treated him exceptionally well with regard to his inheritance. Here we have one version of the story of a rage, engineered over the course of generations, which would later reduce Europe to ashes and rubble.

Attacks of rage are produced by the discord between inner and outer life. Alois, who in the outside world was able to control other people, suffered from the stigma of having been an illegitimate child. When he was 39, he changed his name with the dubious support of his "uncle" (father), to one more reminiscent of his stepfather Hiedler, so that he could inherit from Nepomuk. This money couldn't make him happy: he remained unsettled, restless, and died at 66. At the end, he was still trying without any success to run a large-scale farm. Like many people, he used alcohol and sex as a consolation. His inferiority led him, once he had taken off his police uniform, to become a tyrant to his wife and children. The older children from his second marriage, Alois Jr. and Angela, and Adolf, seven years their junior, were beaten regularly. Alois Jr. was often spanked for little Adolf's misdeeds. At 14 the eldest son left home and moved away for good, breaking off all contact with his family. In the years that followed, his brother became first one of the most admired men in modern history, and then – after 1945, when almost everything had been destroyed – one of the most hated. In 1937, when he opened a pub in Berlin at the age of 55, Alois Jr. was still afraid of his brother's rage. Adolf the dictator hated his family history his whole life, and denied his roots even to trusted friends. When Alois Jr. threatened to go public with their family life, Hitler screamed at him in anger: "He had hidden his personal affairs from the press…the people must not know who he was, where he came from and who his family was" (Zdral 2005 p. 73). Hitler was an upstart, a counterfeiter, a renouncer. Like his father Alois, full of hate and rage. The role model for his hatred was Georg Heinrich Ritter von Schönerer, who developed into a positive father-figure for the insecure Adolf. The apprentice dictator, who was still living in the Waldviertel in Lower Austria, learnt many expressions of hate from him. Amongst his group, which tended towards sect-like rituals and behaviour, Georg Heinrich was addressed as "Führer", and greeted with the word "Heil!" (Zdral 2005 p. 72). The mass genocide perpetrated by the Nazi war criminals around Hitler means we have long been aware of the power of hate, rages and destructive anger to obliterate and extinguish on a massive scale. The following is a story that shows how

How does rage manifest itself?

sudden rages can destroy your own family roots. A few months after the annexation of Austria, in the Spring of 1938:

> "The dictator designated an area of 200 square kilometres in the middle of the Waldviertel as an army shooting ground...The area (Döllersheim Training Ground) was declared a restricted zone and annexed by the Wehrmacht. Some places that had been important to the Hitler family were affected by this: Hitler's father Alois was born in Strones bei Döllersheim, and changed his name from Schicklgruber to Hitler there...This was without doubt an area of great importance in the family's history – and with the stroke of a pen it was transformed into a no-man's-land and closed off to the public...The conversion of the land was undertaken with merciless disregard for its inhabitants ... in total 42 villages, six hamlets ...6,800 people were affected" (Zdral 2005 pp. 75–6).

His hate led him to physically obliterate his real family history, including its psycho-geographic roots. What the dictator, who was 49 at the time, did to his home is what he did over the following years to the whole of Germany and Europe. In this, he had the support of many others who had grown up knowing the hatred and rage of their fathers and grandfathers. The patterns of family and childhood are transformed into a pattern for the masses. Hatred of an oppressor can turn a person's own depression outwards, where it becomes rage-fuelled fantasising. Violence committed as part of a collective results in short-lived feelings of social belonging for its members, which bestow a transient, superficial collaborative warmth on these freezing minds. But the ominous store of aggression laid down in a little boy by his father's sudden rages can be unleashed in an unruly young man, whose rage is sudden, abnormal, and knows no bounds. The civil war in the Balkans between 1991 and 1996 showed the same mass-pattern. The bitter hatred towards the father was carried over onto other people. Intoxicated by power and rage, Hitler had many of his former companions, friends who had financed his rise to power, murdered (Zdral 2002).

"I am justice", says the dictator and tyrant. Instead of engaging with his father, under whose hatred, rage and dictatorial assertiveness Adolf had suffered as a boy, he had other people (who had first been ideologically downgraded to the category of subhuman) killed in a collective homicidal fury. Rage and the hatred of fathers, exercised freely in a mass-pattern of control and domination, is always a cruel social catastrophe. Broken human minds are filled with hate and usually corrupted entirely by this mental poison. They flee from their shattered self-confidence, which was destroyed by their fathers and grandfathers, into a collective megalomania.

In *Fink's War* (1996 p. 290), Martin Walser writes: "Different ways of processing stimuli cause the only differences between human beings worth mentioning". Are the various reactions of anger and rage therefore failed attempts to process stimuli emotionally? At home, parents can use "parental force". In the public sphere, the state – and its leaders – has the Crown Prosecution Service. Once again, this is about rights, justice, honour, worth and morality. What is and is not allowed.

When you are inundated by stimuli, something becomes annoying. Hatred of things can develop through this overload of stimuli, which can't be processed adequately. Communication is impaired. Perhaps in your sleep the stimuli left over from the day can be processed via dreams. Attacks of rage also occur in dreams.

Sudden rages in politics, in politicians, are also considerably more widespread today than they are popularly perceived to be. In times past, it was kings and princes who lived out their episodes of rage with their brutality and excessive debauchery. The King of Denmark, Christian VII, for example, or Ken Livingstone, the former Mayor of London. What actually happens when a politician seeks to hurt and dominate others with his outbursts of rage? Doesn't he discredit himself by doing this? Ragers injure themselves seven times more often than those who are less angry. In his article on cultural policy entitled "Running into walls with élan", Joachim Günter reports on how Adolf Muschg came to grief as president of the Berlin Academy of the Arts, and had to step down. Günter writes: "Adolf Muschg's re-election should only have been due when his three-year period of office expired in May 2006. During this period, his notorious rages and controversial personnel policy created opponents and enemies for him" (*NZZ am Sonntag*, 18/12/2005 p. 6).

The same thing happened to the American gorilla researcher Dian Fossey (1932–85). Professionally she was very successful, with her direct studies of gorillas in Rwanda. With much patience and perseverance, she was gradually accepted by the gorillas. She lived with them and studied their "familial and behavioural structures".

Her articles, published in *National Geographic*, and her documentary films, made her world famous. In private, her life was overshadowed by her relationships with mostly married men, who always finished with her in the end. She often suffered from loneliness, which she tried to bridge by self-medicating with alcohol and by taking antidepressants. Her sudden rages and the stubbornness that came with them thwarted much of what she longed for: a harmonious relationship with a partner, and with her fellow researchers and students. She was depicted as an eccentric who was still engaged in a bitter struggle against poachers, and for the preservation of the national park, even at the end of her life. Tragically, she was murdered in 1985 in Rwanda.

And Donald Duck? Children have never liked him and his temperament: his flaming rages, his miserable greed, his annoying impatience. All the same, we enjoy this contradictoriness in him. As we grow up, it helps us to discover the possibility of incorporating our own contradictions into our overall temperament.

Zidane's Rage

In this day and age, fits of rage can often be observed in sportsmen, thanks to the immediacy of live TV coverage. Thus the former manager of the German national football team, Rudi Völler, "strictly speaking, endangered the team's qualification for Euro 2004 with his egotistical, unconsidered rages" (Jürgen Roth, *Freitag 39*, 19/09/2003 p. 2). Alex Ferguson, Manchester United's celebrated manager, who has determined their first team's fate for over 20 years, is feared by his players, colleagues and the press because of his fits of rage. He's an overachiever, and a leader who just wants to win. Every player, world-famous or not, who has rubbed their raging boss up the wrong way, has had to go (*Welt Kompakt*, 7/11/2006 p. 20; *Tages Anzeiger*, 07/11/2006 p. 39).

Since the 2006 World Cup in Germany, the most famous rager of the moment has been Zinedine Zidane. Described as the King or Buddha of Football, he showed his rage unexpectedly during extra time in the World Cup final, where France played Italy (09/07/2006). The sports journalist Fredy Wettstein, from the *Tages Anzeiger*, writes: "Once again, here is Zinedine Zidane. Once again, here is his poetry, his art" (*SonntagsZeitung*, 09/07/2006 p. 9). He quotes the French filmmaker Stéphane Meunier, who followed France on their way to their last World Cup title, and on the day of the final gave an interview in which he said, "In the current team, he is more than a leader. He is a Buddha. A slim Buddha, who plays football." What must have been going through his mind, Wettstein wonders. Everyone who watched the game, either on TV or in the stadium itself, will have seen the following incident: Marco Materazzi, the Italian defender, was side by side with Zidane, vying for the ball, and coming in from the left, he pinched Zidane's right nipple with his left hand. Zidane got away from Materazzi, who was saying something to him, overtook him, then, when he'd gone a few more steps stopped, turned around, took a run-up, lowered his head, looked angrily in front of him and rammed his head into Materazzi's chest like a bull. Materazzi fell backwards, and Zidane moved off towards his own half. This violent conduct was a complete surprise, and it shocked me. The commentator said he had gone berserk. I immediately thought of the outbursts of rage I have been addressing in this book. The Argentinean referee couldn't have seen what had happened himself, as he was following the ball in the French half. The fourth linesman alerted him to it on the radio. Indignant Italian players did the same. Elizondo, the referee, showed a red card. There was consternation from Zidane, his fellow players and his millions of fans. The Buddha of Football, being sent off in the 110th minute! He had put France into the lead in the seventh minute with a penalty via the crossbar. Just before extra time, he and an opposition player had both gone for a header, they had collided, and he had fallen on his right shoulder, which needed medical attention. With his left hand, he made a turning motion in the direction of the bench, signalling that he wanted to be substituted. His pain was treated by the team medic with a spray, so he was able to play on, injured. It was this injured side of his chest that Materazzi put his arm across, holding Zidane back in the scene that would lead to his outburst of rage. This has to be a contributory factor to his "going berserk" later. Materazzi also verbally abused him. According to some journalists, he made several racist comments about Zidane's family. In my view, Zidane reacted in the same way as he would have as a boisterous young Algerian playing football in the street. He is the child of Algerian immigrants, whose colonial homeland had been brutally terrorised by France during its struggle for independence. The whole world watching on TV, the crowd in the stadium, the World Cup title that depended on that game, his dignified exit as a

How does rage manifest itself?

member of the national team (it was his last game before retiring) – all this provided no ethical support. "It" broke through. In his posture, described as a bull charge, we can see an archaic expression of the power struggle between young bullocks. Wettstein responds to Zidane's dark side: "Why did Zidane, such a quiet, gentle, often melancholy man, turn into a baseless avenger in the blink of eye? We won't get anything out of him on the subject. He'll stay silent, as he usually does. Because of this he had something secretive, inexplicable about him. But we will hang on to this last, wretched picture of him. This too is part of Zinedine Zidane." It may be that Zidane often keeps his feelings to himself. When he scores, we can see him shouting at the world with joy. Wettstein suspects that "his dark side is founded in his childhood, in La Castellane, the poor suburb in North Marseille where he grew up. As a child he played on the street there, when he was still Yazid and not Zidane, though even then he was better than all the others." Zidane himself once said, "Everything I know about football I learnt back there, on the street." He learnt to stand up for himself, even showing his raging side: he could be vicious and short-tempered. "I hate injustice," he said when asked about this. "I come from a hard quarter. I never went looking for an argument there, but when someone provokes you, you can't let them walk all over you. I can put up with it, okay, but then I give as good as I get." And how he does this is something billions of people in our world can experience live. It's a unique spectacle, the way one millionaire treats another millionaire like a child, and stands his ground like a naughty little boy! A god of football shows his wrath and we all watch. On the morning of the final, one of Switzerland's Sunday papers, the *Zürcher SonntagsZeitung*, published an interview with football fan Günter Grass. To the interviewer's statement, "The whole world is waxing lyrical about 34-year-old Zinedine Zidane", Grass added, "Zidane is of course unique in his modesty, and in his mastery of the game, the quiet certainty he has as a player: when he makes a pass, he knows exactly where it needs to go. And the fact that despite his 'great age', he is prepared to play for the national team again, is brilliant. And what he has achieved in a country which doesn't cope well with the large number of immigrants from North Africa, not even in a French way, is brilliant as well. There are probably a lot of French people who see it this way too – certainly people from the Banlieues (council estates) of Paris and other cities, who live under oppressive conditions, where there are outbreaks of violence. There, Zidane is definitely a role model" (*Zürcher SonntagsZeitung*, 09/07/2006).

Once Zidane had passed on his captain's armband, he walked resignedly towards the entrance to the changing rooms. He was crying, and looked dejected. The pride in a sudden rage is an emotional coldness, which cools and controls the turbulence in your mind. Zidane's outburst of rage demonstrates how much can be destroyed in a very short space of time – just nine seconds. All the same, his behaviour was immediately held up as a positive example by others. Hossein Derakhshen "Why Iran loves Zidane" – writes about how "the head of the external relations committee of the Iranian parliament, Alaeddin Boroujerdi, has sent a letter to Zinédine Zidane, congratulating him for his "logical" reaction and "timely" defence against insult to his "humane and Islamic" identity" (*The Guardian*, 13/07/2006 pp. 2–3). The radical paper Kayhan showed Zidane on the front page in two large pictures of him headbutting Marco Materazzi. The headline read: "Zidane's proud farewell – The best player of the World Cup defended his Islamic identity". Zidane, according to his own definition, is a non-practising Muslim, married to a non-Muslim dancer from Spain who doesn't wear a headscarf. None of their four sons has an Islamic name. The journalist from Kayhan and the Iranian MP had no idea what had happened between the two players, but they didn't need to: both were intent on using and misusing this outburst of rage for their own populistic politics. The astounding thing about this outburst is that it made the headlines in many of the most important newspapers. "Zidane: snapped, cracked, lost his head, something exploded, a genius let down by his human side." The Tuesday edition of *The Times* (11/07/2006) had a picture on the left hand side of Zidane gazing into the distance, with the title "What made Zidane crack?" On the sports pages, the journalist Matthew Syed, and Pete Lindsay, a psychologist from Sheffield Hallam's Centre for Sport and Exercise Science, discussed various strategies that would have helped Zidane deal with the triggers for his rage better. They both agreed that it was in the nature of professional sport that intense emotions had to be released in order to achieve sporting greatness. However Materazzi's verbal and physical provocation pushed a really very experienced player over the edge, and made him lose his self-control. Lindsay thought it would be important for the rest of the team, if they knew one of their team mates had an aggressive temperament, to learn the warning signs and try to stop the situation from escalating. Anger is a completely natural emotion in life. A player should however develop a few practical psychological strategies, and wear emotional armour so that a moment of anger doesn't tip over into aggression. When the opposition's players provoke him, they're paying him a compliment, because they're afraid of his sporting prowess. This is one suggestion for turning a negatively charged situation into something that can give a player strength, through "re-framing". Being able to step outside his individual situation can help the player who has been provoked to see the game's bigger picture – there is a World Cup final to be won – and use this to control his emotions. This well-meaning, common-sense psychological advice has no chance at all of being used in an attack of rage like Zidane's. If players like Zidane could control themselves and let the hot air of the opposition's provocation evaporate, they would stay in the game. As soon as players like Zidane lash out, they become a destructive force against their own team. Zidane, the authors of this article write, has the rest of his life to think about this harsh reality. A page further on the chief sports editor of *The Times*, Simon Barnes, writes about his theory that Zidane just couldn't bear the tension between what he was – a gifted, venerated, but ageing footballer – and the "Imago" worshipped by the people – a god of football. In other words, his self-image and his public image were getting further and further apart – something had to give. For Barnes, this headbutt wasn't an act of reason. But neither did he see it as the flame of an aggressive temperament like Wayne Rooney's. It was an act born of a strange dissatisfaction. Zidane's headbutt was an ineffectual protest against the cruelty of the sport, and the even greater cruelty of time. Even a god of football isn't immune. The red card turned him back into a normal footballer.

In Italy, the agent provocateur Materazzi enjoys the status of being one of the hardest defenders in world football (*The Times*, 11/07/2006 p. 67). He has cult status, and a fan club which glorifies his method of defending on their website. 37-year-old Materazzi has a nickname: The Matrix. He is often in the right place at the wrong time. He's seen a lot of red cards himself (three of them just while playing for Everton in the late 1990s), and in this final he was responsible for the penalty which Zidane luckily converted in the seventh minute, with his attack on Florent Malouda. Later he scored the equaliser for Italy, making it 1:1, with a beautiful header. Simon Cass quotes a friend of Zidane's: "In the 14 red cards he has received, 12 are down to him reacting to a foul or an insult. He has told me a lot of times that when people foul him badly or insult him he doesn't know how to get his own back without being seen by the referee. He told me it is not his style. He has a rush of blood, like a bull when he sees red." Explaining his indiscretion, Zidane admitted: "My nervousness and my conduct were due principally to the pressure I've been under. I will learn." Despite his desire to control his darker side, further incidents followed. His final season at Juventus before joining Madrid in a world record £47million deal was tarnished by a five-match ban for butting Jochen Kientz during a Champions' League game with Hamburg" (*Daily Mail*, 11/07/2006 p. 79). In the *Daily Mail*'s picture, taken shortly after the attack on Materazzi, he is wearing a gentle smile of satisfaction – "there, I told you so".

At the high point of a sudden attack of rage, there lurks a heightened pleasure. Then there follows the implosion into misery and the realisation of what has just happened. Wednesday, 12th July: Zidane appears on the French TV channel *Canal Plus*. In the picture of the interview *The Guardian* carried – the same picture was on the front page of *Paris Match* – Zidane has the microphone in his right hand, and the jacket he's carrying over his left shoulder looks like a military uniform. He appears open, but at the same time he is protecting his right elbow, and thus his stomach, with his left hand. He doesn't want to repeat the hurtful things Materazzi said, which provoked his attack of rage. They were of a personal nature and concerned his mother and sister. Zidane says: "He grabbed my shirt and I told him to stop. I told him if he wanted I'd swap it with him at the end of the match. That is when he said some very hard words, which were harder than gestures. He repeated them several times. It all happened very quickly and he spoke about things which hurt me deep down. […] They were very hard words. You hear them once and you try to move away. But then you hear them twice, and then a third time... I am a man and some words are harder to hear than actions. I would rather have taken a blow to the face than hear that." Zidane apologises: "I reacted and of course it is not a gesture you should do. I must say that strongly. It was seen by two or three billion people watching on television and millions and millions of children. It was an inexcusable gesture and to them, and the people in education whose job it is to show children what they should and shouldn't do". When the interviewer asks him whether he regrets his decision to turn round and headbutt Materazzi, he replies indignantly: "I can't regret it because if I do it would be like admitting that he was right to say all that. And above all, it was not

How does rage manifest itself?

right." Sepp Blatter threatened to strip him of the Golden Ball, the honour bestowed on the best player of the World Cup. Zidane says to the interviewer: "We always talk about the reaction, and inevitably it must be punished. But if there is no provocation, there is no reaction. First of all you have to say there is provocation, and the guilty one is the one who does the provoking. The response is to always punish the reaction, but if I react, something has happened. Do you imagine that in a World Cup final like that, with just 10 minutes to go to the end of my career, I am going to do something like that because it gives me pleasure? [...] There was provocation, and it was very serious, that is all. My action was inexcusable but you have to punish the real culprit, and the real culprit is the one who provoked it" (interview transcript published in English translation on BBC Sport website at http://news.bbc.co.uk/sport1/hi/football/world_cup_2006/teams/france/5174758.stm). A cartoon which appeared later shows several youths scuffling and fighting. Next to them stands Zidane with a football in his hand. He says: Have another go, this time with a football. The question is: what did you do, before you did nothing? We can all see how Zidane tried to explain his outburst. Without a trigger there is no attack. Without injustice there is no reaction to try and obtain justice. Thus his attack of rage becomes an act of vigilante justice. The god of football punishes swiftly. Coincidentally, a couple of Borderline Personality Disorder theorists have named their fourth criteria the Raging Bull (Kreisman and Straus 1992 p. 57).

It's a disproportionate, intensive, sudden rage. The person has no control over their rage, and suffers from frequent irritations and repeated physical altercations with their partners. The outbursts of rage in a Borderline Personality are as unpredictable as they are frightening. Behind them, psychologists suspect, lies the fear that somebody will, once again, disappoint and abandon them. The theory of Narrative Psychology suggests that we are constantly engaged in the task of narrating our experiences in terms of known models of experience. At the end of this process, we have narrated our autobiography. Our own story is the factor which unifies all the different aspects of the life we have lived. I narrate my identity to myself and the people around me. According to our age and the stage of life we find ourselves in, we already have a considerable collection of our own stories. This collection tells our main story, of the way we are, and contains the "normative thesis". Galen Strawson calls this the "ethical Narrativity thesis". This proposes that a rich life story is essential to a life lived ethically, and to a true and full personhood. "It's just not true that there is only one good way for human beings to experience their being in time. There are deeply non-Narrative people, and there are good ways to live that are deeply non-Narrative" (Strawson 2008 p. 2). Self-understanding requires an openness which can become restricted by the psychological models a person applies to their experiences, and which in this case has a destructive effect in a psychotherapeutic context. Strawson differentiates between "episodic" and "diachronic" experiences of the self: how we see our selves, temporally speaking. Outbursts of rage are bolts of lightening that illuminate the inner rift in the systems we live by (Strawson 2008). A stumbling-block – and there I am, under certain circumstances, raging at the universe. Megalomaniacs are often mad as all hell at their own helplessness. This unpleasant feeling, mixed with a powerful inferiority complex, can be another trigger for further attacks. Falling into the vicious circle of rage is as certain as night following day. Many perpetrators fall back into a state of despondency and gloom after an attack. They fall into the old stories of their childhood, at least as they remember them. Your own history is different from what appears in your memory. A rager's mantle of self-righteousness is replaced by the rags of contrition, with their own rampant triviality. The fantasy of omnipotence so often produced by an attack of rage crashes down in the simplicity of the everyday. It is seen for what it is: a phoney kingdom of despotic violence. This requires us to pluck up the courage to recognise the devil as an archetype of a brother. The feeling of guilt for having sinned, having revealed yourself, lost face, pushed your luck and lost friends, often comes to the fore in the aftermath of an outburst of rage (Franzoni 1990). How many tears are shed after an outburst, instead of before. Oh goddess of justice, wash my ego and my pride in my own tears – this is an Indian prayer. The proof that their regret is capable of bringing ragers some sort of permanent absolution is yet to be seen. Guilty until proven innocent.

After an outburst of rage, many people experience nervous exhaustion. They feel hurt that they have once again lost control of their emotions.

According to our survey, 13% of ragers suffer in this way after an attack. 16% have a bad conscience, and are plagued by feelings of guilt. 26% see their relationships being destroyed, and feel depressed about this (Table 18). They regret what they have said and done whilst in the grip of their emotions. They are sorry. Standing amidst the shards of their relationships and their beautiful Chinese vases, they feel more than lonely, and are rendered speechless by their actions. Tears might flow due to the fierce counter-attacks their rage may trigger in the people around them. As in war, it is usually more a case of doing damage than achieving anything. The short-lived feeling of relief at having vented their pent-up feelings gives way to the realisation that other people have even less patience with them than before. They are seen as unpleasant people. Their helplessness is hard to endure. They turn from tyrants exercising their power into scaredy-cats who run away and isolate themselves. They are egotists, trying to keep themselves under control, who in the process have got dangerously out of control and now no longer trust themselves to be around other people. And once said, words can never be taken back. Now they have to live with their own disgrace. Some have lost their jobs following a serious outburst of rage, and now feel like a little heap of misery. When they are repeat offenders, nobody can say they learn from their mistakes. As Sigmund Freud remarked almost a hundred years ago: "Nothing in life is so expensive as illness – and stupidity". Your mental wound is bleeding, and nobody is there for you. Even a clown like Grock can find himself in this situation, as he did after a dispute with his variety partner Antonet. The argument escalated to the point when, in a blind rage, Grock laid him out cold in the dressing room with a couple of well-aimed punches. The party was over. The two clowns never spoke to each other again (http://www.clown-grock.ch/1911_1918_05.html). This is not a unique case amongst clowns. The Dutch clown Herman van Veen was sometimes given to rages: "Yes, but only when I postpone my outburst of anger out of a false restraint, and put it off until the next day. Then I can really explode. I get this temperament from my father" (*Welt am Sonntag* 30/10/2005). This insight of van Veen's will be followed up in the third part of this book. In any case, it's an important tip for perpetrators, not to suppress and repress feelings of rage and anger out of a false deference to other people, and to the situation you find yourself in. First show your rage, and then laugh it off.

Victims

"Victim" comes from the Latin *victima*, meaning a person or animal killed as a sacrifice to a supernatural power. The English word retained this meaning from when it was first recorded in the late 15th century, until it also came to mean someone who was killed or injured by another person for their own ends, in around 1650. We now speak of "sacrificing ourselves" for a cause, or for other people. The idea of sacrifice is prominent in Jewish religious history, where we have the sacrifice of gifts to Yahu. A gift to God started an argument between Abel and Cain, who was somewhat given to outbursts of rage. One gift was declined, the other accepted. Here, when we talk about victims of rage, we're referring to people who had to suffer a raging father or mother as a child, or, less frequently, a raging brother or sister. Some of us suffer the sudden rages of a partner or friend who is temperamentally inclined towards these outbursts.

Of the 575 people we questioned on the street or on the phone, 117 said they were the victim of a raging parent. In the street survey alone, 21.8% (105 of 481 people) answered yes to this question, following which 70 of them (30 men, 40 women) gave us additional freely formulated answers on their experiences of rage within their family. These are collated in Table 19, divided by sex and age group.

TABLE 19: Perpetrators and cases of rage in the family

Victim and age	Number of the following answers on perpetrators or cases							Total
	Father	Mother	Partner	Brother	Alcohol	Grew up alone	Other	
Male								
<20		2						2
20-29	2	2						4
30-39	5	2		1				8
40-49	9	1						10
50-59	1							1
60-69	4						1	5
>70								
Female								
<20	4							4
20-29	3	1	1				1	6
30-39	2		3		1		1	7
40-49	4	2		1	1	1		9
50-59	5	1		1				7
60-69	4		1					5
>70	2							2
Total	45	11	3	3	2	1	3	70

How does rage manifest itself?

Amongst the 30 men, 70% of them suffered a raging father, and 23% a raging mother. Amongst the 40 women, 60% cited their father and 30% their mother as the culprit. In total 64% of victims suffered their father's rages and just 15% their mother's. In addition, 2.5% of the women suffered from a partner's rages, whilst in this survey no men suffered from their (female) partner's.

5% of the women were the victims of raging brothers (nobody, male or female, stated they were the victims of a raging sister), and 5% saw alcohol as a contributory factor.

TABLE 20: Perpetrators' views of how others suffer from their rages

Suffering caused	Number (%) of answers from perpetrators
Fear, sadness, helplessness, incomprehension	34 (40)
Verbal abuse	13 (15)
Physical violence	6 (7)
Other	15 (17)
No idea	4 (5)
No suffering caused	14 (16)
Total	86 (100)

Nobody had told Caroline Mathilde of Denmark that Christian VII was suffering from a mental illness that expressed itself through his sudden rages, brutality and excessive debauchery. And so she became a classic victim of an enraged sovereign.

73% of the people who admitted they were ragers answered our question on how the people around them suffered from their rages (Table 20) – a fact I find encouraging. In so doing, they are showing their insight, and their knowledge not only that people around them are affected by their rage, but in what way they are affected.

In spite of this empathetic knowledge, the next attack is sure to come. Knowledge alone doesn't release them or change anything. This socio-psychological knowledge must be integrated into somatic experience.

In his novel *Berlin Alexanderplatz*, Alfred Döblin (1878–1957) depicts life in the central Berlin district of Mitte in the 1920s. Franz Biberkopf beats his lover Ida to death in one of his attacks of rage. He serves a four-year sentence in Tegel prison. Once freed, he works as a cement worker. He tries to live a socially respectable and decent life. Later on, he makes a living as a peddler and newspaper seller. In this novel, Döblin brings together all the important socio-psychological orientations of society in the Weimar Republic. He reflects the confusing emotions of an increasingly disconnected society. Döblin shows us this human experience, of being alienated from your own true self, in his portrayal of a hard life in the big city. Although Franz Biberkopf makes an effort to lead an upright and honest life, he finds himself on a slippery slope thanks to dubious colleagues like the pimp and criminal Reinhold, and Otto Lüders, who robs the widow who has previously paid Biberkopf for his sexual services. Biberkopf keeps a lookout during the robbery of a fabric warehouse without realising it. He is tricked by Reinhold, together with his new employer. On the run from the police, who have caught the crooks in the act, the hoodlums throw Biberkopf out of a moving car. When Reinhold sexually assaults Biberkopf's pretty new girlfriend Emilie, she spends so long pressing him for information that he finally admits to having pushed Biberkopf out of the car. Shocked by his own confession, he then strangles Emilie. The police of course come looking for her boyfriend first. Shortly before he is taken into custody, Biberkopf revenges himself on Reinhold by setting fire to his house on Alexanderplatz.

Franz Biberkopf ends up in a psychiatric hospital. After his release he testifies to Reinhold's good character in the murder trial against him, but Reinhold is put behind bars for ten years for murdering Emilie in a fit of rage. From then on, Biberkopf earns a living as an assistant gatekeeper in a factory. Sudden rages can lead to a downward spiral like this – though they don't have to.

Victims who enter psychotherapy are seeking comfort and freedom from the ever more constrictive and constant fear that "it" – rage – could burst out of their mother or father again. One important negative aspect of these rages is that they destroy so many beautiful household objects, cared for lovingly and signifying home. Four out 100 people in our survey reported this. Mostly the flying objects are plates, cups, knives, forks, food, scarves, pans, glasses, tins, vases, pitchforks, ashtrays, mobile phones, chalk, toys, Lego bricks, shoes, hammers and other tools, chairs, computers, TVs, standard lamps, books, rocks, LPs, bunches of keys, hi-fi boxes, lighters, and so on. In attacks of rage, people are also thrown around, pushed, held down, hit, choked, stabbed, shot. The injuries caused by these various flying objects are deep and often leave permanent marks. There is the story of a man who threw the fork he was eating with so hard that it stuck in his opponent's back. But ashtrays and mobile phones can also cause head injuries.

Virginia Woolf

Roger Poole (1978), who was a reader in English Literature at Nottingham University, wrote a study of Virginia Woolf (née Stephen), which sought to show that she was not "mad" or mentally ill. She spent her whole life suffering from the memory of the sexual assaults she experienced at the hands of her two half-brothers, Gerald (from the ages of six to 11) and George Duckworth (from 11 to 22). She was never really able to speak about this with her husband, Leonard Woolf, or her female friends. These traumatic experiences and the shame she felt in speaking about them often left her in despair, at quite specific moments of her relationships and life. For 16 years, Virginia was incestuously sexually abused. Her life was, in her own words, "stolen" before it could really begin. Wounded for life by this experience, she reacted with extreme anxiety as soon as the affection in a love affair became physical. She withdrew reflexively into herself, appearing frigid in a panic of self-preservation. In her parents' house, she became acquainted with the rages of her half-brothers, George and Gerald. She learnt to cut herself off from her feelings: she tried not to feel anything more in her abused body. She cooled her emotions and divorced herself from them. For this reason she was completely unable to communicate physically with her husband. As soon as she found herself in a sexual situation with him, Virginia entered a state of shock. The pressure on her from both within and without became so great at several points in her life that she could no longer bear it. She had a vegetative nervous breakdown. She never thought of herself as mad or crazy, in the way her husband and others did. Her emotions were kept wrapped up in her. She was scared that if she began to talk about them, everything would flow out of her, like the water in a reservoir, and there would be no way of holding it back. She was very afraid of this kind of emotional inundation. Virginia seldom succeeded in living out her sensual and erotic side. Her sexual anaesthesia was eased somewhat through the vitality of another woman, like Vita Sackville-West or Violet Dickinson.

Her husband, Leonard, experienced difficulties himself with his sexuality and physicality. By the time they returned from their honeymoon, it was already apparent that he and Virginia couldn't be together sexually. Both came to the shocked realisation that even intellectually, they were incompatible and contradictory. And it got worse: Leonard became an intellectual bully towards her. Her self-taught intelligence, which was cultivated by her learned friends; her passionate devotion to her talent for writing; her gift for observing inner and outer worlds so precisely, were her anchor in the storm of her life. Being attacked by her own husband made Leonard into another part of the problem that she tried to solve by writing books. In this remarkable and very convincing study, Poole shows how the "true" Virginia portrays herself in her novels. She describes and explains not only what sees, feels and thinks through her characters, she also simultaneously shows how she views what she is seeing and experiencing. Ronald Laing, a philosophical psychologist, always used this technique in his practice. Leonard was, like his friend G. E. Moore, an extreme rationalist. Every time one of them made a statement, the other would ask: what exactly do you mean by that? The first thing we lose, if we follow this doctrine of emotional control, is our spontaneity. We wall our selves in. When she was a child, Virginia's brother Thoby and her sister Vanessa developed a technique for working their sister into a "purple rage". Two against one: a situation sure to trigger an attack of rage. Both her siblings called Virginia's enraged reaction her "madness". They made life so frustrating for Virginia that the only way she could see to rescue herself from this emotional stranglehold was to have an attack of rage. The emotions she usually kept buttoned up were suddenly opened for a moment. Behind her back, Leonard discussed his thoughts on the matter not only with doctors, but also with her sister Vanessa. When she felt too emotionally constricted in her life with Leonard, Virginia was still capable of flying into a purple rage. Leonard's mind separated facts from one another, dividing them; Virginia's attempted to melt them together, uniting them. She harmonised where he divided. One of the main triggers for her rages was

How does rage manifest itself?

when the doctors, consulted in secret, presented a united front with her husband, saying they didn't know what was wrong with her. Virginia noticed this false front, formed behind her back. However when she addressed this and refused the treatments she was offered, she was branded paranoid. This was the same woman who at such moments repeatedly said to her husband that she had disappointed him by being a failure. What she couldn't explain with regard to this was the fact that she thought she had failed him *as a wife*, because she was unable to have a sexual relationship with him.

Virginia protected herself through communicating indirectly. She could only convey to Leonard who she really was, and what she felt about their relationship, through her books. Secretiveness was a trigger for rages in Virginia's childhood, as it was in her adult life. She often brought this up with Leonard – but he denied making secret agreements with her sister or her doctors. For Virginia, who sought her truth in her inner life, in her relationships, and revealed what she found in her written language like no writer had done before her, this was simply unbearable. Unfortunately for her, and for many other ragers, she wasn't in a position to express the truths of her life, and didn't dare to. Somebody who has been as traumatised and emotionally anaesthetised in childhood as she was will always see the world of emotions as a threat, rather than a possibility. She herself believed her gravest mistake to have been her sexual passivity with her half-brother George. In later life, she saw herself as a victim-perpetrator, who had allowed this intimacy to take place for far too long. In allowing the intimacies forced on her by George, she thought she had destroyed all possibilities for her own sexual life, and for empathising with others. Although she was friends with Lytton Strachey, Freud's English translator, and Freud's first books were published in English by Leonard Woolf's press, she could never submit to psychoanalysis. Then she would have told herself and her therapist how she really experienced her world, and what she made of it – in the light of her past. The stories that were still open would have been seen and heard. In the presence of her analyst Virginia would have seen the state she was in: nervous, tense, not living in the here and now. Once there, fresh and open to physical feelings, it would have been an easy game for such a great lover of words to acquaint herself anew, together with her analyst, with the unconscious language of her wounded mind.

Vanessa's daughter, Angelica (born 1918), got married at a young age to an old boyfriend of her mother's, who had also been her father Duncan's lover in his youth. David Garnett was almost 30 years older than Angelica and was given to frequent fits of rage, terrorising his wife and their four children. Here we see a transgenerational story which is also, emotionally speaking, very incestuous (Garnett 1995 p. 162).

The language of rage shows that reality as we experience it is too strong to be controlled emotionally. Then there are moments where I feel the rage mounting inside me. I push my nose up against the closed glass doors of my locked-up inner life and feel that outwardly, I have no future. My own present, now flaring up inside me, becomes as unbearable as my emotionally anaesthetised past already is. What now? How can I go on? By feeling my own body, as a living being, through which I can express my feelings, and through which I *must* express them, in the form of rage.

The triggers for an attack of rage can act as warning lights. Before I get as far as an outburst, I can recognise what is happening to my emotions, and where inside me this is taking place. Then I can begin to confirm my own feelings and mental perceptions, which will do me good in the long run. There may be repeated conflicts between my inner and outer perceptions. I can either have my emotions confirmed, or not. When our own perception of how we see, feel and experience our inner and outer worlds isn't confirmed – when in fact it's negated – we can fall into an existential crisis. In the story of Virginia and Leonard Woolf, we can see that between 1913 and 1941, psychiatry as a profession was not interested in considering the way it saw things, or in getting to know the point of view of its so-called patients.

The Alternative

He is the victim of his father's rages. By "rages", he means unpredictable, brutal attacks, outbreaks of violence incorporating blows and threats. The trigger for these rages and the yelling and beatings that went with them was imperceptible to him as a child. Why were Father's rages a repeated occurrence in his childhood home? "Firstly, the knowledge that as a child I was weaker, and couldn't

How does rage manifest itself?

defend myself through purely physical means; consequently I wasn't exposed to any more attacks once my physical strength was comparable to my father's. Secondly, my father's ridiculous beliefs about a child's psyche – he had grown up (with the Nazis' 'poisonous pedagogy') in the garden-city of Leipzig, and lived through Fascism during his puberty – 'The child comes into the world like a blank sheet of paper, and character must be acquired.' I wouldn't talk about emotional inheritance, it's more about learning conditioned by socialisation."

The outbursts he experienced were "like a thunderstorm breaking suddenly. I would concentrate on his nostrils, which quivered absurdly, and wait patiently until the air had cleared". By staying silent, escaping, lying to his parents – in that he resorted to an "inner emigration" where he and his brother made fun of his father – he succeeded in mitigating the pain caused by his father's rages. As a victim, he knows only the negative side of rage. "Through the feeling I'd internalised, of always being at the mercy of my father's quick temper, it was impossible to feel unburdened, tranquil, and to develop inner certainty and strength." What does he think is the point of these rages? "Exercising your power, maybe whitewashing a situation when you realise you're actually in the wrong, and you don't have a good argument for doing something." Is he a rager himself? "Not really. I don't want to let myself off the hook completely though, I do have outbursts of anger." As a victim, it was difficult for him to learn to express his own feelings of anger and rage. When he allowed himself to, he was proud of being able to scream and make threats himself for a change. "But I couldn't do that until I was 30. And mind you, I'm talking about outbursts of *anger*." And in these situations, he is well aware of how he looks: "how I am when I'm angry". But in contrast to his father, these expressions of emotion aren't bound up with verbal or physical threats of violence. Even so, the people he lives with react with shock and sometimes turn away from him emotionally.

A victim of somebody else's rages is confused by his own emotions, and as a child has to keep his emotions very much in check. His true feelings are not allowed to be lived out or displayed. This inhibits and stalls his own vitality. For many people who grow up under these circumstances, their path through life leads them into a psychotherapist's office. A few keep ending up in psychiatric clinics. There, if they are supported in the right way, they can show how they are torn apart inside, live out the tears and let themselves be healed. Every patient who comes to me in my psychotherapy practice wants to be whole.

What can we do?

Psychotherapy

Psychotherapy as a Relationship

> Psyche: mind, soul, disposition, state of mind. In ancient Greek, *psyche* meant "the breath of life", from the Greek verb *psychein*: "to breathe, to live".
>
> Therapy: a healing treatment. Loaned from the Greek *therapeia*, really "serving; service", from *therápon*, "servant, companion" (Kluge and Seebold 2002).

These words constantly lead and inspire me as a psychotherapist. Nowadays there are many different schools of psychotherapy (Stumm et al 2005). There are five main modalities: psychoanalysis or depth psychology; humanistic psychology; body-oriented psychotherapy; family or "family systems" therapy, and behavioural or cognitive therapy. My experience lies in depth psychology (after C. G. Jung) and psychoanalytic therapy, humanistic and integrative body-oriented psychotherapy (after J. L. Rosenberg), and I practise a body-oriented integrative psychotherapy. Every sort of psychotherapy is an experience of a relationship where there is immediate contact.

Whilst the English child psychiatrist and psychoanalyst Donald W. Winnicott was having a quick word with his secretary prior to a therapy session, his psychotic patient sat down in the analyst's chair. Winnicott came into the consulting room and observed this power-play. He lay down on his couch and began to free-associate, expressing his thoughts. After five minutes the patient had had enough and asked if they could swap over. The patient had gained a new experience of how he could use the couch and what it meant to express his inner thoughts and feelings, or to witness his own speechlessness. Somebody who hasn't experienced this can only speculate about it. Every theory is based on the phenomenology of experience (from the Greek *theoria*, "to look at, consider"), which means that I was present as a spectator. Reflecting upon what we have experienced and making a theory out of it is one of the tasks of therapy.

"Whereof one cannot speak, thereof one must be silent", wrote the philosopher Ludwig Wittgenstein. But everyone is capable of experiencing something he can't yet express. Every experience is somatic. Then I can begin to feel the relationship between the You and the I, and eventually to describe it. We are related to each other as people by our experience and our behaviour. Psychotherapists are, amongst other things, specialists on human relationships. "Something that you can't know, not yet," writes Martin Walser (2004 p. 86), "shouldn't have words smeared over it, which give the impression you know the thing that you can't know, not yet". Psychotherapy is about openness, creating the space and time for you to feel your own alienation from your inner and outer worlds. R. D. Laing stressed that "Psychotherapy must remain an *obstinate attempt of two people to recover the wholeness of being human through the relationship between them*" (Laing 1967 p. 45). This guiding principle has become central to my therapeutic work. Psychotherapy gives us the chance of becoming healthy, when it's successful; the chance to break free from feelings of lack, and the sense of being lost in an existential hard-luck story. The beginning of this is trusting your mental powers, and expressing them physically – as the Jewish prophet Jeremiah, who knew exactly what he was doing, sang thousands of years ago. He asked Yahu, in a mantra-like prayer: *Sana me Domine, et sanabor; salvum me fac, et salvus ero.* "Heal me, O LORD, and I will be healed; save me and I shall be saved" (Jeremiah 17:14).

Sudden rages and psychosis

As young adults, for a variety of reasons, some people become psychotic (Greek for "intensively animated"). They live with their inner world completely turned outwards. It's like a dream without the protection afforded by a night's sleep. The people around them see their social behaviour as disturbed and disturbing. For them, there is only their inner world, situated in the moment, turned outwards and compulsory for everyone.

When people who have experienced psychosis come to psychotherapy, I can expect a few instances of rage. It usually happens when I express what I sense and observe. A gentle question, ("What do you feel you are lacking?") and compassionate words which get behind the protective shield of their "madness", can become triggers. In German, we also call the madness they are experiencing *Wahnsinn*. As an adjective in Old German and Germanic languages, *wahn* meant "empty, ignorant, lacking".

As a noun, *Wahn* meant hope or expectation, endeavouring to do something, and is related to the Latin "Venus": in other words, love. Many of us know what it is to be in love. And many of the people who are *wahnsinnig* – mad – when they first come to psychotherapy are disappointed in love. They are empty, and using all sorts of dream worlds, fairy tales and religions to protect themselves from this. A gifted musician, who was however not yet the most famous in Switzerland, came to me. He saw himself as an unrecognised composer, and claimed everyone who knew anything about music, at least in America, knew him and wanted to play with him. If I questioned this and thus created a connection to reality, I was not only a philistine, but a disbeliever. He immediately began to boil with rage. I stayed calm, knowing from experience the extent to which this was the "theatre of passion". He was welcome to play the dictator on the stage of my consulting room until he reached the point of disillusionment. I often think of the story Francis Huxley told in the summer of 1979 about his colleague Alec Jenner, after he had, at Jenner's request, spent three weeks working with him in Sheffield. Jenner was interested in linking psychotherapy and anthropology. One morning he was called to the ward. As medical lead at the University clinic, he was tasked with treating a man who had "been" Jesus of Nazareth all morning, and was driving everyone on the ward, both staff and patients, "mad" with his preaching and ceremonies.

Jenner asked: "Are you Jesus of Nazareth?"

The man: "Yes, I am he."

Jenner: "So you're the carpenter of Nazareth?"

The man: "Yes, I am he."

Jenner: "Good, we need a carpenter in our workshop in the basement, please come with me."

The man (astonished): "Yes, lead on!"

And so the two went down from the ward to the workshop, where Jesus was able to spend the whole day working as a carpenter. Jenner had taken him at his word and played along with the game. The patient, as "Jesus", was taken seriously in his need to be different and special, and had to follow the professor's request in order not to drop his mask on the ward. This therapist paid attention to the patient's experience and took what he said seriously. Everyone on his ward got a break from him without him having to be put in isolation or locked up.

In cases where no relationship to the aggressive or raging side of a psychotic person is taken up, and contact remains broken, his dislocation from the world is reinforced.

The 1960s saw some extreme examples of the detachment and segregation of people who were incomprehensible or raging. One patient went about talking loudly and screaming, mostly at his inner "voices". He became so unbearable on the ward of the psychiatric hospital that eventually, after other unsuccessful treatments, he was operated upon. He was given a lobotomy, which cut the nerves between the two halves of the brain. After he had recovered from this operation sufficiently to be allowed back to the corridors of the ward, he resumed yelling at his voices just as loudly as before, though admittedly with the words: "Speak up you rascals, I can't understand you".

From 1960–64, R. D. Laing and his research colleagues investigated the surrounding domestic circumstances in more than 100 cases of incidents where a person had become psychotic. "… [I]t seems to us that *without exception* the experience and behaviour that gets labelled schizophrenic is *a special strategy that a person invents in order to live in an unliveable situation.* In his life situation the person has come to feel he is in an untenable position. He cannot make a move, or make no move, without being beset by contradictory and paradoxical pressures and demands, pushes and pulls, both internally, from himself, and externally, from those around him. He is, as it were, in a position of checkmate" (Laing, 1967 p. 95; Laing & Esterson 1964). Of course, Laing and his colleagues at the Tavistock Institute of Human Relations in London already considered human biochemistry to be highly sensitive to social relationships. A social situation such as this, where people reach checkmate, causes a biochemical reaction – a fact confirmed by modern neuroscience. This biochemical mood in turn causes specific sorts of experience and behaviour, which can again be aggravating or enabling for the person in question. One way of seeking release from this can be a sudden rage; another is to claim to be Jesus, or a dictator, or the devil. Laing also writes that the behaviour of a patient diagnosed with schizophrenia is part of "a much larger network of disturbed behaviour. The contradictions and confusions 'internalised' by the individual must be looked at in their larger social contexts. Something is wrong somewhere, but it can no longer be seen exclusively or even primarily 'in' the diagnosed patient" (Laing 1967 p. 115). For several years now, these considerations have been in danger of being forgotten.

Sudden Rages and Borderline Personalities

People who live on what we call the border between inner and outer often use sudden rages as a defence mechanism. Psychotherapy is about strengthening the control and regulation of impulses, and in so doing, strengthening a person's repertoire of emotions, so that the big emotions of anxiety, fear, rage, love and joy can be tolerated and kept within the body. They can be released somatically without this being an outburst. These people suffer from their emotional dilemma, being pulled in two opposite directions. After a time, unpredictable behaviour becomes the norm for people who live with a BPD sufferer, and it is thus "predictably unpredictable" (Kreisman and Straus 1992 p. 22). One of the most common behaviours, the outburst of rage, usually arrives without warning and seems completely disproportionate to the situation. We shouldn't succumb to the temptation to fight fire with fire. We should try to calm the situation down and keep our own feelings to ourselves. It is enough, when a person is fragmented. In this way we decline any involvement in their attack of rage, and don't take the responsibility upon ourselves for being the trigger of this disproportionate rage. Borderline rages can never be resolved sensibly. There is nothing to discuss: that would only make a heated situation worse. Instead, you should alleviate the conflict by acknowledging the other person's opinion and explaining that an agreement is not going to be reached. A dog only barks for half an hour. Watch out for what comes next, and either sit down or walk away.

It's typical for people affected by BPD to react to depression, anxiety, frustration or rage with a heightening of these emotions. As a result of the perfectionism of Borderline personalities and their tendency to see everything in extremes of black and white, they try to extinguish unpleasant feelings rather than making an attempt to understand and manage them. When they notice that these bad feelings can't simply be washed away, they get more frustrated and feel more guilty. Because bad feelings are forbidden, they feel bad for feeling bad. If the situation gets worse because of this, the affected person falls into an apparently endless spiral. Relatives and therapists must try to make it possible for the person to accept these unpleasant feelings, which are just part of life. The task is to feel out the original emotion in the context of what led to these feelings becoming "forbidden".

A factor in cultivating and raising the tolerance of frustration is movement, in sport and other relaxation activities. The fifth of the Five Tibetan Rites in yoga has a holistic effect. Martin Tschopp describes the physical effects as follows: it stretches and strengthens the muscles, activates the circulation and the collective bodily functions and stimulates the crown and forehead chakras. This somatic experience acts on the mental experience, as mind, nerves and suppleness are connected. Everything negative is driven out and this practice helps us to relieve arrogance, narrow-mindedness and rages (www.entspannungswelten.ch/HTLM%20Tibeter-87.htm).

Other therapists who are oriented towards psychodynamic practices try to use these to help people affected by BPD. They strengthen a person's "I" position, and enable them to gain a workable integration of their identity through deep emotional relaxation. In spite of this, their social relationships with their partners and families must not be forgotten (Rahn 2001; Kernberg 1993).

Rage and Obsession

What was earlier called "sin" is today termed "egocentric obsession".

Sudden rages are an egocentric obsession. I am obsessed with the experience of being the centre of the centre, the thing that holds our social and communal life together. This is the "sin", the addiction to dominating others. It is a constantly repeated attempt – compulsive repetition – to be at the centre of others' networks (family, clan, society), an attempt doomed to failure by the very fact that I am attempting it. Sudden rages are a violent symptom of my own weakness: I will play the dictator and intimidate everyone around me. I covet the centre. I am the centre. I am at the centre of my own rage and let myself descend into "evil". As soon as the attack of rage is over, I am a "heap of misery", plagued by my bad conscience.

Rage is the addiction to power, and to destruction. Rage is a desire born of our own mental and social impairments. Rage is a negative, volcanic appetite for the feeling of being loved. Rage is wanting to grow larger than yourself, and thus the desire to be the triumphator; the illusion of being one-and-all. Rage is wanting to *have*; love is wanting to *be*.

The secondary problems surrounding outbursts of rage can lead to dependence on all kinds of drugs, alcohol, cigarettes – and even compulsive eating. Is there a rager inside every obese person? The mental and physical tension of rage is accompanied by high blood pressure and a permanently heightened state of nervous excitement. This condition often leads to an emotional block, in which a person is no longer able to communicate their mental processes. The outward signs that somebody is caught in this emotional deadlock can be that they dominate conversations and relationships. This is the false self's survival strategy. Drugs and alcohol lower most people's inhibitions. The Janus-faced nature of these substances is that the longed-for relaxation comes at the beginning, and by the end you are no longer aware of yourself. People who are normally closed off are better able to communicate when they're drunk. The compulsion to communicate their pent-up frustration then leads to a loss of social control. Their aggression inhibitors fall away, they start to over-estimate themselves, and they can be quick to start a fight, whether at home with their family or in public.

Attention Deficit Disorder and Rage

One important aspect of Attention Deficit Hyperactivity Disorder (ADHD or ADD), which afflicts many children in western society, is that sufferers are quickly provoked by trivial things, and often react to these triggers with explosive anger or rage. This impulsive release of pent-up emotions and characteristics is one of many possible forms of behaviour. Somebody who doesn't have their impulsive nature under control yet, and has no repertoire of ways to regulate their emotions, is only able either to run away or lash out in any given situation. The possibility of communicating their emotions directly is still unused. We all know children who suddenly fly off the handle in the middle of a lesson. When I speak to one of them about this in a psychotherapy session, she says the tension caused by the people and things around her (classmates, teacher, class work, what's going on at home) is too great to be borne on top of the mental tension that was already there. At the moment they go berserk, young people feel a fleeting sense of happiness, which afterwards becomes shame and sadness that they have reacted in this way once again. They can be helped by encouraging them to express their inner feelings outwardly, and by seeing what can be changed in their learning environment.

I'm sure we are all also familiar with stories of teachers with ADD, who start yelling at pupils out of the blue. When I was 14, I was moved from the back row to the front of the class by our French teacher, to sit next to a pupil with whom I usually messed about during lessons. I was so shocked at this paradoxical intervention by the teacher that as I sat down, I had to laugh. Straight away I got a hefty slap round the ear. The teacher did it impulsively, even though he must have known that he, or anyone else in the same situation, could be reprimanded for it. At first I laughed even more, then got angry, stood up and went home. At that point this was the only way for me to avoid creating a scene. People with ADD are usually afraid of flying into a rage. They feel like, and even describe themselves as, a football kicked around by their emotions. The goal of effecting a change in their own emotional life is to be able to ride the waves of emotion rather than being bowled over by them. This means being able to perceive the signs of approaching rage in their own bodies, so that they don't have to end up in a rage facilitated by their ADD. Sometimes the only appropriate course of action is to change the context of their lives, thereby making the outside factors that were unbearable more bearable. "Think before you act" is a useful piece of advice for adults with ADD. Practise widening the spectrum of your reactions one step at a time, so that you have more than one possible way of dealing with things. Ultimately this results in an improved awareness of your impulses, and allows you to express strong feelings in a balanced, mature way (Claus et al 2005). One expert, somebody with his own experience of ADD, likens the personality characteristics of ADD sufferers to those of men living in a primitive hunting culture. When the hunters had to live in an agrarian culture, their wakeful, agile nature, which they had needed as hunters, disturbed their fellow settlers. In a hunting society, an individual's ability to see everything quickly and precisely, and to notice the smallest of changes in their environment, was important for survival. In people with ADD, who are domesticated, these abilities lie idle. The release lies in recognising what is essential, daring to venture into the unknown places inside you, and letting everything else go (Hartmann 2006).

Rage in the Family

An outburst of rage is always also a shock discovery of feelings that point towards a kind of unconscious possession. Rage is generally a family secret that persists over and terrorises several generations. The unexpected return of the repressed is a double fright in a fit of rage. Repressed rage bursts through the surface of the mind, and at the same time the repression of the bad or evil emotion of rage, which has become a moral obligation within this family, is broken apart. Once again, family members are re-traumatised. The successful repression of rage is an attempt to prevent the wrong that I have experienced from being legitimised and passed on. I can repress it, and forget that I have repressed it. Unfortunately, what happens through this operation is that emotions get neglected. It's not just the bad and difficult emotions that are subject to repression. The good, easy feelings also suffer when emotions are stifled. Grudges, when repressed, and if need be covered with religion, have a tendency to dig their way out of this emotional prison and tunnel through to the outside. We either have a fit of rage or become ill. The scream of rage is generally filled with transgenerational sorrow and indignation at injustices suffered within a family group. The prevailing passive-aggressive mood in families like this poisons the new generation of children, just as their parents were emotionally poisoned. This leads to a penchant for cursing their position in life every time they encounter the least resistance, and beyond this to rages which burst suddenly into everyday situations. This is probably passed on through coding in the unconscious, which communicates with the unconscious of other people. How this transition functions is unclear. Hypotheses like Rupert Sheldrake's "morphogenetic fields" and "morphic resonance" (2003) are encouraging attempts to explain this. The French family therapist Anne Ancelin Schützenberger (2001) tells the story of an Arabian family with a series of daughters. After five daughters, a sixth was born, who the father named Delenda. The following year the family had their first son, and then a second. "Several times, I observed this same configuration of a succession of daughters, with a Delenda before the first son. What does "Delenda" mean? Delenda is not an Arabic first name, but a Latin word, coming from the curse pronounced by Cato the Elder during the Punic Wars between Rome and Carthage: *Delenda Carthago est* – "Carthage must be destroyed." In the area around Carthage, when a farmer or a citizen has "had enough" of a series of daughters, he names the last-born daughter Delenda in a fit of rage: the race of girls shall be destroyed. Nothing bad happens to Delenda, or to her descendants or the other girls, but the series of daughters comes to an end and sons are born" (Schützenberger 1999 p. 125). This 2,000-year-old tradition works. There is no explanation except that the birth of five or six girls warrants the father's fit of rage. And so a blessing can come from a curse (Ancelin Schützenberger 2001 p. 178).

Family therapy seeks to bring this transgenerational coding to light, with its obligations and repetitions. With the help of "reframing" (giving the content of an experience a new frame) it gives these past events a new meaning. In this way, the encoding loses the tendency towards compulsive repetition, and the task is complete.

A Body-oriented Approach to Psychotherapy

In the body-oriented integrative psychotherapy that I practise, there are a few basic principles that must be heeded.

1. Every patient has the answer and carries it within them.

2. As therapists, we offer a place and an encounter in which this inner knowledge can be recognised and accepted.

3. Therapy is an opening for the patient to start freeing themselves, with the transformation from stiff to supple. It is a chance to turn their life around from the dead-end it is heading towards. It is a redirection of emotion. *Solve et coagula.* Where there was hardness, softness shall be.

The art of healing the mind that is practised in the tradition of Asclepius, and which sees the body, mind and soul as an integrated whole, comprises at least three spheres:

- The choreography of the setting, the room and the arrangements for sitting or lying down;

- The paralinguistic messages: the music of the words, their rhythm, tempo, tone and character (warm or cold), and the pauses in a conversation;

- The sensation of movement, the emotion of movement (kinaesthetics): this is the therapeutic ballet of our bodies in movement.

In this way, psychotherapy is related to music and dance. When he first appears on the stage, with his various masks, the patient often doesn't know what to do, or what should be done. He shares this space of the mental stage with his psychotherapist. We start with a conversation. We allow ourselves a second look at things (reflection). We communicate. We give ourselves up to the river of life, which we can never hold back. We are embodied. Seen from the outside, we "have" a body, because we have a mind. Experienced from inside, we *are* a body, which is a vessel for our mind.

"What will happen when I die?" an Indian child asked his guru. The guru took a water glass in his hand, drank the remaining water, put his other palm on the glass and said to the child: "Do you see how the inside of the glass is filled with air?" "Yes," said the child.

The guru made a dramatic gesture and smashed the glass on the floor. "Where is the air that was inside the glass now?" "Everywhere", answered the child. "That's what happens to our souls when our bodies become corpses. Lesson learnt?" he asked the child, and embraced him tightly. The soul's safety is ensured by touch. In integrative body-oriented psychotherapy we consciously let ourselves touch (Itten and Fischer 2002). In a psychotherapy session, the thing that touches me mentally is the touch that can heal. What do people say in the first flush of love? We are one body and one mind. Our bodies can be seen from outside as bodies. Our minds live in this world, on this planet earth, bodily.

In Integrated Body Psychotherapy (IBP), we follow exactly these trans-personal insights. Jack Lee Rosenberg (born 1932) and his team of therapists in Los Angeles developed this method in the 1970s (Rosenberg et al 1989). Rosenberg brought together and integrated the most effective elements of independent British forms of psychoanalysis, Gestalt therapy, Reichian psychotherapy, cognitive behavioural therapy (CBT), and various humanistic psychotherapy processes (Itten 2002). IBP is an eclectic approach to reducing mental suffering. Combining these various psychological and psythotherapeutic methods and the theories that legitimate them enriches and simplifies my daily practice as a psychotherapist. With Rosenberg we consider the following seven areas, which are always present in every psychotherapeutic encounter and situation. First you must perceive your own embodied emotions – what is happening inside you in the here and now, in the face-to-face encounter with the therapist. The body is central to everything that happens in an IBP session.

1. The present, boundaries and inner support. The aspects of being embodied through being in the present moment, boundaries and inner support, help me to sense my embodied-ness, and in the first therapy sessions help me to keep being consciously reminded of it. How do I perceive my boundaries? As a patient I can make myself conscious of these through laying down a boundary. I give myself room to breathe. I respect my boundaries and those of others. How can I keep emotions, impulses, tensions inside myself? How present am I in the meeting with the therapist? Questions that must be clarified.

2. Current everyday occurrences and situations in my own life. Which worries, behaviour patterns, difficulties I have experienced, and emotional issues determine my current day-to-day life? To what extent can variations of a constantly repeated theme be recognised here? After Rosenberg worked on the Basic Fault, together with his wife and colleague Beverly Kitaen Morse, they came to see what appears in this area as an expression of the Basic Fault.

3. Transference and counter-transference. By this we mean the therapeutic relationship between patient and therapist. What each party brings to the therapeutic relationship will be looked at, discussed and resolved. It's about having a discourse and a clarity over what happens in psychotherapy. At the same time it is a meta-log to the therapeutic relationship as a relationship of practice. In therapy I can try out new forms of relationship and release myself from my old relationship patterns (mostly those from my childhood).

4. The Primary Scenario. In the area of the Primary Scenario, we look at what first shaped us when we were born into our family. This concerns our own mental history, and the history of our embodiment. "Secret Themes" and childhood patterns are analysed and the Basic Fault is made visible and experienced. The same is done with the way roles and types of behaviour within the family are delegated down the generations. In a short regression, pre-natal factors can also be brought in – informing a history of our personality that is still open, which has passed its expiry date, but which still by force of habit shows up in our patterns of emotion and behaviour. A great deal of our mental resources and vitality can be committed to this, taking them away from creating a fulfilled life in the here and now.

5. Character style and treatment of others (other agency). Our particular character style is a development from the style of survival strategy we have had to adopt to get on in the family we have been born into. IBP differentiates between three character styles, which are shaped by the quality of a

person's emotional relationship to their primary carer in the Primary Scenario: abandonment; inundation; abandonment and inundation. According to our style, our behaviour is protective, clingy, or avoidant in our interactions with the world. This is where the "Ego Identification" happens, which then matures in the person or character we become in our adult lives. Our treatment of others (other agency) is contrasted with our treatment of ourselves. I must do something to help others (at first this is usually the mother or father), so that they will love and care for me, otherwise I won't be able to grow mentally or physically. Later, when we no longer live with the primary family, this necessary survival strategy becomes a pattern of behaviour, which constitutes a habit. Self-oriented behaviour comes from the innermost core of our being, and is only possible in a family where we are cared and provided for well enough. Patterns must first be recognised for what they are. Only then can we free ourselves from them. With IBP, Rosenberg developed a variety of techniques that enable us to take these steps.

6. Sexuality and the eroticism of emotions. Sexuality and the eroticism of emotions are a wider area which we are always observing, directly reflecting upon and mapping. This is an area of life that directly determines our physical activeness and vitality in our relationships to ourselves and others. Rosenberg established himself as an original thinker and adviser in this area with his books *Orgasm* and *The Intimate Couple*.

7. Existential themes. With existential themes, we are dealing with the realm of myth, religion, and the larger fundamental connections. Here we look at the facts of life: accepting the fact that I am a mortal being, and engaging with the questions of meaning that unfold from this through meditation and the practice of other spiritual disciplines. IBP is also deeply ecumenical.

This short summary of the dynamic models of IBP should help you to better understand my therapy case-studies.

Operating Principles of Therapy

In *Primary Love and Psycho-Analytic Technique* (1952) Michael Balint emphasised the meaning of "primary love", which is occasionally transferred to the therapist in a therapeutic situation. "There is no healing without sympathy" wrote Ferenczi (1988) in his diary, just as love is the beginning of all the healing arts. Hesse (1972 p. 147) wrote: "The worth and scope of art is determined more than anything by the artist's ability to love". Two sets of observations, experiences, ways of life, philosophies of life, two ways of looking at things come together and, over the course of therapy, are brought into harmony with each other. Every situation can be seen in at least two ways. From a romantic standpoint, the sun rises in the morning, and goes down in the evening. Nothing is experienced more clearly than this. From an astronomical standpoint – considered theoretically – the sun does nothing of the sort. We are nestled in the planet Earth in our solar system, just as our solar system is a part of the cosmos. Everything is in motion – at such a huge speed that our human senses not only can't perceive it, but can't even imagine it. There is no practical parallel. In the same way, we reduce the colours to a scale of 20, even though there are over 10,000 colours in nature. We categorise and standardise our perception, in the same way we attempt to gather these types of perspectives as a totality. Laing's principle of indecidability is a psychotherapeutic axiom for me:

> "The fact that we are considering not merely the private unshared autistic inconceivable delusions of single-cut-off crazy minds may mean that more of civilised humanity is still more immersed in deepest darkness than we would like to believe. On the other hand, the laws of what goes on outside our lived world cannot be assumed or be expected to obtain within the world we actually live in. Our human experience is conditional, relative and limited. *Within* this conditional, relative, limited field, as we always are, we cannot determine unconditionally, absolutely or finally the scope of its conditionality, relativeness and limits. Call this *the principle of indecidability*" (Laing 1989 p. 82).

This principle helps me to make use of the distinction between the true and the real world. The "real" personal and social world we live in is and remains finite. The "true", dreamed, prophetic, imagined world is infinite. Over the time we have lived as Homo sapiens, both worlds have had various stories ascribed to them. The "great stories" – our myths – are always a collective memory, showing the continuity of the real world in the true world. They give real world experience a sense of continuity. They allow us to integrate our day-to-day lives into the events of the universe. My biographical story, which acts as a legitimation of my behaviours and experiences, gives me support and direction. The here and now is the desired, present point in time that past occurrences have led up to.

Modern psychotherapy researchers agree that the way in which I as a psychotherapist characterise my relationship to my patients constitutes 30% of the therapy's effectiveness. The "patient factor", the way in which he or she lives, their job, social life and love life, their housing situation, the patterns they have inherited from past generations, accounts for 40% of the effectiveness. The method of psychotherapy that is actually used, in my case Analytic and Integrative Body Psychotherapy, is only charged with 15% of the effectiveness of the process and healing – the same amount as the placebo effect (Lambert and Bergin 1994; Tschuschke and Kächele 1998).

The following report is given of Jesus healing on the Sabbath, when he said to the bystanders:

> "Is it lawful to do good on the sabbath days, or to do evil? to save life, or to kill? But they held their peace. And when he had looked round about on them with anger, being grieved for the hardness of their hearts, he saith unto the man, Stretch forth thine hand. And he stretched it out: and his hand was restored whole as the other" (Mark 3:4-5).

Insights

General Insights into Connections

What I reproach others for, I do myself. What I pass judgement on in others, I pass judgement on in myself. It's called projection. Insight is understanding – of yourself and others. If people who are given to repeated sudden rages can let the answers of their fellow

What can we do?

sufferers, given in Table 17, take effect on them (according to which the reasons for repeated attacks of rage are given as frustration and problems (23%), altercations with other people (22%), and the uncontrollable nature of their emotional regulation (17.5%)), they will already have taken their first steps in psychotherapy. These reasons are mainly difficulties in dealing with their own emotions and their social environment.

I can change how I live through these situations and emotional episodes with the help of psychotherapy (and/or couples', family or group therapy). Not facing up to the rage means it will keep on surfacing.

In an internet forum called "wer-weiss-was: Psychologie" ("who knows what: psychology"), I found the following discussion from 2003, in which sudden rages were seen as a symptom of a personality disorder. From this point of view, rage and the ability to tolerate frustration go together. "So, rages can only appear when you have a low tolerance of frustration, but a low tolerance of frustration doesn't have to result in a rage, it can be expressed in other ways." This is also a possible insight. The theory of personal characteristics sees the tendency towards rage as one of these.

For example, H. J. Eysenck (1970), one of the best-known and most controversial psychologists of the last century, saw the predisposition towards sudden rage as a product of the combination of the two main personal characteristics of extraversion and neuroses (emotional lability). According to Eysenck, people who score highly for neuroses on his personality test's scale exhibit the following characteristics: sensitive, restless, irritable, aggressive, changeable, impulsive, optimistic and active. These various personality traits can occur in different combinations. A raging personality type requires a combination of high extraversion and high neuroticism. Eysenck also call this type "choleric", thus following Galen's typology, which C. G. Jung made great use of. In his personality model, Eysenck tried to trace a predisposition to rage back to an "inborn" behavioural disposition, on the basis of his view of the way the central nervous system worked. Extraversion was supposed to accompany a low level of basic activity in the reticular activating system. Neuroticism was associated with a low excitement threshold in the limbic system. What would Eysenck call somebody who behaves submissively to his superiors, but gives his rage free rein with his family and with weaker colleagues? In this case, aspects of sudden rages as a character trait and as a pattern of behaviour are present. A rage is an aspect of impulsiveness, and impulsiveness is a behavioural disposition. Studies in the 1990s found a probability of 30–40% for the emotional inheritance of temperaments. Impulsiveness, as an aspect of a person's temperament, has a negative correlation with their tolerance of frustration. Ergo sum: a high level of impulsiveness leading to sudden rages is associated with a low tolerance of frustration. Inner and outer factors have a say in determining our characteristics: upbringing, socio-political factors like class, (linguistic) codes and culture, determine how we behave and experience the world.

Ulrich Mees, a researcher at the Institute for Psychology in the University of Oldenburg, gave an interview on the topic of "Anger: a troubling emotion". In answer to a question on the point at which anger becomes pathological or self-destructive, he said:

> "'Pathological' is a difficult concept in this context; people who experience sudden rages are also the victims of their own sustained bouts of anger. They damage themselves and others. You would hope that these people would seek out therapy or undergo behavioural training so they could learn to deal with their rage better. Phrases like 'getting yourself worked up' indicate that the irritation is directed inwards, against yourself. When you put yourself under stress and feel a negative emotion, you are firstly damaging yourself" (The louder he shouts, the better the boss: www.arte-tv.com/de/geschichte-gesellschaft/Wutattacke/826908.html).

Guggenbühl-Craig (1992) writes about the paradoxical nature of psychology. The experienced psychiatrist and analyst makes a case for modesty in psychotherapy. Our minds are autonomous. In Freud's terminology, the Id – the creative activity in us – is a gift which everyone is given at birth, handed across the generational bridge. What you can do is to foster and cultivate this gift. Many people see their Id as a curse. Guggenbühl-Craig's thesis (1992 p. 22) is: "if our destructive side becomes independent, we can easily turn into murderers and killers – witness the Nazi war criminals, Stalin's henchmen, Mao Tse-tung etc. – and when the archetype of the Dragon Slayer behaves independently, in time we become

What can we do?

crazed crusaders and sectarians". Guggenbühl-Craig uses the image of a network in which our mind lives. We are always inwardly and outwardly dependent on what went before, what exists in the here and now, and what will come tomorrow. We are networked into what Sigmund Freud termed the Unconscious. The collective Unconscious appears through messages in dreams, archetypal stories, myths and constellations of synchronous coincidences.

The Unconscious is personal, familial, collective, although the Id – often thought of as the "anima mundi" – is in the "whole". Whether the Id *is* the "whole" remains uncertain. Everything that we humans can think, dream, envision, or fantasise about, is a fragment of a fragment of a fragment. But our longing to "be whole" has existed since the story of the expulsion from paradise, in all cultures and mythologies across the world. My suspicion is that this religious myth was created (in the Torah) because the fundamental experience, the inner knowledge, of never being "whole" had always existed. We on the earth are not really the centre of the universe. Humans are animalistic creatures. We are not God's No. 1 (God: a code word for the true name of the Almighty, which we don't know and therefore cannot speak). Darwin, Freud and Einstein were modest because they knew that, in spite of all their brilliant insights, they were still just a fragment of the "whole".

"God," says Guggenbühl-Craig (1992 p. 26), "doesn't have to justify Himself to anybody. However His moods influence the course of the world. In his rage he sent the Flood. After the Flood He regretted what He had done and promised never to destroy humanity again. But if He *should* become enraged again, nothing could stop Him from, for example, sweeping away mankind with a nuclear catastrophe. We can't argue with God." When humans act like God on earth – something a few of our dictators like to do – they succumb to the "God complex". The God complex is the nagging doubt that, in spite of acting like "God", they are not really God, but human just like everyone else, and unfortunately if you prick them, they do bleed.

C. G. Jung once had two patients who claimed to be the risen Christ locked in a room together for an hour, in the Burghölzli psychiatric hospital in Zürich. Afterwards he had a conversation with each of them separately. "Doctor, it was such hard work being with this other guy. He's completely mad, he thinks he's Jesus. But

I'm Jesus." Both made roughly the same statement. Neither showed any insight into his own insanity.

After Freud's Ego, Superego and Id, C. G. Jung gives us a further differentiation: between Ego and Self.

The Ego concerns itself with the ordering of our inner world, the actual world of the psyche, and coordinating these inner perceptions with the world we live in. Psychology in this case is the sum of all that the Ego knows about mental processes, including dreams. The Self is the centre of the mind, and through it we experience meaning. It is, so to speak, the divine spark in us – that which links our psyche to God.

The devil is God's shadow; a part of the whole. Not, and this annoys him, the whole itself. God's shadow awakens in us the temptation to be like God. Unfortunately for a few of us, fortunately for others, it's just an archetype that lives and takes effect inside us. But caution: in the science of knowledge, the human-designed law of cause and effect – an outmoded axiom of the sciences of the 19th and 20th centuries – does not correspond to the phenomenology of the mind, and human beings' mental worlds. The mind is independent of the real world. How do the mythology and psychology of rage hang together?

> "A large part of our psychotherapeutic work is rooted in mythology. For example we help patients to develop the mythological background of their lives, to characterise their personal mythology. Over months and years of psychotherapy, we transform the *massa confusa*, meaningless chaos, which the patient believes his life and his suffering to be, into a meaningful mythological story, into a novel, a drama, a tragedy – or even into a comedy. This transformation of meaninglessness into meaningful mythology constitutes part of the healing effect of psychotherapy. A life that the patient couldn't understand begins to change into a meaningful biography. The various schools of psychology give their patients various explanations for their suffering, and we psychotherapists often believe we are giving patients causal explanations of their lives, although in actual fact we are only helping to find a mythology that will give some measure of sense to the chaos of their lives" (Guggenbühl-Craig 1992 p. 50).

What can we do?

Almost all the different movements within psychotherapy stem from the school of Sigmund Freud. And so we have a Freudian mythology, an Abrahamian, a Reichian, an Adlerian, a Jungian and so on – out of which further small mythologies grow, like Gestalt therapy, IBP, Systematic therapy etc. Every year new models and myths of psychotherapy come into being. Psychotherapy can be seen as an artistic movement. The art of healing remains embedded in myths, dreams, rituals and places of healing.

Earlier in the history of therapy, we are told that Hildegaard of Bingen's remedy recipes and healing plants came to her in dreams. Her visionary inspiration about the effectiveness of plants, metals and precious stones is well known. The world view of the middle ages, which was still oriented towards a unified cosmology, was formed by the four elements of earth, air, fire and water, amongst other things. Astrology, as a sort of "ancient psychology", was a discipline well-versed in the nature spirits, angels and demons that dwell with us on earth. Hildegaard of Bingen understood sudden rages as a sort of possession – a short, but violent experience of madness. She saw them as a sickness of the nerves and sense-organs, which needed to be healed. She had the following theory: the sun shines and sends its power blazing down to earth. Where it is hottest, in the Orient, jewels and precious stones come into being. Their healing substances thus came from the sun. This is her little creation myth, stemming from an animistic era. Everything is animated. The sunlight, the universe's fire, comes from the east. Thus fire as an element is also in the eastern Anasazi medicine wheel. We orient ourselves, see the sunrise growing in the east and feel the fresh new day. Many people who go about this earth carrying a violent anger or rage within them feel it burning inside. The most often-used metaphor for an outburst of rage is "like a volcano erupting" – fiery rage. A sudden rage is when a tension that exists internally or between people bursts out, creating an equilibrium, a relaxed existence. In the practice of natural healing which can complete a course of psychotherapy, minerals are often used as power factors. The stone chalcedony imparts tranquillity, and lessens irritability and sudden rage (http://www.ananzihealth.co.za/cgi-bin/ananzihealth/search.pl?id:1218564311).

TABLE 21: Steps taken by perpetrators to alleviate their fits of rage

Steps taken	Number (%) of answers from perpetrators		
	Male	Female	Total
None	27 (43)	13 (24)	40
Calming down, meditation, reflection, positive thinking	11 (16)	11 (20)	22
Therapy	5 (8)	6 (11)	11
Sport, movement	3 (5)	3 (6)	6
Running away, isolation	2 (3)	4 (7)	6
Conversation	1 (2)	2 (4)	3
Music	2 (3)	2 (4)	4
Drugs	2 (3)		2
Other	2 (3)	5 (9)	7
Getting better with age	3 (5)		3
Calming down, meditation, reflection, positive thinking and therapy		1 (2)	1
Calming down, meditation, reflection, positive thinking and sport, movement	2 (3)		2
Calming down, meditation, reflection, positive thinking and running away, isolation		1 (2)	1
Calming down, meditation, reflection, positive thinking and conversation		1 (2)	1
Therapy and sport, movement		1 (2)	1
Therapy and drugs			1
Sport, movement and getting better with age	1 (2)		1
Sport, movement and conversation	1 (2)		1
Sport, movement and music		1 (2)	1
Sport, movement and drugs	1 (2)		1
Running away, isolation and music		1 (2)	1
Conversation and drugs		1 (2)	1
Total	63 (100)	54 (100)	117

It speaks to the fifth chakra, the throat chakra (Vishuddha), which is seen as a centre of energy. This chakra has a mental and physical effect and enables us to communicate our feelings and perceptions in our own form of expression. In this vitality and inner independence everyone can and is allowed to verbalise, realise and sense their own self, if they want to.

What can we do?

TABLE 22: Perpetrators' suffering and their attempts to alleviate it

Attempts to alleviate suffering	Number (%) of perpetrators		
	Suffering from their own rage	Not suffering from their own rage	Total
Steps taken	56 (85)	14 (52)	70 (75)
No steps taken	10 (15)	13 (48)	23 (25)
Total	66 (100)	27 (100)	93 (100)

In their study "You can live without Ritalin", the homeopathic doctors Judith Reichenberg-Ullmann and Robert Ullmann (2002) describe how they have used homeopathic remedies to enable "difficult" and enraged children to manage their anger and rage more sustainably. They talk about tackling "rage". Our survey reveals the attempts made by participants to tackle and alleviate fits of rage, and the insights and self-help strategies used by ragers.

Concrete Insights from Ragers

In Table 21 we can see that of the 117 perpetrators, 77 have undertaken something to alleviate their fits of rage. 13 people – 11% – are already using various combinations of activities for this. But only around 8% of men and 11% of women who see themselves as ragers admit to having undergone therapy to alleviate their rage. A few of the men are continually encouraged and sometimes forced by their partners to look into psychotherapy for their inability to deal with extreme emotions. They are trying to change their present way of life.

40 people – nearly a third – have done nothing to alleviate their fits of rage, according to Table 21. Within this figure, the greater proportion of men (43%) is noticeable. For women, this is 24%. Women have a 3% advantage over men in their readiness to undertake therapy. These results just confirm what is already generally known: more women than men go into psychotherapy voluntarily.

In Table 22, if we look at the combination of answers to the question about how perpetrators suffer from their own rage, and the efforts made to alleviate it, it is apparent that of the 66 people who, according to Table 14, suffer because of their own rage, 85% do something to help alleviate their sudden outbursts. A good half of the 27 people who, according to Table 14, do not suffer because of their own rage, still undertake one or another of the activities listed in Table 21. This is great news. Only every fourth person of the total of 93, whether they suffer because of their rage or not, does nothing to alleviate it.

Children and Parents

The Pianist

Her father was a rager, and she sees sudden rages as consisting of: "Uncontrollable outbursts of emotions, which can no longer be kept under control. During an outburst, the person will threaten or attack somebody else verbally or physically with their anger and resentment". She herself isn't necessarily aware of the triggers for her sudden rages, even when looking back after the event. "When my father flew into a rage, it wasn't predictable. Mostly he came upstairs unannounced in the evening – we had been in bed for ages – and checked to see if there was anything under the bed. It didn't matter what and how much, it led to us being caned. My younger sister flew into rages with me when she had the feeling that I was being a know-it-all. Admittedly we were also beaten 'for a reason'. It didn't help that as a musician, my father gave us piano lessons. I'm an experimental type, and he really didn't like that. As soon as I started 'tinkling about' on the piano, the door would open and he would yell at me to stop it." One of the main causes of the rages that occurred repeatedly in her family was the way they dealt with their own aggression, which was not allowed adequate expression. She underwent psychoanalysis for eight years to alleviate her own attacks, and for five years she has been a member of a dream group. With some success, as: "I don't fly into these rages any more. As a child it helped me to laugh at my father after he had beaten us. It was an attempt to disempower him". Whilst she was in the grip of a bout of rage, she felt delivered of her extreme emotions, but had a hurtful effect on others. She often experienced the process as follows: "As far as I can remember, for me it was that I was ruled by my strong emotions. I couldn't see any way out except to scream and give my anger free rein. But it didn't help me any further."

How did her loved ones suffer from her rage? "My son suffered. When I could no longer cope with a situation where there was conflict, and he refused to give in, I got into a rage. I shouted at him and sometimes hit him. Later, when I could look back on it and when he was old enough, I apologised to him for it. I was really very sorry."

Her rages happened when the real conflicts in her life couldn't be resolved, and she was unable to assert herself other than with a fit of rage. Today, through psychotherapy, she is better able to explain herself and help find a solution.

Is rage an emotion which has been passed down in her family? "I suspect it is. But I think you can break the cycle. My son also used to have fits of rage. Back then, he was less amenable to conversations, and he got worked up about what I said. I don't get that any more. I think for him it was important that I showed him I wasn't going to carry on like that, and so I was having therapy. I also explained to him how I came to have these rages – though I called them something else. It was because of my father's beatings." Here we see rages which have been passed down the generations, but can be stopped through psychotherapy. "I noticed that I was having attacks of anger where I couldn't control my emotions. I noticed this happening when I was with my son, and it was horrible to discover my father in me, even in a milder form." Has she become aware of what triggers her rages? "It's when my emotions get wound up until I can't control them any more. I didn't notice the transition to the point where the emotion was the only thing in control, and even more extreme anger was the only way I could express the emotion that was controlling me in the here and now". Now she is able to live with the so-called "insurmountable" differences in opinion she experiences. She is better able to express and regulate her aggression. Why did she keep on having these sudden rages prior to her psychotherapy? "Because I hadn't learnt to keep track of my emotions, and look for other ways of resolving situations. I was adamant about my own point of view without reflecting on it." Today she has other ways of showing the people around her how emotionally important they are for her. One more variation on the theme of her rage: "My feelings get more intense, they wind themselves up, then at a certain point they turn into an overwhelming emotion. The description actually reminds me of orgasm. I think when you're in a rage you can't create contact, and you look for something like an outlet for your feelings. I had a penchant for smashing porcelain, but I looked for the stuff I wouldn't regret smashing afterwards.

Once I turned over a fully laden breakfast table. I have to say, I liked the theatrical part of it. I'd like to turn a breakfast table over again. To discharge the feelings I can no longer control in an outburst of anger. Then to get the same back in answer from the other person, because he was the one who got me into this mood, so he should suffer just as much, or preferably more than, me. I suffered from hurting other people." Shortly before I had finished writing this book, the pianist had the following dream:

> "A man in a big house/palace wants to kill a woman. He knows that she'll come to this house. He installs wire connections from the doorbell to all the metal in the house (radiators, pipes etc), and connects them to the mains. The woman comes to the house and rings the bell – at first the flow of electricity doesn't work, but then it does. She is stuck fast to the doorbell and is begging him to help her. During all this he is standing in a cubby hole and watching what's going on. Half of the woman is paralysed, the other half is normal. She carries on wailing and eventually he sets her free and drags her into the house roughly. The feeling of release spreads through her. However the feeling is just temporary. She knows she can only buy her release by being raped. Somehow she has to get away..."

Her commentary on what happened in the dream is: her husband is imposing because of his power and wealth. The "coach of the football team", the man in the dream, is imposing because of his status, his appearance and his prominence. He is sure of me. He creates emotional dependence without tying himself down. She comes to him, although she knows that the contact will be damaging for her. The doorbell, as a trigger, electrifies her emotionally; she is now wired to him alone. Subservient, masochistic, she begs him to spare her from the pain and set her free from this dependency. For him this creates distance. This is like being semi-conscious. The body and the senses and the possibility of making oneself understood are very restricted. She is submissive and dependent. "The feeling of release is tied to being subjected to rape." Further, she wrote to me in her letter:

"For me the emotional experience and the understanding of being 'connected to the mains was completely new. I know the feeling, but couldn't actively cut the wire. The dream helped me to understand the feeling and myself. The memory of the emotion I felt in the dream enabled me to handle the situation in a different way. Where it comes from: the feeling reminds me of scenes with my father – on a whim, he decided unannounced to try and find reasons to beat us. It always happened in the evening, when we had already gone to bed, and you couldn't predict it. The strokes of the cane on his children's backsides had a sexual motivation. I have to distance myself from this as I describe it. I always pulled myself together and didn't feel any pain, didn't want to feel pain. I didn't want to give him the feeling of having power over me and approving his use of violence. It's like feeling ELECTRIFIED. When he finished the beating and left the room, I started to laugh loudly. I wanted the laughter to sound in his ears, and for him not to forget it. Then I had the feeling of revenging myself and being in control of the situation."

I feel this damaging experience again, and integrate it into myself as an adult or older child. I disperse the emotions I have felt within me. In therapy I'm no longer alone, but alone in the presence of the therapist. So I don't need to be afraid of my boiling emotions – I don't need to withdraw into myself. I can breathe out. Being accompanied in this way on the journey back, going into ourselves, always gives us the possibility of self-discovery. Children – small people in small bodies – are only capable of repressing grievous or injurious experiences, in order to carry on living. When I go back to these emotional nodes and have the courage to resolve them, to release the bottled-up genie of pain, I come to the original reason for my past experience. I can touch the trauma inside me and gain access to the resources I have bottled and bound up in it. I can choose once more.

An adult, normal, balanced mental life is like the movement of a pendulum – in and out, backwards and forwards – in the living continuum of existence. I am not cut off from anything, I am connected to the stories that have taken place within me, and that I have often played out. Conscious and Unconscious, sleep, dreams and waking are all one; the simple multiplicity, the controlled vastness of experience.

Self is the woman. Self is the man. "Self" as a concept in psychotherapy signifies my own innermost being which constitutes my true core. As small children, we learn to want to do something "ourselves".

If the divided Self can come together and be made whole again in psychotherapy, extreme outbursts of emotion become superfluous and unnecessary.

But if I am not really in contact with my Self, then in a fit of rage my words and deeds may conceal

- an elitist claim to being absolute

- a megalomaniacal deed as a dogma of the only true faith

- a negative desire to convert people who have other beliefs.

Words said and deeds done in rage are the wrong tracks of existence. In psychotherapy we hold on, hold back, hold up and hold steady. Hold hands. Look at how you hold yourself. The *topos* of holding things up, pausing – psychotherapy is a pause in everyday life. A place where, if I want to and am able to, I am allowed to take a second look at my life without danger, protected. This lets me declare who I am in the presence of others, with body, mind and spirit. The therapist's art lies in being "other", in being a living other being alongside you. What places do I remember and want to go to. Where are the entrance and exit to the stage of my life's play. If I am suffering because my path through life has been forced upon me, psychotherapy lets me discover the possibility of walking a different path to the one that has been set out for me. If I hold on, breathe out – breathe myself out – my narrow habits will be opened up. Human beings, as every school child knows, are creatures of habit. The power of habit gives us life. It can make your life narrow or it can enlarge it. Francis Huxley (1959 p. 18) said: "Darwin avoided the dilemma by bringing purpose and determinism together under the guise of habit, which to him was really another name for nature". Always make it possible to go in another direction, and keep this option open in spite of the force of habit: this is how to achieve and maintain integration. Maintaining a new continuity. In order to keep my reputation as a musician, I have to practise for four hours a day, as well as learning something new, otherwise the old stuff will be forgotten, according to a Chinese proverb.

What can we do?

The Psychologist

He only had fits of rage as a child. His older brother and his father laughed at him for being the way he was. He couldn't just "swallow" everything. He sensed the agitation growing in him. He started to tell the others off, and began to shout. In order to isolate himself completely from their provocation, he might even kick a door. His heart beat fast, his breathing grew deeper. He needed a lot of breath. His fit of rage was a defensive action. For a brief moment he was taken seriously by his father, mother and brother. Later he would be laughed at for his outburst of rage. His defence was to annoy his father until *he* flew into a rage and beat him. His motto was: if you make me feel small, I will annoy you, and you will get into a rage too, and so I will be revenged.

It is clear here how sudden rages lead to a regression – I am made into a "snail" (a lower life form). Maybe he was missing something, and that's why his father and brother were laughing at him. A developmental gap in the process of maturing can make somebody confused and upset. In a sudden rage all my emotional togetherness breaks apart, and I fall back into the hole. After being loud and making a racket, everything is calm and quiet. He experienced these moments as if in a trance. The impossible paradox of having a fit of rage because he had been laughed at by his father and brother, and therefore not being taken seriously and respected, and after the outburst being laughed at again for it, was solved emotionally whilst the outburst lasted. As long as he remained in a state of rage, he stayed free from the grip of the paradox. Even as a boy he sensed that in the long run, his rages were not an effective way of getting out of this insoluble "double bind". Various courses of psychotherapy enabled him to find other solutions, and to practise effective survival strategies. It always takes a while to see what is glaringly obvious. So what is the deciding factor in my life as a rager that makes me capable of freeing myself from my rages? He found intellectual forms of isolation. Through playing music, he gave himself a new and lasting feeling of self-worth. He didn't "swallow" his feelings any more, but found a new openness through learning to love himself and others, combined with his emotional mood. He considered how he could behave in the future in similar circumstances to avoid having outbursts. He wanted to achieve a great deal professionally, so that he would be admired, seen, heard and read by his father and brother. He has utilised this strategy successfully up until the present day. He gives himself advice and follows it. He tries to plan how he is going to "swim" in emotion, and swims according to his plan. He has achieved a character style in which he knows what's right and what's wrong. He often has a fixed idea of reality. He differentiates, and creates a world of differentiations for himself. Clarity rescues knowledge, until new ignorance comes along. Then the thought-buildings you have constructed often collapse. Collapsing inwards means regressing to an earlier level with its existential modalities (form, content and function of experience), with which you can certainly live to some extent, but without being really socially, emotionally, spiritually and physically integrated and fulfilled.

From Victim to Perpetrator

The Inventor

He is a well-built, powerful 50-year-old man. He has already done a lot to manage his rage, with psychotherapy and self-discovery seminars. Despite this he still keeps having fits of rage, particularly at work. This puts his existence at risk and makes his creative work extremely taxing. A long period of unemployment left him depressed. At this point he didn't want to do anything at all, except stay in bed and listen to music. The only thing that restores his vitality now and again is riding around on his motorbike, and the faster he rides, the more he feels himself. There are days when he wants to stop the world and get off, leave everything on the shore of a lake, walk into the waves and swim out until he can let everything go and sink. Articulating this idea in psychotherapy helps. I take this longing to end it all seriously, though he won't do it. His rages have been with him since puberty. When events in his current social life take an unexpected turn, or don't go to plan, he feels a mighty rage welling up in him. He can't stop this process. He is compulsive. Here is an issue to explore in the therapy he is undertaking: compulsive repetition. When I am suffering from a compulsion to live through something over and over again, I have to do it until my mind has understood the message. I play the trauma out. He believes he's missing certain "software" in his brain. In order to figure this out

What can we do?

and download it, he has at various points in his life undergone a variety of psychotherapies. This has helped him to pay more attention to himself and his past history, and to recognise the character of his life in the here and now. When he has a fit of rage, he pushes away the people who are closest and most dear to him. This is the opposite of what he wants, which is to experience closeness. By this point, he's no longer able to kid himself that he has everything under control. The mental weight which holds his powerful body in its grip is a threat to him and the people around him. It's very rare that he uses force against others. Usually he destroys things that are important and valuable to him. At these moments, his hate is fully directed towards objects. He's observed an inner conflict taking place in his rages. This conflict is carried out between at least two sides in him; sometimes more are conscripted into his mental convulsions. In a desperate attempt to break free of this, he directs the anger and rage that make him powerless against another part of himself. By this point he is desperately hoping for a final rescue mission. For preference, he would like the earth to suddenly open up and swallow him. Never having been born would be a real relief. After an exhausting attack of rage, a deep anxiety, which has been with him since childhood, spreads through him like a mist. The people around him can see this state in his misty eyes. Yet another attack that he couldn't prevent. He is disappointed in himself. He becomes melancholy and feels like a burden on his fellow man. "Why do I keep losing my emotional cool?" he asks himself and me in a therapy session. "Well why did your father and grandfather have sudden rages?" I ask him back. This painful, hurtful way of regulating the emotions has been passed down his father's side of the family for more than four generations. "I think it's about ego-boundaries. About taking yourself seriously, and the feeling of being worth less than other people – so, an inferiority complex," he replies. The boundaries of his ego are lost in the moment his rage wells up inside him. The thing that he wants to protect in his rage is dissolved by it. When he has an attack of rage, he is a great grandson, connected to his forefathers by his emotion. His ego, the "I", melts in the fire of his rage into a "we". Being moderate, moderating himself, would be a by-product of alleviating his existential uncertainty. In a family like this, rages aren't forbidden. Everything which is not forbidden is allowed. He has felt the transgenerational character of his forefathers' rages as an aftershock in his own life. In his psychotherapy with me, he might find a mental peace that would make it possible for him to stay calm at home and at work. This is one of the therapeutic goals he would like to achieve. In addition he is looking for an authenticity, and wants to be fair and truthful with himself and others. He no longer wants to feign something that just isn't there. He also no longer wants to boast that he doesn't boast. He wants to be free of his occasional delusions of grandeur. He knows that these are connected to his inferiority complex.

Delusions of grandeur are like a kite that you let climb into the air: they point back to the person holding the strings that control them, to what are often pathetically small feelings of self-confidence and self-esteem. The true self he is looking for is a somatic experience. In his psychotherapy with me he is given enough space and security. In order for him to transform his life in a way that is positive for him and his mind, he needs to breathe. His own mind needs movement and breath. In our physical selves, breath fills and invigorates our chest-cavity, and with it our minds. If this vitality is no longer possible in our bodies, the soul leaves it with the breath. Then the body becomes a corpse. If a corpse is raised up, you have a god, as the old Egyptian proverb goes. Following his breath, paying attention to his gestures – the Unconscious also (but not only) communicates through our bodies – I listen attentively during our conversations to the content and the text of what he says. He needs a sense of his own boundaries. Thus I recommend to him that he lays out a boundary, a breathing space, around him with stones which I keep ready in a container for this purpose. The stones mark out his space. He can see and feel them. Where in his body does he perceive that the distance he has marked with the stones is correct?

Most of us have an inner and outer tolerance. The issue of proximity and distance is one that can be experienced and discussed with this simple exercise. What we are currently experiencing resonates back to our earliest experience of closeness and the point at which closeness becomes inundation; of distance and the point where distance starts to feel like abandonment. This can be noticed afresh in the here and now. He needs a large space. This can be a hint of emotional inundation experienced as a small child. We discuss this. As a result I encourage him to go and lie on his back on the Japanese futon on the floor of my consulting room. For me, the futon is the logical development of the Freudian couch. It is the Zen place of modern body-oriented psychotherapy. He marks out his boundary again until it's right, and clarifies the distance I should be from him. I encourage him: "Let your breath come and go, be satisfied with what comes, and with what goes. Each time you breathe out, try to let go of a little bit more of what you're bottling up inside. Imagine you're putting it down on the futon. Feel how you are carried and held. This is a steady practice of "giving in to lying down". Try to perceive what you are feeling, and where in your body this feeling exists. It is what it is, the feelings are what they are, they are where they are, in the here and now." He takes 10 full, deep breaths. Then he closes his eyes, to aid inner perception.

All our "big" feelings like passion, joy, misery, love, sorrow and rage, only exist for each of us within our own experience. As expressions of our vitality, all emotions are everyday occurrences and therefore "normal". In our bodies, emotions take the form, intensity, modulation and function that "they" want. We are always in the particular mood that we need at that moment. This is what happens when we trust in our selves. Here, we listen to our inner somato-mental voice. Valuing our emotions in the way they deserve allows us to develop self esteem. "What does your inner voice have to say? What do you perceive?" He answers: "I have a lot of room inside me; I can really feel my lovely big belly. Far down inside, I can perceive a slight sadness." So we proceed cautiously, question by question, feeling by feeling. I let him breathe into the sadness and track what happens and what changes. He uses the vigour that his commitment to his true self gives him. He can discover what this sadness is about. What it has to say to him. So we go from one emotion to another, and to the images which present themselves to him as we go. Deep breathing has a supportive effect: bending my legs, feet a shoulder-width apart, breathing deeply and fully into the upper chest (in sympathy with the autonomous nervous systems). Everything else is as relaxed as possible. When I breathe out, I relax my lower jaw, push into the ground with my whole foot from the heel to the tips of my toes; my pelvis tilts when I am grounded like this. When I breathe in it swings back; when I breathe out, it comes forward and up. We usually practise this form of deep breathing 10 times. Then a pause, and three or four normal breaths – letting the breath come and go – to see what has changed in my body. My eyes are closed. I "look" into myself and take notice of what's going on. My body is the boat of my existence in this world. This sort of breathing directly activates our autonomous nervous system.

We make it easier to access the core of our being. There we sense where the false self covers the true self like a membrane. The false self protects the true self, and through the years as we grow older, makes it more and more into its prisoner. I live in a golden cage – the door is open, but I can't fly out into life. It is necessary to sense this. Here we turn our misery over, like a farmer turns his hay, until it's dry. Then it is brought home. There we are: where and how we were as newborns and as young children. Back when we were with our mothers, living together according to the emotional patterns generated by them and their families. Now, we can touch the trauma or the anguish and at the same time grasp it in an adult way. Thus a momentary regression is made possible, with the transitory reality that accompanies it. Being "good enough" as a therapist means conveying a maternal message to the patient: "I am enjoying you, I am paying attention to you, seeing and hearing you without any effort". The young child (or the patient) is able to draw on his inner world, creating what Winnicott calls the "transitional space", a realm that bridges the gap between inner world and external reality.

Everything that I must be as a father or psychotherapist is "good enough". But being good enough is an art, and it is difficult. Once I've mastered it, it is no longer artificial. The patient, in the "supportive" presence of the psychotherapist, can have a corrective, healing experience. He has begun to be aware of himself. His feelings of "justified" rage in a given situation, whether in the private sphere or his work environment, can be communicated through his vitality. Now he has a choice. Either he takes the old route and flies into a rage, or he tries out the new way. This new way of living, this experience of being able to live differently, takes a while. Doing it over and over again lets his trust in his true self grow and become stronger. Through practising his psychotherapy exercises (experience is practice), he has gained the insight that he is able to change. He experiences his self and the story of how that self was legitimised at first hand. Changing your own beliefs is only possible through the somatic experience of a discipline. Psychotherapy is just one among many. Only when we can take a path that will lead us to a new way of living, one that we have actively chosen, can we give up the comfort of the false self which has protected us and ensured our survival. This requires courage in our own truth and the desire for mental health. An old habit is driven out by a new habit. Once a course of psychotherapy is over, a person is responsible for using his own practises to keep up his new-found integrity. Otherwise the old habits will return and drive out the new ones, which are not yet fixed in the mind. Modern psychotherapy research refers to this as the process of cognitive restructuring. It often requires long-term psychotherapy – 90–120 consultations – to restructure a person's life in a lasting way. Freeing somebody from *symptoms* on the other hand, together with the alleviation of interpersonal difficulties, is often much faster. The success of a course of psychotherapy is dependent on many kinds of factors. Health, level of social functioning, the length of time symptoms have been in place before the start of psychotherapy, age, sex, class, education, religion, work situation, family history etc, are all of enormous importance. In Switzerland, practitioners of Jungian psychotherapy spent eight years conducting empirical tests. Their results have been available since 2004 (Mattanza et al 2006) and are relevant to wider psychotherapy.

As a psychotherapist, I came across a story from C. G. Jung's practice right at the start of my professional training. A woman who had already broken off several courses of psychotherapy came to her first consultation. Jung asked her to tell him what had happened during the previous therapies that made her break them off. She described the start of an episode, and while she was telling this story, she stood up, took a few quick steps towards Jung and hit him in the face. Jung hit back reflexively, and she sat back down in her chair. After this she underwent successful psychotherapy with him.

The other therapists had never hit back. They had never shown her their true feelings and spontaneous reflexes. None of them had pushed her back inside her own boundaries. As a psychotherapist I can and should trust my self, display and maintain my boundaries during therapy, express my real feelings and have integrity in the knowledge that sometimes we shape our lives – sometimes our lives shape us. Jung's patient felt safe with him, because he never deceived her about his own feelings. Where I can no longer be disillusioned, I will no longer be deluded and deceived. Above all, I no longer delude myself. Many patients who have sudden rages at first do not take seriously enough the disillusionment they feel after an emotional explosion: they are disappointed that "it" has happened again. As soon as I stop listening to my own delusions, I have taken the first step to a new trust and confidence in my self. Why should I be somebody different to who I am? What are my rages for? And it's best to write the true answers that come from within down in my diary. This life, which I only have one chance at, is all about how well I can live my own life. This is what Jung meant by "individuation", Gestalt therapy by "maturation", and Laing by his "ontological security". In the system of the false self, we learn to deceive ourselves and others, in order to protect the true self which we are afraid of losing. Then we live by the motto: I am afraid of life, not death. In psychotherapy, we are able to feel how alive we are, and bring the story of the basic fault to a close. Then I can display it in the museum of my life, and take it out of the cupboard from time to time like old figurines from Helvetia, and say: that used to be me. Only the old stories that remain open still torment us.

When we break free from the ties of all today's apparent deceptions, including those of the visual variety – advertising, psychological tricks (Steinmeyer 2003), religion, ideology, Communism, anarchy, revolution, the New Man – the one myth that remains is that of how good, fair and upright we are. The final self-deception. The final disillusionment brings with it an inner knowledge of our moral system.

Why do I do what I do? And to what end? We should keep these questions in mind, without succumbing to a fit of rage, even if we get no direct answers to them. Indirect answers are more likely, because I receive them through dreams and inner visions. The stars of the galaxies – indispensable. The art of healing is just as indispensable.

Resonance – first of all, I take the person as a person, as they appear to me and as they depict themselves. This is their own existential position in life, and this is how I initially understand them. My theories and therapeutic models of experience are always already contained in what I bring to this person with my own empathy (counter-transference – transference). In this way the "science of experience" – as phenomenological, humanistic, existential and depth-psychological thinking – is enriched by natural research material found in the individual patient. To what extent are sudden rages desperate expressions of the combined thoughts and feelings (unwanted, injured, hurt, uncertain) of an inferiority complex? Ragers are for the most part ontologically insecure people.

In personality theory we have four examples for the successful creation of a healing experience. The recipe: create your "own" personality theory and thus become revered and imitated by others in your profession: this worked for people like Laing, Anna Freud and Skinner (Monte 1995 p. 842). As soon as your theory and practice is taken up and debated by psychologists, psychiatrists and depth-psychologists, and the wider public, a healing effect is created. The sudden rages vanish: they evaporate under the force of fame and eminence. Every theory of personality, types, or character style written in this way is a by-product of how our knowledge of human nature is increased. Trying to check whether one theory or another is more or less valid, with all the complexities of human reality, is like trying to examine a sunset through a magnifying glass. A psychological theory is a creative field between me and you. I can "rent" a variety of models. I am always already trying to find a common ground for the self and the other.

In his novel *Jürg Jenatsch*, Conrad Ferdinand Meyer (1825–98) looks at an important episode in Swiss history at the start of the 17th century. Political intrigues, and the trickery inherent in the world of compulsions and masquerades, are described as various factors contributing to the fate of the individual man or woman. Jenatsch causes his own downfall. Meyer describes his rages as the trigger for a tragic romantic entanglement, which ended in Jenatsch being murdered by his true love. Jenatsch is a contradictory character, and rage is in his blood. He learnt the political intrigues, and the deceit and trickery that went with them, from his enemies. Altogether, this was a character-combination that would in the end prove fatal for him. Only the experience of a deep and true emotion can bring a human being out of the world of compulsion, and into a world that constrains neither him nor his fellow man. For Meyer, this great emotion is a fully-realised love. The characters in his works need the cunning and art of intrigue in order to make it out of the shadows and into the light, to the contemplation of the rainbow of love. Peter von Matt's *Intrigues: the theory and practice of skulduggery* (2006) may give us a deeper historical insight here.

Look Back in Rage

In John Osborne's famous/infamous play *Look Back in Anger* (1956), Jimmy Porter, his sidekick Cliff Lewis, Alison Porter (originally played by Mary Ure) and her friend Helena Charles gamble with their young lives and uprightness, their boundaries and feelings of power and subjugation, true and false emotions. The action takes place in the Porters' attic flat. One of the seven titles Osborne played with was *Man in a Rage* (Heilpern 2006 p. 163). In a play about looking back in anger, fits of rage occur several times. Jimmy's rage builds inside him as he speaks to Helena, trying to justify everything he has done for his young wife Alison. At this moment, Alison senses a storm of rage brewing, and willingly confesses how he saved her from the clutches of her family and her former friends. Otherwise she would have rotted away there. Yes, he carried her off. The savageness in her voice unnerves Jimmy, and his rage cools and becomes hard. In another passage, Jimmy gets riled talking about the death of his father, and Alison remarks gently, "All I want is a bit of peace". Jimmy: "Peace! God!" He can hardly get the words out for the rage flaring up inside him. "I rage, and shout my head off, and everyone thinks 'poor chap!'" (Osborne 1956 p. 47) Jimmy says exactly what he's thinking, and his actions are brutal. He resigns himself to his fate at the end of the play, when Alison has left him and Helena has slipped into the position she has left vacant. Jimmy and the other young men of his generation were angry at a world that had murdered their fathers – whether in the slaughter of the Second World War, or in the mines and factories. This generation born in the 1940s showed their rage and their sorrow over what they had lost. The freshness of their rage gave them the power and vitality to try out new ways of living. John Heilpern often felt Osborne (1929–94) to be sensitive and vulnerable. He sees these personality traits as a veil covering Osborne's deep sadness.

When the young John was 11 years old, his father died of tuberculosis at the age of just 39, on 27th April 1940. The premier of *Look Back in Anger* was deliberately planned for his father's birthday (8th May).

Like many artists, Osborne was superstitious about psychotherapy. He saw it as a pillar holding up a life of conformity – another of these was taking medication, in his case antidepressants. Both would curb his writing. But paradoxically the things that restricted his writing and eventually rendered it impossible were his excessive drinking, his depression, and the cruelty he often visited on other people without thinking. As a schoolboy he was humiliated by a teacher and shown up in front of the whole class. When the teacher boxed his ears, Osborne reflexively defended himself by hitting back. As a consequence, he ran away from school. What offended him even more was when the Rector of the school laughed at him for wanting to study at Oxford. Now the boy began to search for a positive father-figure. He was hungry for affection, love and encouragement. His goal was to become a self-made man. After a short apprenticeship as a journalist, he moved into regional theatre. He spent seven years as an unknown, sometimes frustrated, and temporarily unemployed actor. The role that he learnt to play, and play well, during this time was his own role in society. His main character in *Look Back in Anger*, Jimmy, wants to be seen, heard and respected, like the author himself – and like all of us. "One day, when I am no longer spending my days running a sweet-stall, I may write a book about us all. It's all here. (S*lapping his forehead.)* Written in flames a mile high. And it won't be recollected in tranquillity, either, picking daffodils with Auntie Wordsworth. It'll be recollected in fire, and blood. My blood" (Osborne 1956 p. 43). This play about a young man filled with rage, who came from the angry, lost, post-war generation, drew a fresh line in the sand of British theatrical history, as Peter Brook and George Steiner confirmed at a symposium on the play in 1966. Doris Lessing said of Osborne: "He suffered a great deal, and his suffering was genuine...I don't think he could really cope with life. He just wasn't very competent at life...a self-pitying whine...Osborne seemed to have no defences at all...he needed too many allowances made, too much attention paid...He was unable to deal with women...Gentleman John, that was his real nature – and then something deep and spiteful forced him into venom" (Heilpern 2006 p. 247–8). Other women described him as the most complex man they had ever met. He was emotionally immature – unable to make his own decisions – vulnerable, gentle, and yet he could still be scornful. He always needed cheering up, encouraging with attention, and when he got it he was a joyful person. He had a great talent for making a mess of his life and the lives of the people he loved most. He severely traumatised other people, and in the process suffered so much himself that he had breakdowns and a few periods of serious depression. Then Osborne could only lie in bed, staring at the wall and staying silent. He rolled in on himself. The theme was: I hate you, don't leave me. Mother me, but don't make me feel small. My tears will make you feel guilty, and cause you suffering. In the theatre, he had his Luther say: "It's a shame everyone can't marry a nun. [...] Seems to me there are three ways out of despair. One is faith in Christ, the second is to become enraged by the world and make its nose bleed for it, and the third is the love of a woman" (Osborne 1994 p. 116). After he had been divorced for the third time, he was hospitalised with a nervous breakdown.

At such points of his wild life, fuelled by alcohol and fame, he lost all power to heal himself. He sank into his false self. As soon as somebody questioned his loyalty, or conversely was no longer loyal to him, this became a trigger for a severe attack of rage, in which he wore the other person out. After 18 months of marriage to his fourth wife, the actress Jill Bennett, he became aware that their mutual love had crumbled under the battering of their daily power-struggles. In Jill, he had married a female mirror-image. Both of them were immoderate in their dealings with fame, alcohol, the people they knew, and their separate endeavours to control, manipulate and own these people. Jill could shout John down; he punched back. She threw an ashtray at him; he hit her. Rage against rage, a murderous affair. Both were trapped in their destructive selves, and in a destructive "we". After eight years they had had enough. Osborne said: "I was betrayed. Betrayed by myself". He felt like an idiot who had got out of control and lost 20 years of his life (1965–85). Although we can delude ourselves for part of our lives, at some point there has to come an end to this. What then? His theatrical colleague Peter Hall describes him in the following way: "He was a dangerous man, a silly man, a paranoid man, and a man with enormous warmth and wit. He was a charmer, a sweetheart, and really was lovely to spend time with. He was also a bastard and a liar and a shit" (Heilpern 2006 p. 432). This divided character and temperament isn't so surprising when we look at all the other dignified, gentle, charming, sensible and witty people we know who suddenly lose control of their inner choleric, and have to scream at the world. This transition is full of complex processes. It is the site of the physical connection between inner (mental) nature and outer (social) culture. In a spitting rage, Osborne wrote in his 1985 notebook: "To have allowed myself to spend eight years of so contemptible and malevolent ... to have invested such trust in a creature. I despise myself for it to the grave. The fault was mine. The inane, paltry judgement was mine" (Heilpern 2006 p. 364). His feelings of worthlessness and self-contempt were the echoes of his basic fault. He constantly provoked destructive self-fulfilling prophesies in his relationships with lovers and friends. His mother had always laughed at and belittled him and, when afterwards he began to cry, locked him in her embrace. As a dramatist, Osborne was able to write impressively about emotions such as rage, but in his relationships he was emotionally cold.

What can we do?

One afternoon, John and Jill Bennett were in her Mercedes Benz on their way to Sunday lunch at a friend's. They were squabbling, and Jill kept nagging him. A roundabout lay directly ahead. John said, please stop. She couldn't. She said something else hurtful. If you say that again, I'm going to drive straight into this roundabout. She carried on. He slammed his foot down on the accelerator and raced straight ahead at 60mph towards the roundabout. Barry Krost, who told this story to the biographer, was in the back seat: he curled up in a ball and prayed. The Mercedes was stopped by a traffic sign in the middle of the roundabout. Jill had broken her right ankle. In one of those coincidences the higher powers like to arrange for us, a police car happened to be behind them. After the obligatory breath test, Osborne lost his driving licence for a year on the spot. The sort of emotional terrorism shown in this episode is by no means unique to the Osbornes' relationship. We can all sense when we are beginning to destroy each other or be destroyed psychologically. Drawing a line at this point, saying no and stop, and not letting ourselves be wound up until we burst into a sudden rage, is a sign of emotional maturity. Osborne couldn't show his inner feelings. His alcohol consumption caused mood swings which he generally reacted to by having a fit of rage, and punished whoever happened to be around him with hurtful words. He projected a lot onto others, and couldn't find a foothold within himself. Suppressing emotions is something quite different from holding onto them.

What John Osborne gave us in all his plays is a glorious dramatisation of self-pity. He attempted to convey this feeling to us in every facet of his life. He constantly sought out new scapegoats. He raged against his mother his whole life long. His childhood sense of loss was enormous. His father, a frustrated artist who worked for an advertising agency, died early, and like many people in this situation, he spent a great deal of time searching for a father-figure to replace him – somebody who could give him and his life meaning and direction. In spite of his many love affairs, all the sex, champagne, fame and success couldn't fill this emotional hole. His mother, Nelli Beatrice, liked to make a fool of him in public when he was a child, attacking him for his acne, his bed-wetting and his puny frame. In 1983, when his mother died, John Osborne said: "a year in which my mother died can't be a bad year". John Heilpern's extensive biography shows how Osborne's wives, who loved him passionately, regularly hassled and bullied him. He hassled and attacked his own daughter just as much, and eventually chased her out of his house and his life when she was just 17. This fact reveals how little Osborne was able to recognise and change himself and his life: both were determined by rage. His daughter, Nolan, never spoke to her father again after he had thrown her out. Heilpern remarks that it's a miracle she survived being written out of his life, and the devastating letter he sent her in a fit of rage. In contrast to Osborne, Nolan had friends she could discuss this with that same evening. She didn't consider a reconciliation with her father for a second. One rainy evening when she was 23, she was leaving her workplace in the West End of London. She opened her umbrella whilst she was still in the doorway, to avoid getting wet. Hardly over the threshold, she bumped into an older man outside. "Oh, I'm sorry," she said. The man didn't budge. She looked up – it was her father. He looked at her in silence. Then, without saying a word, he walked off in the opposite direction. She thought: "…how stubborn of him. Why didn't he just get out of my way?" (*The Week*, 13/05/2006, p. 45).

When Osborne wrote a weekly column for The Spectator in the 80s, Dominic Lawson, the chief editor, was struck by how little self-confidence this writer had, even then. A further example of Osborne's refusal to acknowledge reality came in 1986, when he and his fifth wife were declared bankrupt. He was over £200,000 in debt. He refused to believe this fact. By this time he had become diabetic, and had powerful, violent mood swings, mixed with irrational behaviour. His self-sabotage was heading inexorably towards self-destruction and death. He hated everything. He cursed himself and others. He was burnt out. His whole life, Osborne had never stuck to a single rule. He was a wonderful, fiery, raging spirit, who knelt to no authority. He did whatever he wanted. At the same time he was often afraid of other people and was always on the lookout for scapegoats. His fate was determined by early loss. In the course of his research, Heilpern discovered that Osborne's sister Faith (April 1928–March1930) died of tuberculosis just three months after his birth. This is his private creation myth, and his "expulsion" from paradise. Right at the start of his life, his emotional security was stolen from him, and this was the origin of his sense of being existentially "lost". We can guess intuitively at this sort of emotional history during our lives, though we can't understand it without undergoing psychotherapy.

What can we do?

Routes Out of Rage

Ragers are not clear about their own self-worth. If their selves were worth enough from their point of view, it would be possible for them to show their own feelings of rage in the moment and express them verbally, when they are present physically. Our emotions play a vital role in us. They take a primary role in our decisions, faster than we think (*SonntagsZeitung*, "Wissen", 06/08/2006, pp. 61-2). Sometimes looking out over the edge of our society and culture helps us to perceive the essential nature of our system differently. Let us therefore turn towards India for a moment. The Indian psychoanalyst and doctor Sudhir Kakar presents two cases of people affected by sudden rages, and how they were healed, in his study *Shamans, Mystics, and Doctors* (1991). Asha, a 26-year-old woman from Delhi, had frequent headaches, stomach aches and constipation, which eventually led to attacks of rage. She lashed out and broke beautiful objects. Once she had even hit her father, something which, as a person who loved and respected her father, she wouldn't have dreamt of normally. Treatments using medication (her uncle is a doctor) and exorcism were unsuccessful. And so she came to the Balaji Temple, 200km south of Delhi. The main god of the temple is Hanuman, the monkey god, who was Rama's principal assistant in his slaughter against Ravana. In keeping with the cult of this place, Asha was possessed by two spirits shortly after she had entered the temple courtyard. The first spirit said that he had been sent by her brother's wife, and was responsible for the stomach aches. His name was Masan, and his home was in cemeteries and crematoria. His speciality was devouring unborn embryos in the womb. The second spirit claimed that he was responsible for the attacks of rage. The tingling she felt in her whole body – which she described as ants walking about – was visited upon her by her fiancé's older brother. After this public confession, both spirits were silent. After being in another state of emotional turmoil, which arose from a dreamlike dance in which she let herself be moved and swayed, Asha felt lighter and generally happier in her own skin. Her skin was no longer as black as it had been at the start of her treatment. It was this darkness – the same darkness she saw on the skin of her dying father – which sent her into rages. What was going on here?

Kakar attempts to explain: "Asha was attempting to exchange her possession symptoms, a pathological reaction to individual conflict, for the ritual trance of *peshi*, a socially sanctioned psychological defense" (Kakar 1991 p. 72). The "spirits" of verbal, sexual, and aggressive/destructive desires thus spoke freely out of her.

Urmilla was an attractive 18-year-old woman from a village in Rajasthan. She sought out the Indian psychoanalyst because of general pains in her body and difficulties breathing. She couldn't get enough air. These constrictions began shortly after her marriage. Consequently she began to have uncontrollable attacks of rage, during which she remonstrated with everyone who happened to be near her. Her husband came off worst, as she used physical force against him. In a rage, she could become so strong that it took two men to restrain her and bring her to her senses.

"When the *Bhuta* comes," Urmilla told the doctor, "I can't remember anything any more."

When the spirit of rage, Bhuta, possesses her, the spirit of her dead father comes with it. He died when she was five. This temperamental spirit, whose name is Pitri, gets her through the periods when she is possessed. It was Pitri who told her to seek out the healer with her husband. During her stay in Balaji, Bhuta came to her a few more times, but he never expressed his desires or disclosed his origins. Urmilla's husband pressed her to go home, but she insisted on staying until Pitri told her when she could leave. This was too much for her husband, and he put his foot down. Then Urmilla was possessed by Pitri, and "he" remonstrated with her husband in the most monstrous way, threatening to break the husband's legs if he left his daughter. The husband gave in. A few days later, Urmilla announced that they would all go to the temple of the mother-goddess Vaishno Devi, two kilometres away from Balaji, to ask the goddess if Bhuta would leave her soon. The following day, Urmilla was possessed by Vaishno Devi. The mother-goddess angrily ordered the husband to go home: she would take care of Urmilla.

When Urmilla came to after this possession, she was freed from her complaints, and said Vaishno Devi could take care of her better than Pitri.

Kakar comments: "The evidence is strong that Urmilla harboured within her a violent rage, which she suppressed till her marriage, until finally her inability to control the rage provoked the mysterious aches and the motor discharge in possession states. In these states, assured of the protection afforded by the clouding of consciousness and the subsequent amnesia, Urmilla was able to give an otherwise forbidden satisfaction to her pent-up fury" (Kakar p. 79). Her rages weren't only directed towards her husband, but at the internalised figures of her parents. She was raging against her own feeling of powerlessness – this is why being possessed by the powerful mother-goddess was such a healing act for her. Now Urmilla had a new inner central figure. Change through life; life through change. Your inner grace, and your own knowledge of what will help you, can enable you to live through changes.

In an interview with the magazine *Der Spiegel* (2006, no. 42, pp. 156-7), the soprano Anna Netrebko was asked: "There can be no great art without suffering. Have you suffered in your life?" Netrebko: "Well, what do you think?" Interviewer: "You don't look as if you have in any case!" Netrebko: "Of course I know what suffering is, like every human being does. I suffer, I'm happy, and then there's another period of exhaustion, when I feel helpless." Interviewer: "So self-doubt, feelings of inferiority – you're familiar with all these?" Netrebko: "Yes, of course! And then from time to time, for no good reason, on some morning in some hotel room I'll have a panic attack: Oh God, everything's awful, my life's over, my career is over, I can't sing any more! After a few hours it dies down." Interviewer: "What helps you when you have a panic attack?" Netrebko: "Practising. I sing for three hours – have a break – sing for another three hours – a break – another three hours. That helps."

This can work for sudden rages too. Once our experience of psychotherapy has shown us how we can live out and display our emotions, all that's left – as Netrebko shows – is to practise, practise, practise, until we feel better. Activating our own abilities and resources helps us to bridge our present feeling of emptiness.

We can gain direct experience of our own worth by spurring our selves into action.

When I asked the *Book of Changes* (*I Ching*) why I was engaging with the issue of sudden rages, it "answered" with no.24, "Fu" (return, also called the turning point). At the top of the symbol is K'un, the earth, the receptive. At the bottom is Chên, the arouser, thunder. The book says: "Thunder within the earth: The Image of THE TURNING POINT. Thus the king of antiquity closed the passes at the time of solstice. Merchants and strangers did not go about, and the ruler did not travel through the provinces" (*The I Ching* 1975 p. 98).

The commentary tells us: "After a time of decay comes the turning point. The powerful light that has been banished returns. There is movement, but it is not brought about by force. The upper trigram K'un is characterised by devotion; thus the movement is natural, arising spontaneously. For this reason the transformation of the old becomes easy. The old is discarded and the new is introduced. Both measures accord with the time; therefore no harm results. Societies of people sharing the same views are formed. But since these groups come together in full public knowledge and are in harmony with the time, all selfish separatist tendencies are excluded, and no mistake is made. The idea of Return is based on the course of nature. The movement is cyclic, and the course completes itself. Therefore it is not necessary to hasten anything artificially. Everything comes of itself at the appointed time. This is the meaning of heaven and earth. All movements are accomplished by six stages, and the seventh brings return" (*The I Ching*, Wilhelm, 1975, pp. 97–8).

In China, the winter solstice – addressed in the *I Ching* as a time to return to nature – is celebrated as a peaceful time. The new year begins with tranquillity. The phrases "take it easy" and "one thing at a time" spring to mind. The life-force rests, and is symbolised by the rolling of thunder under the earth. The Chinese mindset, of letting the power of renewal rest and gather its strength before the Spring, can be applied to every situation, whether it be recovering from illness or reaching a new understanding with somebody after you've had an argument. It's important to grasp the chance to turn things around at the right moment. In an attack of rage, emotions show themselves simply, without any pretence. Emotions are signs of vitality in the body. Now an opening has been created, where before feelings of rage were kept locked away.

The world as we know it is not as neatly segmented as we like to think.

"Our minds," writes Laing, "move between complexity and simplicity, multiplicity and unity. This movement is often felt in terms of going out and forward and in and back. Backwards and forwards in time may be called regression and progression, and the movement between the one and the many may be called recession and procession" (Laing 1982 p. 156). In the experiences of many patients, regression and recession occur together. The same thing can happen with progression and procession. One person can feel incredibly restricted and small (intrauterine regression), whilst another feels unrestricted and lost in space (recession to the loss of most distinctions). This way of looking at the movements of the mind and intellect helps to impart sense to experiences which have no apparent sense.

One person who understood the Tao of therapy as well as any other who walked this path was C. G. Jung. A female patient who suffered from severe depression said of her consultations with Jung, which mostly proceeded in the same way: "I had nothing to say this day. I took my seat (in the library). He pulled his chair close to mine. I did not want to meet his eyes, so we both stared ahead at the books on the wall. I did not speak, so neither did he. Occasionally he reached out to stroke my arm or pat my hand. The hour passed and I became tranquil. I wish that peace would come with me when I leave, but it disappears without his presence" (Bair 2003 p. 381). In this case, her daughter had taken her own life, after her child had died in an accident at a young age. The daughter had laid all the blame for her unhappiness in life on her mother. For several years, the patient sat with Jung like this in his library three times a week. Sometimes her gaze drifted away from the books and out of the window, to the waves dancing on Lake Zurich. Jung's presence as a psychotherapist was very effective. Without using many words, he was able to sense how her life experiences had led to her depression, and he succeeded in integrating this heavy darkness into the totality of her life through analysis and psychotherapy. One day, "she told her diary that 'a great cloud has lifted'. She left Zürich and spent her remaining decade in prayer, fasting, and meditation; living in relative isolation in another part of the country; and sending an occasional greeting to tell Jung that she was well. Her friends remembered her as 'beatific' and 'at peace' until she died" (Bair 2003 p. 381). The harmonious dance of communal silence keeps the mind supple. This masterpiece shows Jung's faith in his own finely-tuned mind, which allowed him to give himself over to the confusions of others and sway along with them. Life heals. This is the first step on the path.

The Cook

For years he suffered from suppressed rage, from the depression that lay underneath it, from a tendency to sabotage his own happiness, and from sudden attacks of rage. As an experienced ship's cook on the world's oceans, he was best acquainted with "kitchen rage". Pans, knives and other hot objects would fly through the air. It took years and various attempts at treatment through self-medication – following a divorce, the closing of his restaurant, the loss of his assets, restricted access to his young daughter, and various somatic complaints – before he came to me for psychotherapy. In total I spent 120 hours with him over several years.

The patient, who is now 48 and was originally from San Francisco, told this story on the theme of sudden rages:

> "My father was a very frustrated individual: my grandfather was a formidable guy. I'm the youngest of three boys. My two older brothers got a lot more of my father's anger than I did. Sometimes after coming home from his job and having a few drinks he would tear into one of us who happened to be close about any number of things that bothered him. But it was always way over the top reactions. My middle brother withdrew himself and was at home less and less as he got older. He went into hiding, so to speak. Mother tried to hide all of us from Father, and she'd say we should be quiet when he was in a bad mood. His rages were often triggered by his drinking – wine, whisky or beer or a combination of all three. On top of that there was his anger about his job, and bad news on the TV. I found his rages really disconcerting: they were horrible. They didn't happen daily but often enough to be wary when I came home in the evenings. As his youngest son, I tried to be close to him and to understand him mostly to no avail. In my youth I smoked a fair amount of marijuana. That made him very mad. Later in his life he had told me that he had always wanted to try a joint of grass but he could not work up the nerve to ask me. I think now – that maybe it would have stopped him from having these tantrums. I believe his rages were an emotional legacy from his father. Once when my grandfather was on the phone, I could hear my father saying, 'Yes Dad, of course Dad, yes, yes' and when he'd finished he slammed the receiver down, then ripped the phone, with the cable and the connection, out of the wall, threw it full force onto the floor smashing it to bits and pieces. Then stomping it like a child. I was shocked. Luckily my father worked for the phone company, so the material damage was minimal. He got a new phone the same day and connected it up again. My

grandfather never treated my father with any respect and would privately put him down as a kind of loser which would set my father off like a bomb. From my point of view he was a total bastard. My father couldn't stand up for himself against him. There was no talk of confronting him with his own thoughts. Once, when my father attacked me for speaking my mind – I was at least 17 – I stood up to him walking towards him instead of running away. I was well-built and taller than him, and at this point he took a step back not knowing what to do as I had never stood up to him so he backed off. After this he certainly thought twice before he attacked me for anything. The way I understand these rages, the way they feel, they're an emotion that can't be controlled. Like a volcano erupting, or a devilish monster that takes me over, like I'm possessed. If I can't suffocate this monster in my belly, it has power over me and I can't stop it any more. Point of no return. My middle brother Tom and I both inherited this monster from my father, my grandfather and great grandfather all on my father's side. So it's clearly a transgenerational thing. On my mother's side the people are sweet, nice and very religious. They never say a bad or hurtful word to anyone. Sudden rages are an emotional legacy. Your own character plays an important role in this. I see what my father did, and I do it as well. Monkey see, monkey do, it's a primitive learning reflex. Everything can become a trigger for rage. The astounding thing is it doesn't have to have anything to do with what's happening at that moment. It can be something in his food, a piece of roast meat that wasn't quite cooked the way he wanted it this particular evening. Then it all happens very quickly, in a whirl. Sometimes I think everything and nothing can trigger an attack. Really disconcerting. Then I sense a feeling in my stomach, which grows quite quickly and then can't be kept inside. It growls angrily, bares its teeth and then it breaks out. It's impossible to hold back an inner fire like this. Personally, when I've had attacks like these, I've looked for something made of wood, so I can break it. That has helped me to get out of the situation, into the shed, and chop wood in there like a madman till I was out of breath. Totally breathless. Then I was 'out' again. I'm an idiot, I'm an idiot, was the musical accompaniment in my thoughts and feelings. Why do I fly into these rages? I think my rage is bound up with jealousy. As I said, this has all been going on for a while in my family. My great-grandfather, so my father says, was the worst of all of us. He was such an angry, bad-tempered, terrible human being. But why? I think it has to do with immigration. This side of the family came from Spain. Mother's side came from Italy. And I came to Switzerland. Something gets left behind and we discover a new world. Our hopes of finding paradise not only remain unfulfilled, we are totally disappointed. That spurs the anger on. And why the whole show of strength? Sure, the deep feelings of frustration that go with these experiences make the rages possible too. I've ignored my problems for a long time. I didn't take care of myself. When someone I knew showed their feelings, like shedding tears of pain, I just ignored it. Sometimes it got so bad, seriously, I could have killed someone. I've never done it, but when I'm in a rage I could be capable of it without a doubt. Whether it's genetic or not, I can't say. What my brother Tom and I swore to each other was that we wouldn't pass on to our children what we'd experienced with my father. I think if he'd had psychotherapy, it would have been possible for him to find out what he was missing, and what was wrong with his way of thinking. His whole attitude to life, his way of life, was called into question from inside by his sons, and from outside by his work and life – we were living in San Francisco after all. His life got more and more complicated. He tried to keep his head above water with the help of alcohol. So he often came home angry, started drinking, watched the news, and then all hell broke loose in our living room. In all these years I've only seen him cry twice, after Kennedy was shot, and when his sister died. I myself tried various routes to reducing my rages. I had to try to stop what was triggering them. Because they were linked to alcohol consumption in both me and my father, I stopped drinking. The Indians had this as well – the Anazazi – when they'd drunk themselves into a stupor, they often flew into such a rage that they'd get their guns out and start shooting. For a while I tried to suppress the feeling of rage. I spoke to my inner monster, and said 'I'm not giving you any room; I'm going to extinguish you'. It's like when a fire breaks out, you have to put it out straight away. Stamp out the inner fire completely. I installed a sprinkler system in my mind. As soon as I noticed the smallest trigger for my rage, I put it out as quickly as possible.

The thing that helped me after this as well was making music. I got myself a guitar and played it like a madman, biting the strings, banging about on it, to let all the rage out of myself. That was my salvation. Suddenly I could do something useful with my emotions. That felt so good. I could channel my rage, and point it in another direction. But even so it still happened now and again. Afterwards I felt like a jerk. When I'm in a rage, I'm not conscious of what I'm saying to other people, I mouth off, as we say. Everything is negative, everything's bad and everyone's an idiot. It's horrible, the people around me really don't like it, and they often don't forgive me for what I've said even though I'm sorry afterwards and I apologize. My father was very despondent after an attack, he felt like dirt – a heap of misery. For a few days he would hardly say a word, he stayed silent and he didn't drink any wine or whisky. He often stayed away from the house for hours. He took himself off to the ocean, to the coast, and sat there listening to the water rushing against the shore. I often did that too, later. It's a comforting noise, this endless repetition of the waves, one after another, shh-shh-shh… Personally I felt secure again, like in the womb. Tranquil, conscious, awake, alert, everything else in the world ceased to be important. Being at the coast, together with my music-making, was always the way I tried to heal myself. But the monster, as I call my rage, is still sleeping inside me. It's just that it no longer strangles me so much. When I have an attack, and I can hardly breathe any more, I feel threatened. That's why I have to scream and shout, to be able to breathe freely again. The other tactic I've discovered is running away. Physically getting out of the place where a rage might happen, as soon as the triggers get too strong, and running, running, running until I'm out of breath. Then I've managed to let my energy out, to let it stretch its legs. Rage is so stupid. I can't see any sense in it, it's senseless. When I see it today in somebody else, I notice how funny, how sinister, how mad it makes them look. A bright red face, jaws pressed together, teeth grinding, raving, throwing everything within reach around like a whirlwind. Then I notice how I draw back and distance myself from this person. He or she loses my closeness. Recently I saw a work colleague throwing whole trolleys around. Frightening, the force that breaks free then. I noticed how my monster stirred a little inside me, as if it was rolling from one side to the other. No, I thought, I don't want to be like that again myself, losing control of my emotions like that. The last time I was really in a rage, when I shattered the windscreen of the work van I was driving with my fist, was five years ago. That was the trigger for starting psychotherapy with you. My colleague was with you already and he tipped me off. At this point I was an emotional wreck. My marriage had fallen apart, the restaurant closed, I was sad, overweight, drinking again, smoking, not getting enough sleep – I was depressed, sometimes suicidal. So I went into therapy with you. What helped me at first more than anything was the way you listened. You were an outsider in my life. You gave me simple tips on how to try going a different route. You asked about my feelings and were interested in my thoughts. I was with another therapist before you, but it didn't work out. While I was in therapy with you I had something like a 'breakdown', where everything in me had to be 'broken down' so that it could be built up afresh afterwards. I had to look at every piece and become aware of my feelings about it. That was what I generally found difficult, to hear how I sounded, to see how I saw the world. You held a mirror up to me and served as my sounding-board. You tried to understand, and to make me understand, the structures behind the situations that I found myself in. You helped me to simply stop and think about what was going on. In this way I became realistic and didn't need to live in my fantasy world so much. I was so good at running away from everything. But I not only saw what it was I was doing when I ran away, but why, and what was missing from the fantasy too. I was looking for a way out. But I would only find one once I had taken a long look at myself and leant to understand my self. I had to realise what my problems and my difficulties were. Now, after five years of therapy, I feel good. I don't smoke or drink any more. I have a spiritual discipline, I've carried on making music, I sing in a choir and do amateur dramatics. Now I've left my rages behind. If I see so much as the smallest sign of its fire, I put it out by expressing the feelings that arise in me, addressing conflicts, or to begin with writing them down. Psychotherapy was a gift. Today I live rage-free, with a deeper sense of self-esteem and plenty of self-confidence."

What can we do?

The Cook, rebooted (2014)

"It's a wonderful feeling to be able to breathe freely again. Over the past few years, since I came to psychotherapy for the first time, I have learned two things that have been important for me. Controlling my emotions is good for my own health, and for maintaining my circle of friends. We might not notice it, but friends do care about us. If I go off the rails emotionally in a sudden rage, friends can turn away. That's a sad experience. Like I said at the beginning, it's good to breathe freely again. Living with anger and sudden rages caused profound changes in my life, which I regret. One thing is clear: even today I still fall back into my old groove of rage now and again. I probably always will. I've learned how important it is to tame and restrain the animal inside me before it takes control. That makes all the difference in my world. Taking a step back, breathing in deeply and letting the fresh air deep into my being. That gives me time to slow down and take back control of my feelings. To feel the power of my own self-discipline, and pull away from what in my old life would have dragged me down, into a temporary emotional meltdown. The sense of being in charge of myself today is an encouraging emotional strength, and it makes me want to do this more and more whenever these emotions try to break out onto the surface. I've also learned that misery loves company. It will always draw in those people who want to bring others down to their own angry level. Understanding the various situations that trigger rages before they happen helps to build up defensive forces. These act like a dam against the negative influence on my sense of self-worth and my own dignity. I keep my head above water, if you like.

In many situations, since my early days, I have found that memories and thoughts of my childhood frustrations triggered volcanic eruptions, which came out in explosive attacks of anger and hurt other people as well as myself. Today I can look back on those moments, knowing they are a thing of the past. That is a sweet relief.

Accepting my own life, as it is for me in the here and now, has never been simple. There were so many frustrated endeavours: marriage, career, other relationships and self-doubt, which almost inevitably led to my own destructive behaviour. Even so, accepting who I am and my current situation in life makes a huge difference. I still harbour ambitions. I'm still looking for ways to advance myself. The most important thing is that if I can't earn or achieve the thing I'm imagining and looking for, I don't let that block me. I leave it as it is, and at the same time try to understand what mistakes were made and look for ways to do it differently next time. Before, my frustrations made me throw myself against the waves, fight the storm, lash out with bursts of anger and pain.

The therapy I received from Mr Itten taught me to breathe again, to become aware of my inner self and cut down the emotional jungle that sprang up during my upbringing. This experience has brought me to a place in my life I had only dreamed of before. Which is to say, I am in touch with myself and have day-to-day control over my emotions. I've broken out of my old routine now – I don't have to force it any more. At the start I had to force myself into this discipline, before I could reach the place where I am now. It wasn't easy. It's never easy for anyone. Resisting the temptation to explode takes extreme determination and clear resolve. I have been successful in the search for peace with and within myself, created a new social life, made new friends. Now I have a fresh view of the world around me. There are a lot of things I can do when I find myself in a situation that triggers a rage. The best thing is to breathe, take a step back, take a few moments to collect my thoughts before I react. That's how we stay in control of our emotions. If I find myself in a situation where I sense my emotions aren't completely under control, it's a good idea to excuse myself and go away for a little while. Don't wait until the feeling of rage grows stronger. Go away. A drink of water helps, splash water on your face, take some deep, slow breaths, until you're aware of your inner emotions again. Slay the beast and think about the fact that self-discipline against unwanted emotional outbursts takes time. Keep the great prize of life clearly before your eyes with hard work and persistence. Climb the mountain until you reach the top. One day you'll enjoy life as never before. I do!"

New episodes of rage

At the second international conference on unruly behaviour by airline passengers – DISPAX World 2014, 10–11 June 2014, London – the aviation community called for urgent measures to combat alcohol abuse in connection with the ongoing increase in "air rage". Crew members were advised to exercise honourable restraint in dealing with unruly passengers, and engage in good, calm, clear two-way communication to de-escalate the situation – both with the enraged person, and with other crew-members. Passengers who spread latent, threatened or (as in outbursts of rage) actual violence should no longer be treated leniently by the legal system. Looking at the change in the sense of space on long-haul flights over the past 20 years, we can see how little room is available. Being restricted or driven into a corner is, as we know, one of the main triggers for an attack or sudden outburst of rage. Seats used to be 48 centimetres wide, and today they are just 43 centimetres: less space, and with it an exasperating restriction of movement. This 5cm-per-seat saving has meant that a nine-seat row in economy could be expanded by one seat. With 20 rows, that's 20 more people on the plane. In business class, meanwhile, the trend is for wider seats: up to 76.2cm. For mere mortals in economy, the space between seats has been reduced from 86 to 75–71cm. In business class, the gap is nearly two metres. This squeeze on the usual space for passengers can be compared with the doubling in the number of cars on our roads, causing more congestion, scarcer parking places, a shortage of time and stress. It is worth bearing this context in mind if we are surprised by the increase in road and air-rage. (Christoph Zürcher, NZZ am Sonntag, 22nd June 2014, pp. 8–11; Simon Calder, The Independent, 10th June 2014, www.independent.co.uk/travel/news-and-advice/aviation-community-demands-action-on-alcohol-to-combat-increase-in-air-rage-9524252.html)

    Naomi Campbell, who makes an appearance in this book as Lady Rage, produced her last great attack of rage at Heathrow Terminal 5 on 3rd April 2008. According to media reports, it was triggered by one of her six suitcases, thought to be overweight, not being put on the plane to Los Angeles. Sitting in first class, she screamed, raged and harangued crew members until they cried with helplessness. She refused to be calmed down by the crew. The pilot called the police. After a final altercation with the police, Lady Rage was escorted off the British Airways flight in handcuffs. The supermodel called the officers "assholes" as they boarded the plane. She is said to have hit and spat at a policeman as he was arresting her. Campbell was taken to Heathrow's police station for questioning. According to British Airways, staff and police did everything they could to help Naomi Campbell. Unfortunately, her outburst of rage had made her lose control and the police had no choice but to arrest her. Eyewitnesses said she had consumed several alcoholic drinks. In June 2008, Campbell was given 200 hours of community service and a £4,500 fine for assaulting two police officers, use of threatening and offensive language and disorderly conduct towards the cabin crew. Although, as I say in this book, Campbell was repeatedly sent on anger-management courses, they didn't enable her to change her pattern of rage. In her view, one possible reason for this destructive behaviour might be that she still felt a fierce rage towards her biological father, who left her mother when she was pregnant with Naomi. She never had a father figure, and had always suffered from a deep and often severe fear of abandonment. Of her relationship with her "surrogate father" Nelson Mandela, Campbell said he was an incredible inspiration who made her reflect on her own life. In him, she found a paternal friend who, even when she had done something wrong – such as expressing her rage in sudden outbursts – never condemned her. But he didn't want her on the stage when he celebrated his 90th birthday. We must also learn to draw up and maintain boundaries. This liberating insight, coupled with her sadness at her public shaming and a life-long ban from flying with British Airways encouraged Campbell, at over 40 years old, to regulate her emotions of rage and anger in a new, socially acceptable way. King (2004) describes the healing power of rage. Well then, it is ok after all. (N Campbell "air rage" interview. http://www.youtube.com/watch?v=f-DFKEQmAKg)

In the world of modern normalising psychology and psychopathology, sudden and severe outbursts of rage are now regarded as an affective personality disorder relating to impulse control. In 2006, when I wrote my book, I was glad that rage had not been categorised in the DSM 4 as a psychological disorder or illness. In the new edition, DSM 5 (American Psychiatric Association 2013), outbursts of rage are diagnosed as Disruptive Mood Dysregulation Disorder (296.99 / F34.8) or Intermittent Explosive Disorder (312.34 / F63.81). The conditions to be met for diagnosis are: verbal and physical aggression in sudden temper outbursts against people or objects, occurring up to three times a week. Interestingly, we find the first of these diagnoses in the "depressive disorders" section. Many people who suffer because of their own sudden rages experience an implosion after the explosion – a deep sadness that they have lost control once again. This is something Campbell says consistently in the interview she gave after her sentencing. This moment of sadness is often a propitious time, which will motivate someone to seek help through psychotherapy. Otherwise, emotional tension will start to build up inside them again, unavoidably culminating in a sudden attack of rage where they will shout down, beat up and destroy the house of love once again.

"What about Charles Darwin?" the English biologist Rupert Sheldrake asked me, as we sat in his Hampstead living room on a mild evening in June 2011, enjoying a glass of wine before the launch of the English edition of this book, and discussing my various theories on rage. "Have you read Darwin's comments on rage in his book *On the Expression of the Emotions in Man and Animals*, from 1872?" "No," I confessed. "The only time I brought Darwin up was in a quote from Francis Huxley's long essay Charles Darwin – Life and Habit (1959). Huxley says there that The Origin of Species might just as well have been called The Origin of Habit." Rupert got up and went upstairs to fetch a 1917 copy of the book from his well-stocked library. He began to read out one of the 39 passages listed in the index under Rage. The gap in my knowledge was gently closed. Afterwards I promised him that when I revised the book, I would include a taster of Darwin's thoughts, and now that time has come. Darwin describes the various physical reactions caused in us by the emotion of rage.

Our hearts beat much faster, our faces turn red from the increased blood-flow and raised blood pressure, our breathing becomes more intense and our nostrils flare. We tremble all over, and our voices become loud and screeching, and higher-pitched. Our entire musculature is put on a state of high alert through intense, almost frantic, autonomously driven actions. All these symptoms of rage and more are, according to Darwin's thesis, probably triggered in the muscles in large part as a direct effect of the agitated senses. Mammals of all species and their ancestors, when attacked by a predator, have often managed to defend themselves or struggle free thanks to the physical power unleashed by rage. Rage is useful for the ultimate self-defence. This emotion is an inherited habit. Darwin reminds us of the gorilla's terrible screams of rage, as he beats his chest like a drum; the lion's powerful, fear-inducing roar; the dog's growling and barking – all physical actions designed to send an enemy fleeing in terror. We humans often gesticulate wildly with our arms when we are in a rage, to make ourselves appear larger and more frightening in a situation that threatens our existence (Darwin 2009).

In the not-too-distant future, up to 80% of Europeans will spend the majority of their lives in cities. In the hot days of rage – for example in England in August 2011, and in Egypt in August 2013 – we have seen how the various arenas of alienation such as youth poverty, racial tensions, violence, unemployment and neglected neighbourhoods promote anger and a propensity for rage. In both places, the triggers for a wave of enraged protests were the brutal actions of the security services. Population density and the reduction of economic resources for sports and social clubs play a decisive role. Rage expressed in public (enragement), is often a result of serious disagreements over how the public sphere can be used for the politics of the street (Rabinbach 2012). Members of the political elite often speak disparagingly of the younger generation, who are at the start of their social and career integration and the arduous acceptance of their given circumstances, largely dictated by others – and who, in the democratic tradition, raise their voices in order to be heard, as a mob. This kind of thinking, and words like these, signal the start of the season when the powerful and their police hunt the youth, who have been forced into a realpolitik position of powerlessness. The latter defend themselves with the anarchic energy of their rage. Sebastian Borger (St. Galler Tagblatt, 6. 8. 2012, p. 6) reports that while the Summer Olympics were taking place in London, the wounds of that summer of rage had not

New episodes of rage

yet healed. No, those in power just went on with their repression. Kagan (2012), a retired psychology professor, remarks that politicians in Washington gave billions of dollars to banks and car companies to shield them from the ruinous consequences of the extreme risks that had been taken by their chief executives. But after the 2008 crisis, very little money was handed out to save millions of poor families, no longer able to pay their mortgages, from the certainty of bankruptcy. Many had taken the risk of buying a house although realistically, they couldn't afford it. The mortgage brokers had sold them a pup in full knowledge of these risks. Most lost all their hard-earned savings. Reason enough for healthy rage and indignation.

Since the publication of this book, I have been happy to discover and buy new books whose titles include the issues of rage, feelings and emotions – always with the desire to learn something new about sudden rages, and to broaden my psychotherapeutic repertoire. From a wealth of books, the following seem particularly important to me. Luc Ciompi und Elek Endert's book Gefühle machen Geschichte (Feelings make history, 2011) describes collective emotions first and foremost. These were vehemently expressed during the days of rage we have seen over the last few years in England, North Africa, Brazil, Turkey and Ukraine. Such powerful collective emotions are the catalyst for radical social and political changes. Mixed with the poison of nationalism and fascism, social conflicts and dogmatic tensions can degenerate into war. Sudden, explosive rages and healthy rage are not considered in collective affect-logic. Frenzied anger, as a consequence of collective helplessness, powerlessness, purposelessness, disenfranchisement in the socio-cultural and political process of negotiating definitions, and of the annihilation of the way you yourself give and experience meaning is a powerful collective guiding emotion. At such moments, in the here and now, lively communal communication is the matrix – the breeding ground, in fact – for an effective, fair and peaceful capacity to resist. In his postdoctoral thesis, Johannes Lehmann (2012) places the emotion of rage as a theme in literature at the centre of a wide-ranging investigation. But sudden rages make no appearance, except in one quotation. A similar collection of essays on anger and rage in culture and literature was published in 2013, edited by Bozena Anna Badura and Kathrin Weber. Rage here is often mixed with anger, to which annoyance is the precursor. All the same, the book does illustrate some psychoanalytic approaches to treatment and attempts to find solutions. This study is silent on the issue of sudden outbursts of rage, although the frenzied actions of some angry or raging characters do represent a transformative power, for good or ill – and, as already mentioned, this must be analysed in context. Anton Bucher (2012), a religious educator, looks at the seven deadly sins in therapy and pastoral care. Since he carried out a recent study on the seven deadly sins, of which rage (wrath) is one, using 376 people (one-third women, two-thirds men) in Salzburg, I hoped for new empirical data, and for the author to look at my own study. There was no mention of it – surprisingly, since we share a publisher. When the deadly sins are listed from worst to least severe, rage comes after greed, sloth, lust and envy, coming joint second-to-last with pride. Gluttony is ranked in last place. When rated by the damage it does, rage takes bronze, after greed and envy. In terms of gender, rage is seen as more masculine than feminine, although 38% of those surveyed saw both sexes as capable of rage. The confusing and disappointing thing in this study is that Bucher quotes extensively from American studies of anger, which he presents as studies of rage. Here, he makes a categorical error. His suggestions for cognitive behaviour therapy interventions, which are commended both here and elsewhere as more efficient than other forms of psychotherapy, are amusing.

Emotions are always where body and mind meet. Margit Koemeda-Lutz's study Intelligente Emotionalität (2009) explains how we can deal with our various and abundant feelings in an intelligent, elegant way. We can approach the repertoire of our own and other people's emotions with care, certainty and liveliness, devoting our energy to the task, if we trust our own inner voice. Moods, affects, physically manifested or even obviously illuminating emotions reveal our true self. To know an emotion in and of itself, you have to experience it. It can never be completely, comprehensively understood, because our human psyche as a whole is not something that can be grasped with consciousness alone. And so showing your psyche in your own feelings and emotions can often be a thoroughly honest social and inter-personal risk. Even Sigmund Freud tried to master his emotions – although we know that in intense emotional debates with male colleagues who were important to him, he sometimes came close to passing out. This was his organism's way of protecting him from unleashing his emotional passions. "He would not explode in anger or expose his pain. He would not shake his fist or walk away"

(Donn 1990, p.155). This was in November 1912, when the 56-year-old Freud had a theoretical and personal argument with his designated successor, the 37-year-old C.G. Jung. Donn suspects that Freud experienced this fainting fit (being overwhelmed by his own feelings) because he was unable to express his intense emotions – which I suspect were rage, sadness, disappointed love. Even psychoanalysts are only human. Our understanding of emotions such as rage, the well-thought-out theories that have been provisionally tested in the social sciences, and the psychotherapeutic approaches that result from them, remain perennial difficulties. The enlightening effect remains unsayable, inexpressible and hopeless until we say what we are feeling, thinking and imagining. What we cannot yet say, we may experience. A feeling arises. A fundamental trust strengthens our guiding emotions and our physical and mental health. The particular emotional path we take through life depends on our culture, the age in which we live and our beliefs. Rage experienced in a healthy way evaporates along with the ferocity it brings out here and now in our bodies. Suppressed rage, on the other hand, becomes hard, bitter and often explodes violently in the form of a sudden outburst. As soon as I dare to feel, imagine and think of the eternal as a process, I sense in the heart of my feelings the transpersonal miracle of existence that reaches beyond me. For me as a psychotherapist, it is important not to let my own feelings of annoyance, anger and rage become a taboo subject. Howard's study on the emotions (2008) describes how as psychotherapists we admit rage, fear, loss and love into psychotherapy as the heart and soul of therapy. These emotions are a part of what I, as a coherent being, can bring to psychotherapy. I have feelings that patients cannot yet release in themselves. As our young colleagues train to become psychotherapists, and experience therapy themselves, one thing I would like them to learn from us seniors is to give authentic expression to their own difficult feelings, from a slight irritation to nagging doubts and annoyances, all the way to the more intense waves of anger, rage and sudden rages. Then they will no longer be afraid to be a human being; they will have no fear of their own emotions or of other people's. Our old Viennese master, Sigmund Freud, is credited with the brilliant remark that psychoanalysis and psychotherapy can help us to stop being ashamed of what and who we truly are, and who we will become.

"The only way to measure progress is by the decline of domination" (Walser 2013).

Tips for therapy and self-empowerment

Many readers of this book's previous two editions expressed a desire to both publisher and author to see a summary of the therapeutic aspects of self-empowerment that are scattered throughout the text. For the third edition (2nd English edition), I am pleased to accommodate this request, and to augment the book with new experiences from my own psychotherapeutic practice. In the following chapter, I will present the first four steps to take out of rage. They are: to get help; create an emotional scale; agree a code word with our partners; practise the courage to express strong emotions, and learn to argue in a healthy way. At the end, there are some tips for victims, and a tentative conclusion.

Help!

Confessing to yourself: "Yes, I have fits of rage, and things can't go on like this," is the first important, courageous step that must be taken to bring about change. When you acknowledge your own unhealthy, immature way of working off this strong emotion, the way is clear for you to deal with your own emotional impulses in a healthy manner. When we express our rage suddenly, we always lose our impulse control. We experience these emotions as if we were trapped in a prison of our own habits. This is one of the important insights that my study has afforded. Sudden rages are a veritable plague, and each fit of rage frightens, saddens, upsets, harasses, hurts and completely unsettles other people, mostly our nearest and dearest, our families and partners. Often, after one of these fits, a person who tends towards sudden rages will promise never to let things get to that point again – and that promise is then broken, shattering trust in them.

If we are prepared, at last, to seek professional help by confiding in a psychotherapist, then in my view, this is a step towards adulthood. We realise that we can move away from the childish belief that we have to do everything on our own, and that no one can help us. This thinking, learned in childhood, shaped our survival strategy in the immediate and extended family into which we were born. Seeking help from outside can, perhaps for the first time in our lives, allow us to move into a new situation where we feel emotionally secure. Here, in the psychotherapist's consulting room, where patient confidentiality is the highest commandment, we can explore our own character and lifestyle without prejudice and with excitement, for what it is: protection. Psychotherapy is an investigation of our own lived, unlived or fantasised biography. It means engaging with our own inner power. The questions to be answered are: what am I doing, for whom, in whose name, why, when and to what end? How do I feel when I exercise the dictatorial power that I am able to enjoy for a short while during sudden outbursts of rage? Am I ready to take the first step away from the great ego show, towards emotionally regulated, consensus-oriented relationships?

People who tend towards sudden rage are often unable to argue in a socially acceptable manner. They are not vicious per se; it is just something they haven't learned from the family who brought them up. They usually come from a house where there was arguing and violence; they swore to themselves as children that they would never grow up to be like their parents. This was tantamount to a ban on arguing. And later, in young adulthood, it means that they prefer to swallow annoyance or anger, and these tensions build up inside them until, unfortunately, they run over and explode. Then, as I have described in this book, they reach the limits of what can be tolerated and controlled. Inwardly, they feel the disappointment of not quite having themselves under control after all, the manipulated emotions, the masquerade that allows them to present an image of themselves as tolerant and relaxed people, people who don't really exist. This shield for their own inner turmoil, their own psychosocial identity, is dropped for a short while during a fit of rage.

After every outburst and the psychosocial crisis that follows, which is often accompanied by depressive moods, a new chance presents itself to get professional, psychological and psychotherapeutic help. A person can do this on their own initiative, or at the renewed prompting of a partner. This important first step towards a new way of dealing with rage is often regarded with disdain for too long, mocked and made to seem ridiculous. "Come on, I'm not a psycho – why don't *you* go and see someone first, it's all your fault. You're the one who makes me angry." Externalising one's own feelings and facts is a common pattern. The people affected by someone's rages are always grateful when that person dares to take this step, to move away from the plague of rage. When everything is threatening to fall apart, then often (but not always) a new breakthrough comes into view.

The writer Christa Wolf (1929–2011) was seven years old when her four-year-old brother began to have severe fits of rage that the whole family came to fear. "Oddo is in a rage, my mother said, quite astonished that one of her children should have such a flaw. And Oddo did get into a rage, he kicked his feet and yelled horribly, and for the first time, one of his gestures made me suspicious that this attack might be a piece of theatre, staged to get his own way, and I felt cheated. I was gripped by rage myself; we tussled bitterly with one another, writhing on the floor, destroying our prison system, panting and trying to hurt each other" (Wolf 2014, p.92).

That was when Wolf began to think about these strong emotional experiences. In her stories, painful childhood patterns of this kind are distilled into useful knowledge. In *Kindheitsmuster* (Patterns of Childhood), she outlines, among other things, how difficult it is for a wounded soul to speak and write about these emotions (Wolf 1977). In a fresh language of healing emotions, which gently detaches itself from the language of our parents and grandparents – a kind of transgenerational rescue mission – we can find words that describe, as precisely as possible, how our emotions make our bodies feel. In this way, we can de-identify from our learned behaviour, and finally speak about what we lack and what oppresses our minds from an interior and previously unexpressed place. We thereby make ourselves newly communicable, and release ourselves from the old fear that was bound up with old articles of faith. That fear is what prevented us from allowing ourselves to express emotions, including strong and difficult ones. This is a new kind of support, and it feels like a breath of fresh air.

Empirical fact 1. Seeking help is the first step away from rage.

Creating a scale of emotions

The second step for a successful therapeutic experience lies in becoming aware of your own emotions and the physical movement associated with them. This (again) requires a language of emotions with which to express the feelings you are perceiving. Let us begin to let go of our fear of being human. Emotions are the expressions of our vitality.

Take a blank, white sheet of A4 paper. If you use a diary, this emotional scale can be kept there (Figure 2). First, draw the baseline of calm along the bottom edge. Then draw the tension build-up line, perpendicular to it along the left-hand edge. Then, starting in the bottom left-hand corner, draw a line rising up to the top right. I call this the emotional excitation line.

Now, place markers along the emotional excitation line. These are labelled with the kinds of tension that you can sense in yourself and describe. For me, it starts with the feeling of being disturbed or bothered, as in: "You're disturbing me. Could you leave me alone, please?" If I consciously acknowledge my emotion, I can make a mark at this point on the line. My tension ebbs away, and I return to the basic mode of relaxation. In layman's terms: I calm down.

Further emotional markers, rising with inner tension, are: irritation, stress, annoyance, resentment, anger, fit of anger and (sudden) rage. The important thing is to recognise and understand each of these escalating emotions as "I-messages". "I am experiencing you as bothersome." This means that I am not viewing the other person as the cause, or placing the blame on something external; instead, I share the message of my inner experience with the other person. We communicate how we are experiencing their behaviour towards me (or someone else). The other person's behaviour becomes my internal experience of it. In experiencing one another *through one another*, our interpersonal situations and communication are enriched by three subjective interpersonal parts (at least six, then, in an interpersonal perception). Firstly, the image I have of myself, or my self-image; second, the image I think other people

Tips for therapy and self-empowerment

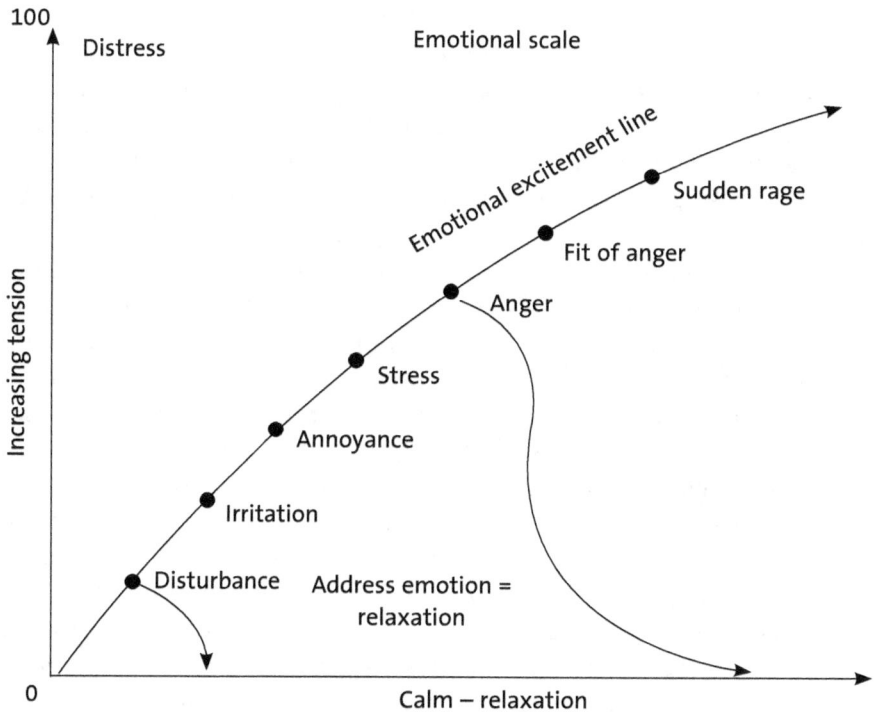

have of me, or my public image; and third, the person I truly am: my authentic existence.

Utilising the emotional scale means that every time I express a feeling that appears on it, I can make a mark beside that feeling. I give myself feedback, record a result. Have I admitted to one of the emotions that I have felt today and put on the scale? Have I dared to say something, rather than swallowing that emotion down? If the answer to that is "yes," then I make a mark on the scale and spend a moment recalling how, after addressing this emotion I used to keep quiet about, I returned to the baseline of calm. The further down the scale I begin to express myself, the less risk there is of ending up in the higher "danger zones" of anger and rage. When we used to swallow our feelings and keep quiet about them, we held the physical and emotional tensions inside, and thus perpetuated them. Sensing that her husband is tense, a wife asks: "What's wrong?" He replies: "Nothing, what should be wrong?" That "nothing" contains within it the statement: "I don't want to talk about it". Repeating the emotional-scale exercise over a long period guarantees a continual, empowering reduction of those inner tensions.

Most of us are aware that rage builds up gradually until it reaches the "point of no return". If we don't turn back before then, there will be no avoiding an attack. Using the emotional scale, we can practise being conscious of our own range of emotions, being aware of annoyance or anger backing up inside us, and we can re-learn how to communicate this directly rather than indirectly. This allows us to assert ourselves, to say – if we can and want to – "I stand by my emotions. I am now truthful, upright and authentic." Socially emotional interactions thereby become clearer. If someone's behaviour towards me oversteps my boundaries, I can, for example, resurrect that boundary by expressing my annoyance. Thanks to this daily practice, we will be tempted to go blundering beyond the point of no return much less often, and avoid entering into the cruel stupidity that comes with it. Afterwards, the emotions we are left with are an overwhelming, isolating mess of "I'm afraid it's happened again."

Utilising the emotional scale allows us to express being annoyed, stressed, feeling anger in our bellies and (in the very last instance), rage, in a new way. We also gain a greater ability to perceive the triggers for each feeling, and the emotion of rage, with more care and nuance.

The great advantage to communicating my emotions as "I-messages" is being able to stand up for myself and my experience of a situation, or of another person. It conveys the experience of self-awareness, self-confidence and self-assurance. The other person, to whom I communicate these things, takes what I have said less as an attack or personal criticism, and more as my own realisation. My inner emotional tension, which is often experienced as distress, is diffused, and I become even-tempered and calm again.

When we succeed in spotting and naming the triggers for our rage, we have taken the first step towards escaping from emotional storms that – in visual terms – are sudden and dangerous like volcanic eruptions. The aim is to stop being ruled by my emotion, and rule over it instead.

It's like learning a musical instrument: the more I practise, with the instrument here being my mind and its emotions, the better and more experienced I become. I reveal myself in my emotions, and summon up the courage to express them. After a week, I can look back at where I have been able to make the most marks. Each time I acknowledge an emotion and express it in words, I come back to the baseline, to a place of calm and composure. More marks are added week by week, and the self-efficacy I have experienced is reinforced.

But maybe I don't want to do this, and I fall back into old habits – after all, in my typical character style, no one can tell me what to do (including myself). I get further and further up the emotional-excitation line, and what happens then? Up at the top, I reach anger, having swallowed everything down as I always used to do, and at this point it takes only a minor irritant from the bottom of the scale to trigger an angry outburst. As ever: too much is too much! Relapses are not forbidden; they will happen naturally if we neglect this practice.

It might be that we experience something that triggers an immediate and powerful feeling of anger. Then it is healthy to express this anger, first verbally, as a warning (in the way that other animals also do), and then – if we are ignored – physically, as a way of defending and maintaining our own mental and physical integrity. A thug grabs a biker by the arm. The biker gets angry at once and warns him: "Let me go or I'll knock you down." The thug first laughs, clings on, and seconds later finds himself lying at the biker's feet, bleeding and with a broken nose. "You idiot, I warned you," the biker says, angrily. The old saying, "He who will not hear must feel" is not always a stupid, threatening part of the harsh pedagogy that is based on obedience and punishment.

Empirical fact 2: We can face up to our emotions without the world coming to an end.

The code word

Another tip that has proved useful is for everyone affected by someone's rages to take time, while you are in a good mood, to agree on an easily remembered code word. Words like: "Stop" or "enough" are not really suitable: they are socially charged and often produce resistance. Using a code word is also a way for a couple to build mutual trust. All of us who are affected know well enough that, after every outburst, someone who tends towards rages usually promises that they will do everything they can to stop it happening again. In the triangle model of domestic violence, this is what is called the "honeymoon phase". The other two parts are the build-up of tension and the discharge of violence. Now, once again, we hear the perpetrator asking the victim: "Please give me one more chance." Following each incident, the latter feels deeply shaken and often says: "That's enough, get out! Get out of my life," (or "our lives", if children are involved). Many people agree a code word such as "fireman", "bell" or "dragon," and promise to heed the warning when one or the other of them uses this word, if the first triggers should appear. Many people affected by rage say how effective this practice is.

As soon as one person has said the code word, everything that has happened up to that point is subject to the agreed "time-out". Ideally, this means that the interaction between the triggers and the person given to sudden rages is interrupted. From then on, there is no further discussion or potential taunting. Talking can wait until both people have calmed down, each in their own way. Only after that should questions be asked. "What went wrong there? And why?" Each person goes either to another room, or out of the house altogether. Some like to walk a few laps of the garden in the fresh air, others even leave the property completely. Moving around outside releases the muscular tension that builds towards anger or even rage, and is usually discharged in an "attack". One possibility, if there is any woodland nearby, is to walk there, find an old, fallen branch and hit it against a tree trunk, ridding yourself of a few screams in the process. Give your imagination free rein as to what might help you, and make use of these possibilities.

The person who remains behind can go back over what they have contributed to the situation in which the code word had to be uttered. What has caused their own frustration and annoyance? Now, thanks to the time-out, they are able to think about how these emotions feel, and where in the body they are felt. Have I been heard, seen and respected by the other person, or not? Have I ignored myself? If you have a diary to hand (and I recommend you get yourself one), these thoughts and feelings can be recorded there. First, write down what emotions accompany the interior aspect of your experience, presenting them as fact. Writing these down will help in the conversation that is still to come, to clarify what led to the code word being spoken. I recommend the same to the person who has gone outside. When they get home, they should first go to their own room and write down their thoughts and internal experiences. In so doing, we feel more precisely the emotions that accompany such a critical situation. This is where your own introspection begins. I take what I have expressed back into me. This is how the crucial insight happens. The issue lies within me; it relates to me and my emotional history, or the history of this emotion in my life. My current partner, wife or girlfriend is not the cause; they are not to blame. They are merely contributing to, or are involved in a situation that has been stirred up until it almost results in a fit of rage. If we go ahead and take this code-word-led time-out, then these terrible, emotionally excruciating interpersonal situations, which often involve violence against objects or people, will arise very infrequently. Some patients report that to begin with, it is difficult to respect the other person when they say the code word. "No, no, I'm not anywhere near the 'point of no return' yet." But all the time, he is getting louder and louder. We know from experience, however, that self-righteousness is like dirty clothes. This third step, too, is all about mutual trust, and knowing that the other person is using this word in good faith, for the good of everyone involved.

During the Covid-19 pandemic (since March 2020), code words were introduced in France and Spain to allow women to seek help outside the family safely, without being hit and humiliated by their husbands again for doing so. This assistance from women's refuges and family advice centres has been very successful.

When we learn to reflect on our own feelings of rage, and find other solutions for difficult life situations, we gain more options for expressing and reflecting on our emotions. Our sense of self-worth, self-confidence and self-reliance are fed by recognising the truth of our feelings. Fairness within the family and living freely within a community require that we do not use psychological or physical violence to assert our view of things. But danger lurks everywhere: some groups of people, and the world of politics, are not immune to tyrannical posturing. Rage can often produce brutal counter-rage, as many couples have told me. And that is a genuine, reliable guarantee that you will destroy yourself and your relationship. When we communicate what we feel inside, we find a double balance. First in our own emotional world, and second in the shared, interpersonal order of things. The ethical principles of fairness, compassion, freedom, justice and empathy with the suffering of others, lead to a transformation of attitudes and to a new life.

Empirical fact 3: using the code word together works wonders.

Expanding the repertoire of your own emotional regulation

We can regulate our emotions – and in our particular case, rage – in various ways, depending on how emotions and feelings have been cultivated within the family we grew up in. Jean Briggs, an anthropologist who studied the Utku Eskimos near Hudson Bay, found in the course of her research that Eskimo parents and relatives fell silent whenever a child over the age of two showed any signs of anger or rage (Briggs 1970). A good indication that the expression of emotions is dependent on social conditioning and social respectability. This behaviour is accorded no attention other than silence. The reaction is neither a positive nor a negative one. The psychoanalyst Michael Eigen (2002) mentions that one of the worst aspects of rage is the affinity between this strong emotion and a sense of righteousness. Sudden rages are attempts to fill the inner void. This is doomed to failure. The inability to acknowledge our own emotional life and show our emotions is masked by rage. The results of our questionnaire show that seven out of every hundred people who suffer from sudden fits of rage don't want to be cured of them. They don't want to enter into any process of change.

When we summon up the courage to express our own rage, if need be, healthily and passionately, without falling back into the habit of sudden rages – to expand our repertoire of emotions, in other words – this is proof of our own psychological and social maturity. As I have said before, curing sudden rages begins in each case with becoming aware of our own feelings. If we accept rage as a part of our natural, animal life, we can allow ourselves to feel our own vitality in the power of this basic emotion.

When I reach the limit again, what then? When I don't know how to go on, where do I seek help this time? The personal is political, and outbursts of rage are mostly the consequence of violence in the family. This habitual behaviour can make a person become addicted to ruling over themselves and others like a dictator. For many people, as in the monumental Homeric stories, the politics of

Tips for therapy and self-empowerment

experience in sudden rage is a mythical guide of available options for how we could behave differently, if we were permitted, willing and able to. This requires our human capacity for empathy, far-sightedness, love, and mutual support in a relationship we want to maintain. Since all we humans are vulnerable creatures, it is valuable and important not to do intentional damage to ourselves. In future, our own experience of being able to argue in a healthy, adult way will be important to us.

Standing up for our feelings, dreams, desires, thoughts, experiences and the resulting insights takes courage. If we don't live alone, there are always social situations in which it is important for us to assure ourselves of what our standpoint is in a quarrel or conflict. We have a showdown – with ourselves, and with the other person. Here, if necessary, is where an argument can happen in order to find a new consensus. If this should be unsuccessful at first, then this search for the third couple-dimension can be adjourned. Better to wait and have a cup of tea than allow an argument to escalate into violence. In this situation, one person wants to prevail over the other because they want to feed and maintain the little dictator within them. "I know what's what here. We're going to do things *my* way." Asserting your will means playing by the same rules that other, political dictatorships use: making threats to body and soul – stopping at nothing – to destroy the other person's life. Psychological and physical violence serves this purpose. Violence often arises when one person in a relationship feels powerless. They fear losing their influence. When I run out of words in a discussion or an argument, then "my fists do the talking". That is where the danger lies, because it begins with resounding, verbal humiliations.

We must continually learn empowering emotional behaviour, in order to know when the feeling of rage is rising up inside us, so that we can avoid exercising it in a violent and hurtful way. We can build up a repertoire that allows us to exercise our emotions well enough (as you might exercise a horse), depending on the occasion and situation in which we find ourselves. We know from past experience that the more agitated we get inside (the pressure-cooker image), the more tense our muscles grow; our whole body has an urge to release the tension.

In taking these steps away from rage, the crucial thing is to be able to express ourselves in nuanced language. To listen well enough, to take on board other people's perspectives – which doesn't mean adopting them ourselves. According to Katz Anhalt (2017), Greek myths can be seen as cautionary tales, instructions for changing our emotional behaviour. Violent outbursts provide a short-term emotional satisfaction, but unfortunately they have no lasting effect. The limit to our tolerance is important, and if we can or have to extend it from time to time, that is a good thing. The same goes for the limit to our frustration.

Empirical fact 4: Communicated feelings reinforce our self-confidence.

Tips for victims of rage

I must admit how shaming it is for the male sex as a collective that in the private family home, usually seen as a place of trust and protection, domestic violence against women and children rose by 30–50% during the Covid-19 pandemic, from China to Germany, Johannesburg to Glasgow. Dirk Behrendt, Berlin senator for justice, remarked on this with outrage at a press conference (25 March 2020). Graham-Harrison et al. (2020) give a more nuanced report of the facts. In his study on violence broken down by gender, Michael Meuser (2010) itemises the typical profile of a violent offender in the police's criminal database. More than 80% of physical injuries and murders are perpetrated by men. This is a statistic that remains constant over years and decades. Gender is the strongest predictor of violent crime. There is also an unequal gender distribution when it comes to victims of violence. Meuser outlines how violence – physical, sexual or psychological – is "admitted into" social gender relations in a huge variety of ways. Every man who undergoes psychotherapy for his rage, or undertakes self-help with friends or a men's group, is a brave person, who has chosen to renounce and disassociate himself from male violence as an instrument of power and oppression.

If you experience violence at the hands of someone who has rages – the perpetrators are often suffering from ADHS (Meuser 2010, p.126) – and you don't have a black or brown belt in one of the various self-defence disciplines, then as soon as you are able, get out. Retreat to a safe place, such as a women's refuge, a friend's house,

Tips for therapy and self-empowerment

or the police station. Don't believe that there will be no repetition of this violence. It will happen again and again, unless and until the perpetrator is finally prepared to seek effective help to escape from this "vicious circle". Protection is always better than the illusory, often romantic faith in your ability to heal the other person with your love. The daily, disappointing facts of personal experience, social and psychological studies, the full women's refuges and the many reports written about domestic violence speak against romanticising what is later revealed to be deception or cunning on the part of the perpetrator.

It is also important for victims not to hesitate to get help. Expert assistance can help people who are suffering to stop tormenting themselves with the feeling that they are to blame for their partner's aggressive outbursts. What can be done? The hurtful experience needs to be revisited and integrated into the present. In the presence of a therapist, I no longer need to be afraid of my surging emotions. I can breathe. If I have the courage to look again at the knots of emotions, to untangle them and to let the genie of suppressed pain and anger out of the bottle, I will come to the source of my past experience of violence and abuse. In the regression that accompanies this, I access the earlier situation that has been stored within my emotions, and at the same time, I am aware of myself as an adult, in the healing presence of another adult (in the role of psychotherapist). With advanced practice, I can later recognise that, as in the image of a horizonal number 8, I can be equally in the past situation, and in the "here and now". In touching the great wound (trauma) on the one hand, and using my own adult source of strength on the other, I glide around that endless 8 to my emotional recovery with a newly calm attitude towards what happens. Of all the feedback from this process, let me cite just one comment:

"I wanted to get in touch to thank you for the therapy. My wife and I are now doing really well as a couple. I have you to thank for that to a large extent. And I must confess that I miss my sessions with you a little, even if the reason for them was a terrible one. I am managing to use your tips well in my everyday life, and the methylphenidate is helping with that, as well. I no longer lose control, and we can discuss the things we disagree about. Yes, we can even have an argument that stays at a healthy level. My wife and I are very glad and grateful for my development. In my case, you told me I had to 'rebuild the burned-down roof' – and that is what I have done. My heartfelt thanks to you for that."

I have now set out four tips for self-empowerment that I give to people in my practice. Patients who use them regularly report that they suffer from fits of rage much less frequently. After the second edition of this book was published in 2015, several couples got in touch with me because they both tended towards a level of rage that was fundamentally endangering their relationship and their love for one another. That doesn't have to be the case.

If we practise the four steps (get help, regulate your emotions, use a code word, help yourself), we will suffer much less from severe emotional outbursts. We will become active, rather than remaining passively at the mercy of our own dogma surrounding the politics of helplessness we have learned. We can practise new maxims, such as: "I am not bad, I can do this. I see and hear myself. I love myself for what I am, and not for what I do. I will not abandon myself when I need my own support the most."

A few remarks on psychotherapy

When we begin a course of psychotherapy, we often wonder how long this treatment is going to take. Modern research on psychotherapy describes the process of healing the mind as a cognitive restructuring of the personality. In discussing the results of their eight-year investigation, Mattanza et al. (2006) come to the conclusion that long-term psychotherapy (90–120 consultations) is necessary for a person to restructure their life in a lasting way – for the therapy to have a curative, emancipatory effect, in other words. Short-term psychotherapy (8–12 consultations) is very often enough to free someone of symptoms and alleviate interpersonal difficulties for the time being.

The success of psychotherapy is contingent on several factors: physical health, the degree of a person's own ability to function socially, the duration of symptoms prior to the start of therapy, age, sex, social and economic class, education, religion, work situation, family history etc. All these variables are of tremendous significance. With an emphasis on the practice of evidence-based psychotherapy, the Swiss Charta für Psychotherapie carried out a wide-ranging, naturalistically oriented sociological study between 2007 and 2012. The "naturalistic psychotherapy study on outpatient treatment in

Switzerland", called the PAP-S-Studie for short (Psychotherapiestudie Ambulante Psychotherapie-Schweiz) was conceived as a process-outcome study. It looked at 86 therapists from nine different psychotherapeutic institutions, and recruited a total of 362 patients (238 women and 124 men) aged between 17 and 72. The many outcomes achieved show how the role of patient compliance with the therapists, their professional experience, their therapeutic alliance and the severity of their clients' psychological problems are dependent upon one another if a positive outcome is to be achieved (Von Wyl et al. 2016).

For the eight different therapeutic concepts investigated, a good 30% used interventions that adhered to the concept (were specific) and up to more than 73% used non-specific interventions. Psychotherapy is a highly complex interpersonal process, in which the individual concepts behind the treatment (e.g. Gestalt therapy, body psychotherapy, psychoanalysis, behaviour therapy) are applied to a lesser extent than has previously been assumed. What certainly makes psychotherapeutic treatment successful is a good match. The more the patient is suffering, the greater and more complex their sufferings, the more important the therapist is. The therapist is a crucial key to effective psychotherapeutic treatment. The therapeutic relationship is a vessel for curative and emancipatory successes. The study shows how aspects of sex and gender influence the treatment: in general, and fundamentally, the female therapists in the study are more markedly empathetic, and their interventions more supportive than their male colleagues.

Alongside psychotherapy, making your own music can change people in a healing way. We are all musical creatures from the moment we are born. Another healing option for regulating your own feelings healthily, and exercising an age-appropriate level of impulse control, is the practice and method of the "inner team". This is a personality model put forward by the Hamburg psychologist Friedemann Schulz von Thun. The plurality of human inner life is represented in the metaphor of a team and its leader. This practice is designed to support what he calls "self-clarification" in ambiguous situations, and thereby create the conditions for clear and authentic communication with others (Pörksen and Schulz von Thun 2014). In this model, the raging person is only one among many, and can thus communicate inwardly in a different way. This raging character no longer needs to be hidden or suppressed – and doesn't have to oppress others, either. Most of us are familiar with Galen's old model of personality, with the four types of temperament. In this model, people given to fits of rage would be the choleric type. The team then also includes the melancholic, phlegmatic and sanguine. These are two helpful personality models for dealing with a complex social and psychological reality.

Another crucial question is how my sociological research can support other psychotherapists in working with patients who suffer from attacks of anger and rage in the best, outcome-oriented way. I think it is important to summon up your own courage, your own emotional vitality, and to cultivate the experience and knowledge that accompanies our psychotherapy training.

As Herman Hesse (1986, p.198) puts it in his poem "Steps", in words that bring my suggestions for practice to a close:

> A magic dwells in each beginning,
> Protecting us, telling us how to live.
> [...]
> Courage, my heart, take leave and fare thee well!

Appendix

Questionnaire used in the 2006 rage survey

1. Age group
2. Sex
3. Do you come into contact with rage in your family? (yes/no)
4. Do you have outbursts of rage? (yes/no). If no, go to question 6
5. When did you first realise that you tended towards these outbursts?
6. Are you the victim of a raging partner? (yes/no)
7. Were you the victim of a raging parent? (yes/no)
8. Any comments on question 7
9. What do understand by "sudden rages"?
10. Are you aware of what triggers your rages? (yes/no)
11. Any comments on question 10
12. Why do you (or people you know) fly into a rage?
13. What do you (or people you know) do during a rage?
14. Why do you think your rages are/were a repeated occurrence?
15. What have you done to alleviate these attacks of rage?
16. What are the negative sides of rages?
17. What are the positive sides of rages?
18. What do you generally experience during an attack of rage?
19. What do these outbursts mean?

20. (If you are a victim of rage) Do you have rages too? (yes/no)
21. Comments on question 20
22. When question 20 = yes, proceed to question 22;
23. When question 20 = no, proceed to question 25, if participant is a rager
24. Where do you usually experience fits of rage?
25. In what ways do you suffer from your own rages?
26. In what ways do the people you know suffer from your rages?
27. Over how many generations of your family can these outbursts be traced back?
28. Are rages an emotional legacy in your family? (yes/no)
29. Comments on question 26

Acknowledgements

For Rage

I wholeheartedly express my gratitude to Ruth Martin, who lent me her excellent vibrant, and sagacious English in translating *Jähzorn* in the first place, and now has done these additional new chapters from the second (2015) and third (2020) German edition.

As author I feel honoured and thankful, that the present editorial board at Libri Publishing, John Sivak, Celia Cozens and Roger Amos, have decided to produce a second English edition, ten years after. Many thanks to Raphael Grischa Itten, Berlin, whose art I deeply appreciate, for the cover painting.

It is my pleasure to thank Paul Jervis who dared to take this book first into Libri Publishing, merci beaucoup to Celia Cozens for careful copy-editing and Pat Graham, who aided its leaving, back in 2011, this author's harbour.

For their various encouragement, hospitality, wisdom of heart, good humour, and generosity in seeing the English version into gestation, I would like to thank my friends the late Deirdre Bair, Brian Evans, Bob Henley, the late Francis Huxley, Ron Roberts, Rupert Sheldrake, and Emil Stutz (who opened generously his deep purse).

For Jähzorn

The following people have helped make this book a reality, for which I extend my heartfelt thanks.

Raimund Petri-Wider, publisher at Springer Verlag, who gave me the chance to describe the phenomenon of sudden rages in book form.

Franziska Brugger and Renate Eichhorn, publishers at Springer Verlag, who found my manuscript appealing and were happy to see it through to publication.

Thomas Redl, my wonderfully serious editor at Springer, who cherishes the principle of accuracy, and whose corrections enriched the book. I couldn't have wished for a better proof-reader.

Evelyne Gottwalz-Itten, my wife, who gave me an inspiring place to write in her book-lined study in Hamburg. As a critical, kind reader, she provided me with a great number of helpful suggestions for essential improvements to the text.

Adolf Holl and Inge Santner, who gave me friendly encouragement in writing this book. Their brilliant, voluble suggestions for developing the text were a gift.

Eva Kutschera, who copy-edited my original text elegantly and clearly.

Thomas Schwemer, a fellow researcher, who undertook an exchange of thoughts with me in the area of social sciences, helped create the questionnaire, compiled the research statistics and took care of the computer back-up.

Dimitrij Itten, who analysed the raw data from the empirical study, helped form the sets, thought things through with me and scrutinised my variation of qualitative social research.

Natalie Weber, who turned my hand-written drafts into texts quickly and reliably, and shared her feelings about the book as it developed.

The street-survey team: Dimitrij Itten (lead), Jasmin Häne, Jan Tisato, Jerry Zimmerli.

Anne-Hélia Nidecker, who carried out the evening phone survey.

Everyone who participated in my personal survey, the street survey and phone survey. I have them to thank for the empirical data for this study.

Those patients who suffered from their own rages, or their parents', who have started on their route through psychotherapy in my consulting room.

Thomas Scheibler and Ludwig Westmayer, who gave me helpful, appreciative tips after reading the manuscript.

The late Jost Gross, Joseph Gomes, Johanna von Renner, Ulrich Heiniger, Peter Lehmann and Ljiljana Filipovic, who shared their experiences, dreams and thoughts with me.

Bibliography

American Psychiatric Association (2013) Diagnostic and statistical manual of mental disorders: DSM-5. American Psychiatric Association, Washington DC

Ancelin Schützenberger, A. (1998) The Ancestor Syndrome. Brunner-Routledge, London

Anhalt, E.K. (2017) Enraged – why violent times need ancient myths. Yale University Press, New Haven, CT

Apuleius (1997) Golden Ass or The Metamorphosis and other philosophical writings. Trans. Thomas Taylor, The Prometheus Trust, Somerset

Asbridge, M. Smart, R. G. & Mann, R. E. (2006) Can We Prevent Road Rage? Trauma, Violence & Abuse 7:109-121

Bachofen, J. J. (1975) Das Mutterrecht. Suhrkamp, Frankfurt am Main

Bair, D. (2005) C. G. Jung: eine Biographie. Knaus, Munich

Balint, M. (1952) Primary Love and Psychoanalytic Technique. Hogarth Press, London

Balint, M. (1968) The Basic Fault - Therapeutic Aspects of Regression. Tavistock, London

Bandura, B. A. & Weber, K. (Hrsg) (2013) Ira – Wut und Zorn in Kultur und Literatur. Psy-chosozial-Verlag, Gießen

Barnes, M. & Berke, J. (1988) Meine Reise durch den Wahnsinn. Fischer-Taschenbuchverlag, Frankfurt am Main

Berger, K. (2005) Paulus. 2nd Edition. C.H. Beck, Munich

Berger, K. & Nord, C. (1999) Das Neue Testament und Frühchristliche Schriften. Insel, Frankfurt am Main

Bertaux, P. (1981) Friedrich Hölderlin. Suhrkamp, Frankfurt am Main

Bibel (1981) von A bis Z. Wortkonkordanz zum revidierten Luthertext. Stuttgart, Deutsche Bibelgesellschaft

Bircher, U. (2000) Mit Ausnahme der Freundschaft: Max Frisch 1956-1991. Limmat Verlag, Zurich

Bleuler, E. & Bleuler, M. (1983) Lehrbuch der Psychiatrie 15. Auflage. Berlin, Springer

Bloom, C. (1996) Leaving a Doll's House. Little, Brown, Boston

Borger, S. (2012) Tollster Tag meines Lebens. St Galler Tagblatt, 06.08.2012, S 6

Breuer, T. (1992) Café Jähzorn. Wunderhorn, Heidelberg

Briggs, J.L. (1970) Never in anger: portrait of an Eskimo family. Harvard University Press, Cambridge, MA

Buber, M. (1952) Moses. 2nd Edition. Lambert Schneider, Heidelberg

Buber, M. & Rosenzweig, F. (1992) Die Schrift, Vol. 1: Die fünf Bücher der Weisung; Vol. 3: Bücher der Kündigung. Deutsche Bibelgesellschaft, Stuttgart

Bucher, A. (2012) Geiz, Trägheit, Neid & Co. in Therapie und Seelsor-ge. Springer, Heidelberg

Burkert, A. & Kippenhahn, R. (1996) Die Milchstrasse. C. H. Beck, Munich

Calder, S. (2014) Aviation community demands action on alcohol to combat increase in 'air rage'. The Independent, 10.06.2014. http://www.independent.co.uk/travel/news-and-advice/aviation-commuty-demands-actionon-alcohol-to-combat-increase-in-air-rage-9524252.html

Campbell, N. (2008) Air-rage Interview. http://www.youtube.com/watch?v=f-DFKEQmAKg

Camperio Ciani, A. (2000) When to Get Mad: Adaptive Significance of Rage in Animals. Psychopathology 33 : 191-197

Cau, J. (1985) Croquis de mémoire. Julliard, Paris

Ciompi, L. (1982) Affektlogik. Klett-Cotta, Stuttgart

Ciompi, L. (1997) Die Emotionale Grundlage des Denkens. Sammlung Vandenhoeck, Göttingen

Ciompi, L. & Endert, E. (2011) Gefühle machen Geschichte. Vandenhoeck & Ruprecht, Göttingen

Claus, D., Aust-Claus, E. & Hammer, P.-M. (2005) ADS - das Erwachsenen-Buch. ObersteBrink, Ratingen

Colli, G. (1993) Nach Nietzsche. Europäische Verlagsanstalt, Hamburg

Damasio, A. R. (2000) Ich fühle, also bin ich: die Entschlüsselung des Bewusstseins. List, Munich

Darwin, C. (2009) The expression of the emotions in man and animals. Oxford University Press, Oxford

De Waal, F. (2006) Wir sind gemeiner als alle Tiere. SonntagsZeitung, 22nd October 2006, Diogenes, Zurich

Deutsche Bibelgesellschaft (1981) Bibel von A bis Z: Wortkonkordanz zum redivierten Luthertext. Stuttgarter Nachschlagwerk zur Bibel. Deutsche Bibelgesellschaft, Stuttgart

Donn, L. (1990) Freud und Jung: Years of friendship, years of loss. Macmillan, London

Dürrenmatt, F. (1986) Der Auftrag oder Vom Beobachten des Beobachters der Beobachter. Diogenes, Zurich

Dürrenmatt, F. (1990) Das Hirn. In: Turmbau – Stoffe IV-IX, S235-266. Diogenes, Zurich

Edelman, G. M. (1992) Bright Air, Brilliant Fire: On the Matter of the Mind. Basic Books, New York

Edelman, G. M. & Tononi, G. (2001) Consciousness. How Matter Becomes Imagination. Penguin, London

Edmonds, D. J. & Eidinow, J. A. (2005) Wie Ludwig Wittgenstein Karl Popper mit dem Feuerhaken drohte. Fischer Taschenbuch Verlag, Frankfurt am Main

Ehrenreich, B. (1998) Blood Rites: Origins and History of the Passions of War. Virago Press, London

Ehrenreich, B. (1999) Blutrituale. Ursprung und Geschichte der Lust am Krieg. Rowohlt, Hamburg

Eigen, M. (2002) Rage. Wesleyan University Press, Middletown, CT

Erikson, E. H. (1972) Young Man Luther. Faber and Faber, London

Eysenck, H. J. (1970) The biological basis of personality. Penguin, London

Fazel, S. & Grann, M. (2006) "The Population Impact of Severe Mental Illness on Violent Crime". American Journal of Psychiatry, Aug. Vol. 163 pp. 1397–1403.

Ferenczi, S. (1980) The Dream of the 'Clever Baby', in Further Contributions to the Theory and Technique of Psycho-analysis, Ed. Rickman J. Maresfield Reprints, London

Ferenczi, S. (1988) Ohne Sympathie keine Heilung: das klinische Tagebuch von 1932. Fischer, Frankfurt am Main

Foer, J. S. (2003) Everything is Illuminated. Penguin, London

Franzoni, G. (1990) Der Teufel – mein Bruder: Der Abschied von der ewigen Verdammnis. Kösel, Munich

Freud, S. (1993) Der Moses des Michelangelo. Fischer, Frankfurt am Main

Garnett, A. (1995) Deceived With Kindness. Pimlico, London

Graham-Harrison, E., Giuffrida, A., Smith, H. & Ford, L. (2020) "Lockdowns around the world bring rise in domestic violence", The Guardian, Sat. 28 March https://www.theguardian.com/society/2020/mar/28/lockdowns-world-rise-domestic-violence

Grandin, T. & Johnson, C. (2005) Animals in Translation: using the mysteries of autism to decode animal behaviour. Bloomsbury, London

Graves, R. (1969) The Greek Myths, Vol.1. Penguin, Harmondsworth

Grigson, G. (1978) The Goddess of Love. Quartet Books, London

Grossman, D. (1996) On Killing: The Psychological Cost of Learning to Kill in War and Society. Little, Brown, Boston

Guggenbühl-Craig, A. (1992) Vom Guten des Bösen. Schweizer-Spiegel-Verlag, Zurich

Hartmann, T. (2006) Eine andere Art die Welt zu sehen: das Aufmerksamkeits-Defizit-Syndrom. Schmidt-Römhild, Lübeck

Heilpern, J. (2006) John Osborne: A Patriot for us. A Biography. Chatto & Windus, London

Hell, D. (2002) Die Sprache der Seele verstehen – Die Wüstenv.ter als Therapeuten. Herder, Freiburg im Breisgau

Hesse, H. (1972) Lektüre für Minuten. Suhrkamp, Frankfurt am Main

Hesse, H. (1986) Das Lied des Lebens. Die schönsten Gedichte. Suhrkamp, Frankfurt am Main

Hobhouse, J. (1993) The Furies. Doubleday, New York

Holl, A. (2002) Brief an die gottlosen Frauen. Szolnay, Vienna

Holl, A. (2003) Weihrauch und Schwefel – Ein Monolog. Styria, Graz

Holl, A. (2005) Wünsche können nicht irren. Abteilung Z/11, Medienservice, Bundesministerium für Bildung, Wissenschaft und Kultur, Vienna

Holl, A. (2006) Om & Amen. Eine universale Kulturgeschichte des Betens. Gütersloher Verlagshaus, Gütersloh

Howard, S. (2008) The heart and soul of the therapist: rage, fear, desire, loss, and love in the psychotherapy relationship. University Press of America, Lanham, MD

Huxley, F. (1959) Charles Darwin – Life and Habit. American

Huxley, F. (1976) The Raven and the Writing Desk. Thames & Hudson, London

Huxley, F. (1990) The Eye – The Seer and the Seen. Thames & Hudson, London p. 56

Huxley, J. (1960) Religion without Revelation. Max Parrish, London

Itten, T. (2002) From R.D. Laing to Jack Lee Rosenberg. In: Itten T, Fischer M (Ed.) Jack Lee Rosenberg. IBP-Books, St. Gallen, pp.52-69

Itten, T. (2006) Interview with Professor G. M. Edelman. Psychotherapie Forum 14 Supplement: pp.143-147

Janson, T. (2006) Eine kurze Geschichte der Sprachen. Elsevier, Munich

Kafka, F. (1998) Letter to the Father. Trans. Karen Reppin, Vitalis, Prague

Kagan, J. (2012) Psychology's ghosts: the crisis in the profession and the way back. Yale University Press, New Haven, CT

Kakar, S. (1991) Shamans, Mystics, and Doctors. University of Chicago Press, Chicago

Keenan, B. (1993) An Evil Cradling. Vintage, London

Kerényi, K. (1972) Mythologie der Griechen. Deutsche Verlagsanstalt, Stuttgart

Kernberg, O. F. (1993) Psychodynamische Therapie bei Borderline-Patienten. Verlag Hans Huber, Bern

Kierkegaard, S. (1941) Fear and Trembling (first published 1843) Trans. Walter Lowrie, Princeton University Press, Princeton

King, R. (2004) Healing Rage: Women Making Inner Peace Possible. Sacred Spaces Press, Berkeley, CA

Kluge, F. & Seebold, E. (2002) Etymologisches Wörterbuch der deutschen Sprache. Walter de Gruyter, Berlin

Koemeda-Lutz, M. (2009) Intelligente Emotionalität. Kohlhammer, Stuttgart

Köhlmeier, M. (1998) Sagen des Altertums. Piper, Munich

Kozorovitskiy, Y., Hughes, M. Lee, K. & Gould, E. (2006) Fatherhood affects dendritic spines and vasopressin V1a receptors in the primate prefrontal cortex. Nature Neuroscience 9, 1094–1095. Published online: 20 August 2006.

Kreisman, J. J. &Straus, H. (1992) Ich hasse dich – verlass mich nicht. Kösel, Munich

Kurnitzky, H. (1981) Ödipus: ein Held der westlichen Welt. Wagenbach, Berlin

Laing, R. D. (1967) The Politics of Experience & The Bird of Paradise. Penguin, Harmondsworth

Laing, R. D. (1972) The Politics of the Family and other essays. Vintage, New York

Laing, R. D. (1974) The Divided Self. An Existential Study in Sanity and Madness. Penguin Books, Hamondsworth

Laing, R. D. (1982) The Voice of Experience. Allan Lane, London

Laing, R. D. (1987) The Use of Existential Phenomenology in Psychotherapy. In: Zeig, J. K. (Ed.) The Evolution of Psychotherapy, S.203-211. New York, Brunner/Mazel.

Laing, R. D. & Esterson, A. (1970) Sanity, Madness and the Family. Families of Schizophrenics. Penguin, London

Laktanz (1919) Vom Zorne Gottes. Bibliothek der Kirchenväter, 1. Reihe, Vol.36, Munich, www.unifr.ch/ patr/bkv/ kapitel.php?ordnung=0&werknr=58&buchnr=132&abschnittnr=501

Lambert, M. J. & Bergin, A. E. (1994) The effectiveness of

Lapide, P. (1994) Ist die Bibel richtig übersetzt? Vol.2. Gütersloher Verlagshaus, Gütersloh

Lapide, P. (1996) Er wandelte nicht auf dem Meer: ein jüdischer Theologe liest die Evangelien. Gütersloher Verlagshaus, Gütersloh

LeDoux, J. (1996) The Emotional Brain. Simon & Schuster, New York

Lehmann, J. F. (2012) Im Abgrund der Wut: zur Kultur- und Literaturge-schichte des Zorns. Rombach, Freiburg im Breisgau

Lessing, T. (1983) Geschichte als Sinngebung des Sinnlosen. Matthes und Seitz, Munich

MacLean, P. D. (1990) The Triune Brain in Evolution: Role in Paleocerebral Functions. Plenum, New York

Mattanza, G., Meier, I. & Schlegel, M. (eds.) (2006) Seele und Forschung: ein Brückenschlag in der Psychotherapie. S. Karger, Basel

Mayring, P. (2002) Qualitative Sozialforschung. Weinheim, Belz

Meuser, M. (2010) "Gewalt im Geschlechterverhältnis", in: Aulenbacher, B., Meuser, M. & Riegraf, B. (eds.) Soziologische Geschlechterforschung. VS Verlag – Springer Fachmedien, Wiesbaden, pp.105–123

Meyer, C. F. (1988) Jürg Jenatsch. Insel, Frankfurt am Main

Mineka, S. (1992) Evolutionary Memories, Emotional Processing, and the Emotional Disorders. Psychology of Learning and Motivation 28: pp.161-206.

Mithen, S. (1996) The Prehistory of the Mind. Thames & Hudson, London

Möller, H.-J., Laux, G. & Deister, A. (2001) Lehrbuch der Psychiatrie und Psychotherapie. Thieme, Stuttgart

Monte, C. F. (1995) Beneath The Mask. Harcourt Brace College Publishers, Fort Worth, TX

Öhman, A. & Mineka, S. (2003) The Malicious Serpent: Snakes as a Prototypical Stimulus for an Evolved Module of Fear. Current Directions in Psychological Science 12: pp.5-9

Osborne, J. (1956) Look Back In Anger: A Drama. Samuel French, London

Otto, E. (2006) Mose. C.H.Beck, Munich

Panksepp, J. (1998) Affective Neuroscience: The Foundations of Human and Animal Emotions. Oxford University Press, Oxford

Poole, R. (1982) The Unknown Virginia Woolf. Humanities Press, Atlantic Highlands, NJ

Rabinbach, A. (2012) Violence and the city. Times Literary Supplement, 05. 08. 2012, S 7–8

Rahn, E. (2001) Borderline. Ein Ratgeber für Betroffene und Angehörige. Psychiatrie Verlag, Bonn

Reichberg-Ullmann, J. & Ullmann, R. (2002) Es geht auch ohne Ritalin. Michaels-Verlag, Peiting

Rilke, R. M. (1919) Neue Gedichte. Insel, Leipzig

Rosenberg, J. L. (1973) Total Orgasm. Random House, London

Rosenberg, J. L. & Kitaen-Morse, B. (1996) The Intimate Couple. Turner Publishing, Atlanta, GA

Rosenberg, J. L., Rand, M. & Asay, D. (1989) Body, Self and Soul: Sustaining Integration. Humanics, Fort Worth, FL

Roth, P. (1993) Operation Shylock. Vintage, London

Roth, P. (1999) I married a communist. Vintage, London

Rowley, H. (2005) Tête-à-tête. Simone de Beauvoir and Jean-Paul Sartre. HarperCollins, New York

Schröde, W. (1992) Traktat über die drei Betrüger. Meiner, Hamburg

Schultz von Thun, F. & Pörksen, B. (2014) Kommunikation als Lebenskunst. Carl-Auer, Heidelberg

Sheldrake, R. (1995) A New Science of Life: the Hypothesis of Morphic Resonance. Park Street Press, New York

Sloterdijk, P. (2006) Zorn und Zeit. Suhrkamp, Frankfurt am Main

Smart, R. G. & Mann, R. E. (2003) Causes and Consequences of Air Rage in Canada: cases in newspapers. Canadian Journal of Public Health 94: pp.251-253

Smolker, R. (2001) To Touch A Wild Dolphin. Doubleday, New York

Steinmeyer, J. (2003) Hiding the Elephant. Carroll & Graf, NewYork

Strauss, A. & Corbin, J. (1990) Basics of Qualitative Research: Grounded Theory Procedures and Techniques, 2nd Edition. Sage Publications, Thousand Oaks, CA

Strawson, G. (2004) A fallacy of our age: not every life is a narrative. Times Literary Supplement 15th October 2004, pp.13-15

Stumm, G., Pritz, A., Gumhalter, P., Nemeskeri, N. & Voracek, M. (Hg) (2005) Personenlexikon der Psychotherapie. Springer, Vienna

Tschuschke V, Kächele H (1998) Was Leistet Psychotherapie?

Tschuschke, V., Von Wyl, A., Crameri, A., Koemeda-Lutz, M. & Schulthess, P. (eds.) (2020) "The Impact of Patients' and Therapists' Views of the Therapeutic Alliance on Treatment Outcome in Psychotherapy", in: The Journal of Nervous and Mental Disease, Vol. 208, No. 1, January 2020, pp. 56-64

Turnbull, C. (1976) The Forest People. Picador, London

Von Matt, P. (2006) Die Intrige: Theorie und Praxis der Hinterlist. Hanser, Munich

Von Wyl, A., Tschuschke, V., Crameri, A., Koemeda-Lutz, M. & Schulthess, P. (eds.) (2016) Was wirkt in der Psychotherapie? Ergebnisse der Praxisstudie ambulante Psychotherapie zu 10 unterschiedlichen Verfahren. Psychosozial-Verlag, Gießen

Waleczek, L. (2001) Max Frisch. Dtv, Munich

Walser, M. (1996) Finks Krieg. Suhrkamp, Frankfurt am Main

Walser, M. (1999) Über die Schüchternheit – Zeugen und Zeugnisse. Edition Isele, Nussdorf

Walser, M. (2004) Der Augenblick der Liebe. Rowohlt, Reinbek bei Hamburg

Walser, M. (2013) Messmers Momente. Rowohlt, Reinbek bei Hamburg

Werner, J. (1999) Die Sieben Todsünden. Deutsche Verlagsanstalt, Stuttgart

Wilhelm, R. (1975) Translation: The I Ching. Routledge & Kegan Paul, London

Wolf, C. (1977) Kindheitsmuster. Aufbau-Verlag, Berlin

Wolf, C. (2014) Nachruf auf Lebende – Die Flucht. Suhrkamp, Berlin

Zdral, W. (2002) Der finanzierte Aufstieg des Adolf H. Ueberreuter, Vienna

Zdral, W. (2005) Die Hitlers – Die Unbekannte Familie des Führers. Campus, Frankfurt am Main

Zürcher, C. (2014) Klassenkampf über den Wolken. NZZ am Sonntag, 22. 06. 2014, S 8–11

www.ingramcontent.com/pod-product-compliance
Lightning Source LLC
LaVergne TN
LVHW021659060526
838200LV00050B/2427